INQUIRY INTO BEING

Joseph J. Sikora, S.J.

Loyola University Press
Chicago, 1965

Library of Congress Catalog Card Number: 65-26034

PREFACE

In order that this work be judged fairly, it is necessary at the beginning to explain its purpose and method. It is, as the title says, an inquiry into being. It is not an inquiry into the history of philosophical thought about being; it is not even an historical inquiry into being. The two preceding types of inquiry are, of course, quite legitimate; but they ought not to be allowed to rule out all possibility of a more direct approach to the problem of being.

I do not suggest that the contemporary philosopher may proceed in ignorance of the long tradition of philosophical thought; this has certainly not been the case in the metaphysical reflection preceding and accompanying the composition of this work. But after history and the dialectic of systems have been allowed their say, there is still need for mere philosophical reflection and meditation on the problem of being. The present inquiry is simply the setting down in print of such a meditation, made in a comparatively brief period after some twelve years of philosophical study, teaching, and reflection upon the problem of being. The disputes of the schools of philosophy have been put into the background; recollection, reflection, and meditation upon being itself occupy the center of attention.

The method is primarily analytic, proceeding by a gradual clarification and distinction of the original datum of being. Demonstrative argumentation is at a minimum, although some is necessary, especially in the movement of transcendence from limited to infinite being.

As has already been suggested, this philosophical reflection does not begin in vacuo. The author could not help but begin within the Thomist tradition. But this tradition, in its present state of preservation and development, cannot but appear even to many Thomists to be in need of much further growth by means of assimilation of many new insights which have themselves been gained outside the Thomist tradition. This is not the place to argue about whether many of these things were or were not already known to Saint Thomas himself in some manner or other. What is necessary at the present moment is that Thomists of the present day come to the fuller appropriation of being that does indeed seem possible. The purpose of this inquiry is precisely to move beyond some conventional limits of Thomism by a confrontation of diverse traditions. The work is limited, just a beginning; but there does seemingly result some enrichment of the Thomist idea of being. Some might prefer to say that some of this "enrichment" is really non-Thomist after all; but I believe that the metaphysics of existence which is here presented is in fact only a development of, not a substitution for, Thomism.

Lest the non-Thomist reader begin to fear that this inquiry is not so much an inquiry as an esoteric treatise for the initiates of the Thomist school, I hasten to add that the development of ideas proceeds from analysis of the data of being and not from the already accepted tenets of a philosophical school. The above remarks about Thomism are for the Thomists who happen to read this book.

But although this inquiry is non-historical in nature, it still seems appropriate at this point to say a few words about the historical background. The principal sources out of which this inquiry grew may be reduced to six: the Thomist tradition, the positivist tradition, contemporary phenomenology, the idealist tradition, contemporary existentialism, and contemporary scholasticism. A few remarks may be made here about each of these.

What constitutes the most authentic Thomist tradition is strongly debated among Thomists. Without wishing at this time to enter into a controversy on this subject, I merely say that I understand this tradition to extend backward from Saint Thomas to Aristotle and forward through John of Saint Thomas, Cajetan, and other commentators to its leading contemporary exponents in Gilson and Maritain (here there are, unfortunately, many dissenters).

Contemporary scholasticism is a much wider term, but I have here in mind principally those scholastics who comprise the "Thomist school," in a somewhat wider sense than that of the last paragraph. Some of these deny that those mentioned in the preceding paragraph are the best representatives of the Thomist school. (Indeed, even Gilson has been rather critical of Cajetan as a Thomist.) But again, I wish to avoid argument, and merely state which of these have been especially influential in my own work, without establishing any scale of degrees of proximity to true Thomism. Maritain and Gilson have already been named. The Jesuits, Fathers De Finance, Hayen, Lonergan, Klubertanz, and G. Smith, have been most important to me. Also Monsignor Journet, Father Garrigou-Lagrange, O.P., and V. E. Smith should be mentioned.

The positivist tradition here refers principally to Hume and to the members of the Vienna Circle and their sympathizers. But also to be included are Comte, Duhem, and a variety of philosophers of science who understand the strength of positivism in regard to the understanding of modern natural science. Hume and the positivists have made it impossible to ignore sensible phenomenality in the enumeration of the fundamental dimensions of being.

Contemporary phenomenology is a widespread movement, and I do not claim thorough acquaintance with it. But Husserl and Sartre have brought to me a deeper awareness of psychic phenomenality as a distinct dimension of being.

The idealist tradition I understand to include all those who have focused upon the reality of transphenomenal essences without grasping the even greater importance of the exercised act of existence as a co-principle of being. By this criterion, Plato, even Aristotle, Saint Augustine, Saint Bonaventure, Descartes,

Kant and his idealist school, and Cassirer must be included. (Aristotle was also included in the Thomist tradition, insofar as his idealism is not closed but open, in virtue of his very method, to further development along Thomist lines.) It has been the special importance of the idealist school to focus attention upon transphenomenal essence, however misconceived at times, as a distinct dimension of being, and on the role of *a priori* construction in the understanding of being.

Existentialism, like phenomenology, is a term of wide application. But the existentialists of particular importance here are Marcel and Heidegger. Their insights have been confirmed for me by the reading of Buber, of Saint John of the Cross, and of the ancient Indian *Upanishads*. The principal contributions of this group have been toward a better understanding of subjectivity and of createdness as dimensions of being.

But most fundamental remains the characteristically Thomist contribution of the understanding of the existential act of things and of that superabundance of existential act which is activity. The firm grasp, in Thomism, of these two fundamental dimensions of being makes of Thomism, in my view, the perennial metaphysics of existence and being, the vital metaphysical organism to which other valid philosophical insights should be assimilated.

Special acknowledgment and thanks are due to Messrs. Robert Grib, S.J., James Vorwoldt, S.J., Paul Zook, S.J., Robert Weickert, S.J., and Daniel Liderbach, S.J., who compiled the index.

North Aurora, Illinois

TABLE OF CONTENTS

Part 2. TRANSCENDENT BEING

Chapter 1

THE DIMENSIONS OF BEING

The question of being for modern man

There have been times and places in the history of philosophy in which the givenness of phenomenal reality--that spread-out and ever-changing field of reds, blues, whites, noise, musical harmonies, odors and savors, hot and cold, smooth and rough, pleasure, pain, emotion, imagination, etc. in which we find ourselves immersed--has been put in doubt. As far back as Parmenides, we may find the phenomena regarded as essentially illusory and luring man along the way of opinion as opposed to the way of truth. True being is considered by such thinkers to be found in the line of pure thought, in the realm of ideas. Here the absolute primacy of spiritual reality is assured from the outset; the problem is to give a foundation for such knowledge as we have of what is called the material world. Of course, Plato is the foremost representative of this school of thought; but his followers are to be found throughout the history of philosophy.

There has always been, to the uninitiated, a certain appearance of unreality in this kind of philosophy. It seems to disregard the obviously given in order to penetrate into the obscure and esoteric, and it not infrequently ends in a pseudo-mysticism. To the analytic thinker, this philosophy is a scandal. When metaphysics proceeds in this manner, the analytic thinker can only regard it as an intermediary stage between mythical thought and positivistic thought, in the manner of Auguste Comte.

Let us not deny the possibility that profound aspects of being may have been discovered by such Platonic philosophers (although they should be criticized for the radically deficient mode of conceptualization of their insights, insofar as they do not do justice to the necessary dependence of all such insight on the sensible given). But it remains true that it would be better to rediscover these aspects of being through the use of a self-consciously analytic method. This would allow them to be incorporated the more easily into a philosophical system which has that consistency and harmony which the analytic thinker demands.

Another reason for beginning philosophy with the analysis of the phenomenal given is that in contemporary America, and indeed throughout the Western World and wherever else the Western influence has penetrated, it is practically impossible to gain a wide hearing in any other way. There is today a positivistic prejudice at the heart of most of Western philosophy outside Christian philosophy, and indeed it has penetrated into Christian philosophy itself in many places. Idealism itself may be viewed as an attempt to put some intelligibility into a being that has first of all been conceived in a positivistic manner. It is because they fail to see any intrinsic intelligibility, but only bare phenomenality, in being that idealists turn to a consideration of transcendental a priori's and absolute spirits, which might enable them to impose an artificial intelligibility on the essentially chaotic phenomenal flux.

But there is no pretense in this work of discovering within the phenomena the non-phenomenal aspects of being. Rather, in the examination of the phenomenally given we hope to find that it has more than phenomena, that it has other "dimensions" as well. At this point there is, of course, a great divergence from the well-trodden positivistic path; but it may be hoped that even the positivistically inclined may follow at least a little way, and perhaps be tempted to venture a good deal further.

The question of being, then, for modern Western man is not "Are the phenomena being or illusion?" but rather "Is being anything at all more than phenomena?" "Are there also transphenomenal depths in being?" Of course, many have ceased to ask this question any more at all. However, simply refusing to ask it is not a philosophical attitude but a pre-philosophical act of faith in the meaninglessness of being. The reflective person must ask the question, even in the midst of our positivistic culture; or he will be guilty of bad faith.

The question of being for modern man reconsidered in more detail

I have been speaking of phenomena and phenomenal reality. Perhaps it is good to set in a little clearer light the meaning of these terms, in order the better to understand the question of being.

What is phenomenality? Phenomenality is the world as it is given in sensation. But this formula is full of obscurity, for both "the world" and "sensation" need further explanation. And if it be said that the world is the sum total of all that is, this itself needs explanation; for what is this "is"? Is it not necessary already to understand the meaning of being in order to understand phenomenality? This is, of course, true in a profound sense; and yet, so long as no attempt is made to settle the question of being completely, being may be regarded merely as some unspecified something which in fact does give itself to us in sensation. It would be useless to try to explain "given in sensation" at this point; and yet in a way we are all aware of its meaning, at least in a global way.

However, it is possible to point out in some detail some characteristics of what is given in sensation. First, this given is a manifold, or rather a double manifold; it has a multiplicity of parts given simultaneously in space and a multiplicity of parts only given successively in time--thus it may be called an extended flux, of both coexisting and non-coexisting parts. Second, this given is a factual given and not an ideal given: it is a given in which each part is confined to its own here and now, not one in which any part transcends its own here and now, as would be the case with a universal idea or an absolute value. Other aspects of sensible phenomenality will emerge later; these may suffice for the present.

Some philosophers have distinguished two stages in human intellectual life: the stage of mythical thought and the stage of rational thought. The stage of mythical thought is characterized by the dominance of the imagination over the reason in conscious life, even in that of the reason itself. This stage is said to be that of primitive man (it might also be added that this is the stage proper to the child). The stage of rational thought, on the other hand, is characterized by the dominance of the reason over the imagination in conscious life, even in that of the imagination itself. This stage is said to be that of the civilized man (and it might be added that it is the stage proper to the civilized adult, although it remains true, as St. Thomas Aquinas said, that most men follow their senses rather than their reason). Of course, one never finally leaves behind for good the stage of mythical thought; there is always the danger of regression, both in the individual and in whole nations--as Ernst Cassirer has pointed out, and as the temporary success of the Nazi racist myth makes vividly clear.

Now it should be evident that in the stage of mythical thought, it is the phenomenal real which dominates the life of the intellect. And yet even here the tendency of the intellect toward the trans-phenomenal real is manifested in the evolution of explanatory myths. These explanatory myths stand as symbols of the real causes and principles of things, causes and principles which are properly accessible only to rational thought. Ancient religious and quasi-religious mythology was meant in a way to give reasons for the way things are and for their coming to be at all.

We stand now at a point in the history of human thought which enables us to distinguish two ways of passing beyond the mythical level in our intellectual life: the way of positive science and the way of philosophical reflection. In historical fact, it was the way of philosophical reflection which was first followed up in a thorough manner (although the possibilities of positive science were not left entirely unexplored even in ancient Greece).

To the ancients and medievals, the existence of nature and natures beyond the phenomena, producing the phenomena, and manifesting themselves through the phenomena was an utterly self-evident fact, as Aristotle indicates in the first chapter of his Physics. It was this given nature, in some mysterious manner abiding and stable, in and yet beyond the phenomenal flux, subject to and yet also in some way above change, which fascinated philosophers from Socrates and Plato down through the great medieval thinkers. And the study of nature, or physics, was found to lead beyond itself to metaphysics, the general study of being as being. Just how physics leads to metaphysics necessarily depends upon one's notion of what being is, of what pertains to it above and beyond merely having a determinate nature. If being is nothing more than what has a determinate nature, the movement from physics to metaphysics is as simple as it was for Aristotle. But if being has other aspects, other "dimensions," then matters may become a bit more complicated. In any event, some distinction is made between physics and metaphysics, the study of nature and the study of being; but both are considered to be legitimate fields for philosophical reflection. And as one penetrates more and more deeply into the principles of nature and being, he rises higher and higher beyond the level of mythical thought, acquiring the wisdom which enables him to consider the whole universe and its ends instead of being dominated by the here and now of phenomena.

But to modern Western man, the existence or knowledge of determinate natures beyond the phenomena, producing the phenomena, and manifesting themselves through the phenomena--far from being a self-evident fact--is highly problematic. If nature for the ancients was a given to be investigated more fully, for the moderns nature may or may not be a given, but at all events is to be ignored so far as scientific thought is concerned. Philosophical reflection about natures and being is now considered to be a lapse backward into a quasi-mythical thought, springing from a mysterious optical illusion of the intellect.

Why has this scepticism, or at least indifference, regarding the problems of natures and of being arisen? In part, this can be traced to the spectacle of the continuing disagreement of philosophers concerning just about everything--a spectacle which can only be a scandal to the uninitiated. The fact of this disagreement can, however, be philosophically understood in the light of the fundamental obscurity of any knowledge of natures and of being, as compared with the knowledge of phenomenal reality. (Of course, one must grant that there are clear and distinct ideas about nature and being; but their reference to the reality of nature and of being is by no means always so clear.) Yet this very obscurity can only reinforce the conviction of the non-philosopher--already there by reason of the disagreements of philosophers--that the object of philosophy is somehow illusory and not worth the effort expended on it. And to all this must be added the apparent unfruitfulness of the knowledge of nature and of being in an age determined to dominate matter and to use it for the ends of man. I have deliberately said, "apparent unfruitfulness"; for in fact the sciences of matter could not exist without at least obscurely given insights of metaphysics and the philosophy of nature (such as the conviction that there is order in the universe, and that there is some permanence behind the flux of phenomena), which regulate the development of these sciences almost without the sciences even knowing it. Other reasons also come to mind for the loss of interest in natures and in being in the modern world--the loss of the Christian faith which gave the greatest stimulus to philosophical reflection, the consequent immersion of man in his own concerns and the resulting disposition to ignore the questions of transcendent truth and the absolute, the brilliant success of the new positive sciences of phenomena (although even in the twentieth century some scientists are found mixing up philosophical concerns with these positive sciences). As a result of all this, the phenomena monopolize the attention of modern man. "Nature" is now only the assemblage of phenomena, and to be is to be a phenomenon. All attempts to penetrate beyond the phenomena, whether to nature or to being, in the older sense, are branded as "metaphysical" and dismissed as a waste of time and energy. Positive science reigns supreme.

In positive science there is another surpassing of the mythical level of thought, but quite different from the rational thought of philosophy. Positive science aims to dominate the phenomenal flux, not by a consideration of the non-phenomenal causes and principles of phenomena, but rather by imposing a rationally constructed order on the phenomena, as in the concepts, laws, and theories of physics. This rationally constructed order represents no penetration of nature or of being but only an artificial organization of the chaos of phenomena, that they may be aesthetically contemplated and physically dominated by man. Idealists and positivists differ as to the source of the impetus toward this artificial construction. But they are at one in affirming it as the fundamental work of the intellect, as opposed to what has above been called philosophical reflection. They are at one in denying to what we have called philosophical reflection the power to achieve a knowledge of being in itself, of absolute being and of transphenomenal natures.

Parenthetically it may be noted that even in our world of positive science the tendency of the intellect toward the absolute manifests itself in a resurgence of mythical thought, in the construction of "world-images" suggested by scientific progress, and in the concern lest such constructions be rendered impossible through the continuing evolution of physical theory. It was seen above that this effort of mythical thought does in fact spring from a deep desire of coming to understand the transphenomenal principles of phenomena. But it remains true that philosophical reflection cannot feel welcome in the modern Western world, at least any philosophical reflection aiming to penetrate transphenomenal being.

The positivistic spirit carries with it a number of serious difficulties for modern man. In the order of pure knowing, the speculative order, he is left with a truth which simply cannot satisfy the thirst of man--a truth that is purely relative and incapable of meeting man's need for the absolute, a truth that is at best only a partial a priori ideal organization of a depthless multiplicity without any ground of unity, a hopelessly fragmented and limited truth in which one can never rest but which can only tantalize us the more as we broaden our grasp of it. Even success in dominating the chaos of phenomena through an ideal synthesis does not mean the attainment of a transcendent truth, a truth greater than man, which he can serve in order to escape his condition of finitude. Here he has only a truth to serve him; but he must remain alone and in fear at his radical weakness, darkness, and finitude. Man, with the positivistic spirit, must find in himself frustrated desires and his deepest longings unfulfilled.

And if there is no grasp of the absolute, no truth for us to serve, then, in the practical order, the order of action, there are no permanent values or any natural, necessary, and eternal norms. And if there are no permanent values and norms, then fact alone matters, might makes right, civilization cannot hope to endure, man is always and everywhere the "useless passion" of Sartre, a "useless passion" whose annihilation would be desirable, insofar as it would at least bring to an end that burning <u>pain of loss</u> of the absolute and of God.

If follows then that we must make the effort, the inquiry to determine whether being is more than phenomenality or the mere ideal synthesis of phenomena. The alternatives are the transcendence of phenomena or the annihilation of human personality in the despair of the individual and the collective destruction of civilization, at least morally in despair and perhaps physically in modern war.

I do not wish here to suggest that the transcendence of phenomena, among the leaders of mankind in the significant areas of human life, is itself enough to bring ultimate peace to men and nations; that is not to be attained by man alone, but only in his acceptance of the grace of Christ. Indeed, one may well suspect that the transcendence here spoken of will not even take place on any large scale apart from the helping grace of Christian life. But we must do everything possible to prepare the way for the advent of grace by restoring to our culture, so far as possible, the "sense of being, " through the transcendence of phenomena and mere ideal syntheses of phenomena. Positivist despair of reason is in fact a most serious obstacle to the will to believe in a revelation of God. In the very lowly work of philosophical reflection the way is prepared for the coming of the Lord.

We pose then the question of being. But the question may be further clarified. "Being" is simply what is. This is an intrinsically mysterious notion, since no man ever understands the totality of what is. And yet even to common sense it has some intrinsic intelligibility. But the common sense intelligibility of being is itself mysterious; common sense sees being only in a global way--the inner diversity and structure of being remain obscure to the unreflective man. The very question here asked concerning being, whether it is more than phenomena, presupposes that there is this initial obscurity in its givenness to us. For the moment, then, let it be said only that being is what is found polarized around "me" and "not-me." This manner of describing being very well suits our present position concerning being, since it serves to point out where being is but in no way prejudices the question of being which is being asked.

This question can be asked in another way. This new formulation of the question in fact goes some distance toward pointing out the method by which one can proceed in answering the question. We ask: Is being multi-dimensional? Does being have more than one dimension? By such a dimension of being is meant a distinct aspect of being presented or presentable to the intellect in a distinctive manner. If there are several distinctive manners of presentation of being to the intellect, grounded in some diversity in being itself, then being has several dimensions. One distinctive manner of presentation has already been pointed out, namely that of objective sensible phenomena, which is known not only to the senses but also to the intellect, through its concepts of phenomena.

But here has occurred the distinction of sense and intellect. Does this not itself presuppose something more than a positivistic standpoint? Is not the intellect by its very nature the faculty of the absolute, and is this not just precisely what yet remains to be seen? It is true that in the preceding paragraph we momentarily adopted the position of the already well-advanced metaphysics of being, but that was only as an hypothesis. It was pointed out only what a dimension of being would be if in fact being were more than phenomena. If being is indeed more than phenomena, and known as such, then it will be attained in its transphenomenality by what we call intellect rather than by the senses. The senses are necessarily faculties of the relative, of the unstable and flowing and consequently what is non-opposed to nothingness and essentially relative to nothingness; for the senses are the faculties of attaining phenomena. If there is in fact more to be attained in knowledge, it is not attained by the senses. But even the positivist acknowledges implicitly the existence of another faculty, a mysterious organizing intelligence making use of concepts to bind together the multiplicity of phenomena in an ideal synthesis. Now the abstractions employed by this organizing intelligence are in fact of a quasi-absolute character, a fact which has sometimes resulted in their being regarded as more really real than phenomena by some modern Platonists. It would seem clear, then, that if there is indeed any true faculty of attaining the absolute, of knowing transphenomenal reality, it must be sought on the side of the intelligence rather than on the side of the senses.

Now a further point concerning the life of intelligence must be noted, which reinforces the conviction that the multi-dimensionality of being will be discovered in the life of the intelligence. The intellect not only formulates concepts to organize the phenomena; in some mysterious manner it must possess an insight into these phenomena as such--how can it reflectively organize what it does not know? The concept is here the formulation of one or a group of insights. But if such insight is given (to be formulated conceptually), then we cannot rule out on any a priori grounds the possibility that other modes of insight are also given, insights which may be formulated in what have traditionally been called abstracted concepts as well as those which are formulated in constructed concepts, insights which may be formulated in the meta-concepts of metaphysics as well as insights which are formulated in the concepts of other sciences. If in fact new modes of insight beyond that into phenomena can be detected, then there are other dimensions of being, regardless of the problems to be raised concerning the conceptual or meta-conceptual formulation of these insights.

Note that these dimensions of being are not to be confused with the transcendental attributes of being studied by the metaphysician. The transcendental attributes of being are meta-conceptually formulated in dependence on the various special modes of insight demanded by metaphysics <u>all taken together</u>, as will be seen much later. We are speaking here rather of those aspects of being which give rise to these special modes of insight, <u>taken separately</u>. We are asking whether there are not given several radically diverse cognitive unions with being, and inquiring about the diversity in being itself (its multi-dimensionality) which grounds this diversity of cognitive unions.

Note that it is in principle impossible to discover the other dimensions of being through an analysis of one of them, for example, of sensible phenomenality. What is required is original insight, irreducible to other insight. This original insight is essentially non-predeterminable in character; no a priori conditions can be laid down for it. Here can be seen the essential error of the positivist criterion of verifiability, or indeed of any so-called universal criterion of verifiability other than that of being itself, which may prove to be quite multi-dimensional.

By now, it may be hoped, the question has been sufficiently clarified for us to discuss in some detail, not yet the answer, but some possible methods of getting an answer.

The method of answering the question

The first problem to be considered is, Where to look to find the dimensions of being? In the ancient world, the transcendence of phenomena was achieved in the study of the merely physical and merely biological worlds first of all. But it does not seem promising to begin with the physical world; for the dimensions of being are in all probability even less evident here than in the biological world, since even the phenomena themselves are less rich, less diversified. There seems to be less of being in the physical world, and therefore the multi-dimensionality of being should be manifested less clearly in this domain. And it is also true that modern Western man seems in great part to have lost the ability to look at physical nature in any but the scientific manner. Either other forms of analysis are not even tried or they are fumbled and confused in a sophisticated mythical thought, as in the case of philosophizing scientists such as Jeans and Eddington. The philosophy of nature is cultivated today only with the constant danger of its becoming nothing but a mythical construction taking off from the sciences of phenomena.

What has just been said of the study of physical nature is of course also true of the study of biological nature. We tend to look at the biological world in a positivistic manner, dazzled as we are by the success of the positivistic physical sciences. But still the mystery of life continually suggests that in fact there is more than the flow of phenomena involved here; above all is this the case in that being who is the summation of the physical and biological worlds, as well as something more, namely the human being. If there are in fact dimensions beyond phenomena in being, they should be most evident in man.

But, in considering human being, we must be careful to try really to grasp human being in its fullness, not just to stuff it into the Procrustean bed of physical and biological science. We must retain an attitude of docility, a willingness to acknowledge the more that there is in man, if this more should manifest itself.

If it be found that there are other dimensions than sensible phenomena in man, the next step will be to look for these other dimensions in other things as well. The comparison of diverse multi-dimensional beings will in fact reveal at once the fundamental unity and analogicity of being. The dimensions we discover in man are in fact also present in other things, but they are not present in the same manner. Each being is being according to its own mode.

We shall begin then with an analysis of the being of the me, and in the light of this analysis turn to the comparative analysis of the not-me. But there still remains the question of the method of analysis to be employed. Many have used the historical method, a careful enumeration, examination, and comparison of the positions of preceding philosophers, in order to gain a fuller understanding of the meaning of being. Indeed, the very fact of philosophical pluralism has led many to distrust completely their own powers of independent analysis. But in fact the method of historical analysis alone must ultimately of necessity fail to come up with genuine answers to properly philosophical questions. For by itself it is only a dialectical method, one which does not end in an understanding of being in its intrinsic intelligibility but rather in an understanding of the way men have thought about being. I do not mean here to deny the value of the historical method in philosophy, but it is essentially a supplementary method, which must presuppose direct analysis of the intrinsic intelligibility of being if it is to be at all fruitful in philosophy as opposed to the mere history of philosophy. At most, the historical analysis can only confirm direct analysis or suggest new lines for the direct analysis of being in itself.

The fundamental method to be employed in this work is that of reflective recollection, directing attention to our own life in all its aspects so as to achieve a conscious self-appropriation, in order to see whether in this self-appropriation aspects of being other than sensible phenomena will manifest themselves to us. In this self-appropriation it is of course possible for one to learn something without a teacher, but one cannot value too highly the presence of a Socrates or of a modern existentialist calling upon us to know ourselves. The purpose of this chapter is mainly to provide some similar aid in the process of self-appropriation which each must carry out for himself.

One final point remains to be considered here regarding method in the analysis of being, concerning the difference between insight and conceptualization. It is quite possible that there may not be an adequate conceptual expression of every insight. It is also possible that there are quite diverse modes of conceptualization corresponding to quite diverse modes of insight. It is impossible to set down a priori limits as to the type of conceptualization which is to be allowed as valid --this would be only to refuse to push the inquiry concerning being beyond an arbitrarily determined point. But it is not at all necessary to become involved in the questions of the modes of conceptualization right now. Such logical and psychological questions, however tempting, may be put off for some time; all that is necessary now is to come to recognize the presence of genuinely diverse modes of insight in our cognitive union with being.

So much for method; it is time now to begin the analysis of being itself.

The dimension of sensible phenomenality

Sensible phenomenality has been already described above, but it is possible here to add a few points in the hope of illuminating further this aspect of reality and of leading to a fuller understanding of it as a dimension of being. This reconsideration of sensible phenomena also provides the starting-point from which to move reasonably to the consideration of other dimensions of being.

Sensible phenomena have been characterized as an extended flux, a double manifold in space and time. They have also been described as mere here and now fact without any intrinsic ideality or transcendence of the here and now. They are therefore radically contingent without the remotest trace of necessity about them. Therefore, no true notion of causality can ever arise out of a consideration of phenomena as such. It was perhaps the greatest merit of Hume to have disengaged the phenomena as such, and to have pointed out the complete absence of all necessity and causality from the phenomenal given. It was the merit of Kant to have seen that, nevertheless, a science of this phenomenal manifold is possible through the imposition of a priori forms of intelligibility upon it by the understanding. This possibility is the necessary basis for the existence of all the modern positive sciences of phenomena. Of course, we need not conceive, nowadays, such a priori forms as Kant's, or regard them as natural and necessary givens in our intellective life.

Sensible phenomenality was of necessity the first aspect of being discovered by the inquiring intellect, since being is first manifested to us in sensation. But even in the prerational stage of thought it was impossible to rest in pure sensible phenomena. The natural drive of the intellect forced it to penetrate beyond phenomena and to symbolize the results of this penetration in the myths of primitive, and even civilized, man.

Unfortunately, it has been a frequent event in the history of philosophy for a philosopher to go back to acknowledging sensible phenomena as the only given or at least the only clearly given aspect of being. This has been true of all empiricists, and especially of the positivists, as was seen above. It is also true of Kantian idealists, insofar as they share with the positivists the denial of any intrinsic meaning, accessible to our intellects, in being beyond the phenomena and consequently wish to impose upon the phenomena the forms of the a priori.

For positive science, of course, the purification from concern with the non-phenomenal has been a great gain, a great help in the achievement of its own proper nature. This purification achieved by positive science has also been very instructive to the philosopher of being, since the fact of conceptualization of the phenomenal as such, of the intellective grasp of phenomena in insight, should reveal to the philosopher that phenomenality is a distinct dimension of being. This is a most important acquisition for philosophers, who often fail on their own side to appreciate phenomenality as such just as much as others may fail to appreciate any other dimensions of being besides phenomenality.

Sensible phenomenality is, then, a genuine dimension of being. But as we examine the domain of sensible phenomenality, a most interesting characteristic emerges--the polarization of phenomena around the <u>me</u> and the <u>not-me</u>. This is a fundamental datum which not even the positivist would ordinarily care to deny. We next ask ourselves, What is the immediate ground for this distinction between the me and the not-me, and the consequent polarization of phenomena? This ground must itself be a given, since there is question here of the immediate ground. The clarification of this ground brings us face to face with a new dimension of being--that of <u>psychic phenomenality</u>.

The dimension of psychic phenomenality

In contemplating the distinction between the me and the not-me, I am forced to admit that this distinction does not receive an adequate ground, even an adequate immediate ground, from the mere multiplicity of being-in-itself (I borrow this and some following terms from Sartre, although not always with the same meaning), or sensible phenomenality. I am not myself a mere multiplicity of being-in-itself, as is the sensibly given not-me. The immediately given I is a mysterious union of being-in-itself (sensible phenomenality) and being-for-itself (psychic phenomenality); it may indeed be even more than this, but it is at least a composite of the in-itself and the for-itself.

This being-for-itself, or psychic phenomenality, is the conscious manifestation of consciousness as my consciousness. This consciousness is also the consciousness of some thing; and from this latter point of view, being-for-itself is also being-for-another. "Being-for-another" here refers to consciousness precisely as tending beyond itself toward some being distinct from consciousness. This is not the meaning given by Sartre to this term.

Several remarks about psychic phenomenality are now in order. First, the clarification of the for-itself and for-another does not at all mean losing sight of that in-itself which is also a part of the composite me. What is in fact given is a mysterious union of these quite disparate elements. The immediate ground of this union is considered in the next section. But at present it is good to see yet more clearly the traits of the for-itself-and-another, and consequently its sharp distinction from the mere in-itself.

There is a strong contrast between the clarity with which sensible phenomena, or the in-itself, are presented and the obscurity with which psychic phenomena, or the for-itself-and-another, are presented. As phenomenon, the in-itself can contain no obscurity. Of course, there still remains the obscure domain of possible phenomena, which exists whether we know it or not; but so far as actual phenomena are concerned, the in-itself is given with clarity insofar as it is given at all. On the other hand, the psychic phenomena of the for-itself-and-another are invariably given with obscurity. It may be said that the latter phenomena are given with regard to their existence but not with regard to their nature. And this is with good reason; for these are the phenomena of consciousness itself, which does not have a nature but is a mode of existence.

Yet this mysterious existence which is consciousness is at the same time the existence of a peculiar kind of objectivity, of objects which are essentially and totally relative or intentional, such as the concept of a man, the concept of a dog, the concept of blindness. Psychic phenomenality is a phenomenality of intentionality, of intentional being. The scholastic notion of intentional being can itself be the object of a long treatise, but here it is sufficient merely to indicate some essential points in order to get on in the discussion of the diverse dimensions of being.

It is in the nature of intentional being to refer beyond itself, and it is in the nature of the intentional which is here discussed to refer beyond itself in two directions simultaneously. If I am here aware of consciousness as my consciousness, the intentionality of consciousness (at least of this self-conscious consciousness) is a reflexive intentionality--whatever else it may also be. And as reflexive, it is a means by which I spiritually possess myself as subject, as a self.

But if I am also aware of this consciousness as consciousness of some thing, a thing which--though object of my consciousness--is in itself indifferent to my consciousness, then the intentionality of consciousness is asymmetrically binary. As asymmetrically binary, this consciousness is the means by which I possess the other as other. This intentional possession of the other as other has diverse modes. The ordinarily discussed modes of objective knowledge by no means exhaust the possibilities. There is also the intentional possession of the other through affective connaturality, through the very act of love itself precisely as superadded to the act of simple objective knowledge. And again, there is also an intentional possession of the other arising from a lived connaturality of existence or operation--but we shall see more of this later.

Let us now summarize our results before going further. Psychic phenomenality is the phenomenality of consciousness to itself. Since this consciousness is manifested as my consciousness, as essentially reflexive intentionality, it can be called being-for-itself. Since it is also manifested as consciousness of some thing, as essentially an asymmetrical binary intentionality, it can also be called being-for-another. Hence, it has been above called being-for-itself-and-another.

The next question to consider is whether this dimension of psychic phenomenality is in any way attainable by me in the world of the not-me. In order to answer this question, it is necessary to return to the dimension of sensible phenomenality for a moment to consider what it is in itself and what is added to it in virtue of its coexistence with or dependence upon psychic phenomenality.

First, while it is true to say that the world of sensible phenomena is a world of the purely relative, insofar as it is in itself essentially unstable, impermanent (therefore non-absolute), it must also be added that this same domain can be further characterized by the lack of any intrinsic relations. Each point or instant of the phenomenal flux is what it is, factually given; but there is no intrinsic relation of dependence of one point or instant upon another, no intrinsic relation of any kind, to be discovered by the senses within this phenomenal domain itself. Such a relation would immediately mean that the point or instant possessing it is elevated above the plane of the merely here and now; but sensible phenomena have already been described as mere here and now facts without any intrinsic ideality or transcendence of the here and now.

On the other hand, in the world given existence through psychic phenomenality is a multitude of relations and relata. It is not necessary to run through the various types of relata and relations to be discovered existing in this world--some of them cannot profitably be discussed until other dimensions of being beyond the merely phenomenal have been seen. Nor is it yet possible to understand the ultimate origins of this world of relata and relations existing in the field of consciousness. But the fact that such relata and relations do exist is undeniable. Three examples will suffice.

First, ordinarily even the most sceptical of thinkers is prepared to grant that mathematical relations exist, at least in the field of consciousness, relations which give rise to a body of mathematical truth. Second, the possibility of using these mathematical relations and truths to construct theories resulting in a logical unification of the phenomena of physical nature, and even to a certain extent of biological nature, is too obvious in the present-day world to dispute. But this means that there are a priori physical relations as well as mathematical relations. Finally, in the utilization of knowledge of phenomena to bring about a state of things more favorable to our life and more conducive to our comfort, enjoyment, and profit, as well as in our general organization of our own lives, we either perceive or create hierarchies of means-ends relations concerned with our projects and goals.

One may then contrast intrinsically unrelated sensible phenomenality with the countless relations encountered in the field of psychic phenomena. However, when I consider that portion of sensible phenomena which is in some mysterious manner co-existent with my own psychic phenomena, I notice that the psychic hierarchy of means-ends relations has a projection on the plane of sensible phenomena, which may be called purposive behaviour. There can be no doubt that this purposive behaviour is immediately linked to psychic phenomena; no inference is required since the link is a given. Sensible phenomena, themselves intrinsically unrelated to any other sensible phenomena, have in this case an extrinsic relation of dependence with reference to some psychic phenomena.

With the preceding analysis in mind, whenever there is seen an instance of purposive behaviour on the plane of sensible phenomena of the not-me, I may immediately infer the coexistence of some psychic phenomena. This inference, as I have said, is immediate. I "see" the existence of psychic phenomena, or something else to which psychic phenomena are similar, in the not-me, in the very act of seeing the existence of purposive behaviour in the sensible phenomena of the not-me. This is so because purposive behaviour itself has an immediate, intrinsic, intentional reference back to the psychic phenomena which are its source. So it is that we come to understand something of the thoughts, desires, and plans of other men.

If reality is viewed from the exclusive perspective of sensible and psychic phenomena, one is confronted with an apparent welling-up of the flux of phenomena from an abyss of nothingness and again a recession into this abyss of nothingness. But surely there is more to be seen. There is given a unity of the in-itself and the for-itself in me and in other persons. What is the principle of unity--itself also given in some way--grounding this fusion of two so disparate components of reality? There is also given a unity even in mere sensible phenomena themselves, or rather a whole multitude of such unities unifying and dividing the plurality of the sensible phenomena of the world. What is the principle of such unity or unities? Again, what is this apparent abyss of nothingness whence well up the phenomena and into which they recede? The prolongation of the analysis of being in an attempt to answer these questions brings us to a consideration of <u>transphenomenal being</u>.

Transphenomenal being

In both psychic and sensible phenomena, what is most striking is the multiplicity and flux. And yet in both domains analysis reveals a clustering and a mysterious permanence. In the domain of the psychic phenomena of the me, in particular, while states may change continually, still there remains some connection between them; and also there is an "apperceptive mass" formed gradually from the succession of psychic states. This is the psychological personality, known to one first of all in its inwardness and manifested to others through the sensible phenomena with which it is interfused and which it uses as its instruments of expression. Similarly, the psychological personalities of others are revealed to one, this time only in their outwardness, through the sensible phenomena with which they are interfused and which they use as the instruments of their expression and communication. But now it may be asked, What is the real ground of the unity and permanence in the midst of the psychic flux?

The same question occurs again in considering more closely this actual interfusion of psychic and sensible phenomena in oneself and in others. Two quite diverse domains, and yet they not only coexist but coexist in an interfusion. So much is this the case that it is necessary for me to acknowledge that I am more than my consciousness, that I am more than a spirit, that my body (so far known only as a special segment of sensible phenomenality) is as much a part of me as is my consciousness. This body is not simply an instrument for the expression of my thoughts or a mere receptor instrument utilized by the real me of consciousness. Indeed, it is not that the sensible phenomena of the body are seen as mine with any difficulty; the real difficulty for most men is in coming to know that psychic phenomenality does indeed exist in us in distinction from the sensible phenomenality to which it is conjoined. The "mind-body" problem is a problem, not for those who are fully conscious of the actual flow of life, but rather for those who leave this actual flow of life in order to find the truth in an analysis of mere conceptions.

The fusion of the quite disparate domains of psychic and sensible phenomena in the unity of the me must mean that I, and other persons as well, am more than the simple sum of phenomena. This conviction is further reinforced by a consideration of the continuity and permanence of the psychological person, as noted above.

But even when one leaves the reality of man, of oneself and of other persons, and turns to consider the infra-human world, he finds a similar clustering and permanence in sensible phenomena. The phenomena are indeed a multiplicity in flux. And yet one is compelled to distinguish between the phenomena of this thing and the phenomena of that thing. It is not possible to look long at the flux of phenomena without discerning certain permanences and stabilities in space and time. And yet there is nothing in the phenomena themselves, as such, to justify this--they are only a multiplicity in flux. Whence then arises this perception of permanence and stability in the midst of sensible phenomena? Again, we are forced to acknowledge that the nuclei of permanence and stability are more than the simple sum of sensible phenomena.

All that has been said so far in this section comes to the acknowledgment that, in addition to phenomena, there is also given transphenomenal being. It is not that the reality of transphenomenal being is inferred from the existence of phenomena; rather, in the multiplicity and flow of phenomena is seen something more, which unifies and endures.

Now we have not yet said a great deal in the line of philosophy. The awareness of transphenomenal being was required for the very beginning of pre-Socratic Greek thought. And yet we have said a very great deal from the viewpoint of much of modern thought, tied down as it is by phenomenalist or idealist presuppositions. For if being is more than the phenomena, and if it is indeed known as such, then it is quite possible that the ontological speculations of the past history of philosophy should be reinstated and be entitled to a hearing again. But this is moving much too rapidly. It is necessary to resume the somewhat plodding analysis and see to what it leads us.

It was noted above that transphenomenal being presents itself, not as one homogeneous mass, but as divided into the various nuclei of unity and stability which are the persons and things of the world. The distinction already made between persons and things must immediately suggest that these diverse nuclei are not all simple "chips" from one "block." Besides mere diversity, there are also found differences in transphenomenal being. But before this insight can be followed up analytically, some observations are necessary concerning the relations between the phenomenal and the transphenomenal.

First, the transphenomenal is really prior to the phenomenal. Transphenomenal being has some stability and permanence; it endures, while the phenomena come and go. Also, the unity of the transphenomenal nucleus holds together the diversity of the phenomena. If the phenomena did not in some way depend upon the transphenomenal nucleus, they would remain a pure multiplicity. But in this case they could not manifest the unity of the transphenomenal nucleus, as they actually do. It is not the multiplicity of being which is primary; it is its unity. But this is to say that phenomena are being only in a secondary sense, that being must be said primarily of transphenomenal reality. The phenomena then are only the first manifestations of being, but the being which is manifested is preeminently transphenomenal being.

But then the phenomenal multiplicity and flux must in fact be dominated, controlled by, the transphenomenal nucleus. Thus the differences in patterns of phenomenal flux associated with diverse things must manifest differences in the transphenomenal nuclei themselves. The difference in the behaviour of a dog and a man manifests that there is some deeper difference in the transphenomenal reality of a dog and a man. The difference between the observable laws of organic and inorganic phenomena manifests some deeper difference between the transphenomenal realities of living and non-living things. The difference in observable properties between uranium and iron manifests that there is some deeper difference between the transphenomenal realities of uranium and iron.

And so also, the similarities in patterns of phenomenal flux associated with diverse things manifest similarities in the transphenomenal nuclei. Thus we know that there are indeed other persons like us, and that several samples are all of the same element, and that several dogs or cats have been seen during our walk in the park.

But in all this it must be remembered that knowing that there are differences is not at all the same as knowing in precise detail what the differences are in all cases. Who can put his finger on the precise transphenomenal difference between a dog and a cat? Who is able to distinguish sharply between all the varied types and individual characters of men? Still, it remains true that the differences and similarities in the patterns of phenomena manifest transphenomenal differences of one kind or another. We shall see much more concerning such transphenomenal differences later.

These differences and similarities of transphenomenal things are known by insight into given reality. Such insight is expressed in concepts, which, since they express attributes that are at least capable of being found in more than one individual thing, are called universal concepts. The validity of such a concept as a representation of transphenomenal reality is seen in the light of the insight itself, which stimulates and dominates the production of the concept.

What has just been said does not eliminate the need for a thorough metaphysical critique of universal concepts, to determine more clearly just how they do in fact refer to reality, as well as to understand more deeply their limitations in giving us a knowledge of reality. But we are only at the beginning; the critique can only be made profitably after one has progressed some distance in metaphysics. Such a critique may be found in the *De Ente et Essentia* of Saint Thomas Aquinas. Here we only recognize that such concepts do in fact express knowledge of similarities and differences of transphenomenal reality. Such insight and conceptualization unveil a new dimension of being beyond sensible and psychic phenomenality--the dimension of *transphenomenal objectivity*. This dimension is considered in more detail in the next section.

Transphenomenal objectivity

In order to understand the dimension of transphenomenal objectivity, it is helpful to compare it to phenomenal objectivity, that is, to sensible phenomenality. Phenomenal objectivity is equated with sensible phenomenality because the other phenomenal dimension (psychic phenomenality) is in itself not directly objectifiable. Psychic phenomenality is, in fact, nothing but consciousness itself, manifesting itself as consciousness.

Sensible phenomenality may be viewed either precisely as known to the senses or as considered by the intellect in immediate dependence upon the data of the senses. The object of the intellect and the object of the senses even here exhibit certain notable differences with respect to their *mode* of presentation; but since the immediate object of such an intellectual consideration is nothing other than sensible phenomena as attained by the senses, since, in other words, the object at each of these levels of consideration has the same general formal content, the discussion here may focus upon sensible phenomena or phenomenal objectivity, precisely as known to the senses.

Let us now summarize the characteristics of sensible phenomenality. It is, first of all, quite vivid in its appearance. For most men, the evidence of sensible phenomena is what is solid and clear, as opposed to the abstractions of speculative thought. This is the "real" for that vast majority of mankind dwelling in the cave of Plato's *Republic*. This is why Saint Thomas Aquinas declares that most men follow their senses rather than their reason.

Second, this vivid evidence is always of what is here and now; and yet the spatial and temporal instantaneousness is embedded in a "spread-out" field of space and time, a field that may thus be regarded as intrinsically multiple.

Third, the temporal extension and multiplicity arise from the fact that the evidence of phenomena is in a continual flux.

Fourth, this continual flux manifests the radical contingency of phenomena, their complete lack of stability and necessity, their mere factuality devoid of all intrinsic reason (at least so long as we consider them only in their manifestation to the senses).

Finally, as was emphasized earlier, the field of sensible phenomena shows no intrinsic relatedness between the various elements of the phenomenal manifold. It is true that one may discern relations of order, of similarity, and of difference in phenomena; but these relations are not perceived as such by the senses themselves. These relations become known only when the intellect considers in its own way the phenomena offered to it by the senses.

At each of the five points just enumerated, a notable contrast is found at the level of the transphenomenal object. First, in contrast to the vividness, the solidity and clarity, of sensible phenomena, the transphenomenal object, always known in an abstract way, must seem tenuous, obscure, and even mysterious. In the understanding of the transphenomenal being and nature of things, we gain insights that are only partial, that call for further analysis, that are possessed only in an unstable manner, with an instability in direct proportion to the difficulty of gaining the insight in the first place. (Yet it cannot be denied that these attributes of tenuity, obscurity, and mystery also have a certain place even in the intellectual analysis and organization of sensible phenomena--in the development of the positive sciences.)

Second, the transphenomenal object is not necessarily confined to the here and now; and yet what is known here is not "spread-out" in space and time. The transphenomenal object is a unit, which nevertheless is capable of realization in many diverse places and times.

Third, this unity of the transphenomenal object with independence of time or place means that in some way this object endures throughout the phenomenal flux. As will be seen clearly later, this immunity to change is not absolute as regards the transphenomenal objects of the physical world; but still they may be characterized as enduring, in opposition to the flux of phenomena.

Fourth, if such endurance is manifested, then these transphenomenal objects must partake of some degree of stability and necessity, and possess some intrinsic reason for their "resistance."

Finally, in contrast to the intrinsic unrelatedness of sensible phenomena as such, transphenomenal objects are everywhere permeated with relation. The abstract unities are essentially related to the concrete individuals in which they are realized or at least capable of realization. Between these unities themselves, many relations are seen or discovered in the course of time, not merely relations constructed by the mind but relations intrinsic to the very nature of these unities.

Despite the fact of these sharp contrasts between sensible phenomena and transphenomenal objects, the fact remains that both are objectivity, the former primarily on the plane of sense knowledge and the latter properly on the plane of intellectual knowledge. Moreover, even the sensible phenomena can be known in an objective manner by the intellect, both in insight and in conceptualization. For the moment, the "objective" is whatever is capable of being known through concepts or expressed in concepts. At this point, then, sense knowledge may be called "objective" only because it can be considered in some way in the intellect itself and there expressed in concepts. Later on, a deeper understanding of the meaning of objectivity will be possible; then it will be seen that sense knowledge is intrinsically objective, independently of its susceptibility to conceptual formulation by the intellect.

While it is true that phenomenal objectivity has been the center of attention for modern science, and therefore for the modern world, during the greater part of the history of Western civilization the primary interest was in the investigation of transphenomenal objectivity. In early Greek philosophy, the two dimensions of reality were not clearly disengaged from each other; but in the time of Socrates and Plato there was not only a disengagement but even a tendency to separate them into two quite distinct worlds. The same might be said of the Eleatic school, but it would be necessary first to examine critically the Parmenidean notion of being.

Above all in Plato is seen the sharp separation of the "unreal" world of phenomena from the "really real" world of Ideas (corresponding to transphenomenal objects), with the consequent epistemological distinction between opinion and true knowledge.

But the two worlds could not remain apart. Aristotle tried to put together the two types of object with his conception of concrete natures which manifest themselves through the phenomena. This synthesis generally corresponds with the analysis made here thus far, in which transphenomenal objectivity has been seen as governing the mode of phenomenal manifestation of transphenomenal being.

(Whether or not this transphenomenal being is in fact even more than mere transphenomenal objectivity still remains to be seen.)

Yet this Aristotelian synthesis labored under two difficulties. The first seems to have arisen because of the teaching of Aristotle's master, Plato. Plato's distinction between the "unreal" phenomena and the "really real" Ideas had its effect on Aristotle. His whole interest was focused on the dimension of the transphenomenal object. Phenomenal objects for him were only a means through which he could learn more of transphenomenal objects. But this meant that the possibility of a scientific knowledge of the phenomenal world as such was to be in general overlooked by Aristotle.

The second difficulty is not due to any oversight on the part of Aristotle but rather to the very nature of reality itself. Even supposing that we understand clearly the relation between transphenomenal objects and sensible phenomena to be one of conjunction rather than one of separation, still the problem remains of understanding how the intelligible units of transphenomenal objectivity become realized in a multitude of instances. What is the precise relation of the intelligible unity to the concrete individual? This is nothing else than the classic problem of universals. The problem has been treated in the long Aristotelian-Thomist tradition, especially by Saint Thomas Aquinas and his followers. But the solution of the problem is of necessity precarious; it is difficult to preserve the delicate balance between the intelligible unity and the concrete multiplicity.

At the moment, however, it is useful to consider the two most radical solutions that have been offered. Each proposes to eliminate the problem by eliminating one of the two poles. The fundamental direction of Plato's thought has been followed by the long tradition of idealistic philosophers. Some of these, such as Saint Augustine, have tried to keep some semblance of a balance; but the general tendency has been to minimize the value of phenomenal reality and to consider transphenomenal objectivity as the true reality which is alone really worth knowing. Some have even placed this whole domain of transphenomenal objects in the mind of God, so that all our knowledge becomes ultimately a knowledge of God. Others will speak of a priori syntheses or of an evolving world-spirit, but the basic direction remains the same.

On the other hand, the pure empiricists (now generally logical positivists) deny any except illusory status to transphenomenal objects and insist that the phenomena alone are really real. Heraclitus, Occam, Hume, and the Vienna Circle are separated by many centuries but are one in spirit.

From a merely dialectical point of view, it seems that one lesson should stand out as a result of the continuing philosophical traditions of idealism and empiricism--that neither of these can represent an adequate solution to the problem posed by the co-existence of transphenomenal and phenomenal objects. Neither of these so much solves the problem as ignores it. Exaggerated realism (idealism) and nominalism (empiricism) must both be rejected, and this leaves the field clear for a more moderate realism.

But before passing on, it seems worthwhile to add that, even if the empiricist rejection of transphenomenal objects were seriously entertained, it would not eliminate the problem of the relation of the intelligible unit to the sensible multitude. This problem only rises again, when we attempt to understand how a positive science (using intelligible unities such as concepts, laws, and theories) of sensible phenomena is possible. The positivist does not really eliminate the problem of universals but only transposes it to another level, a level at which Aristotelians and Thomists have been so far somewhat deficient in their analysis.

So much for the moment concerning transphenomenal objects. It is now possible to carry the analysis of being one step further. It has already been pointed out that the knowledge of both phenomenal and transphenomenal objects can be formulated in concepts. Such concepts must then be formally identical with the objects themselves; for what exists in the knower is the known precisely as known. But then what is it that constitutes the difference between a mere idea and a physical reality? What distinguishes the world of objects in the mind from the world of objects in reality?

And this is no time for anyone to object that the two worlds may after all be one and the same in every way, that the world may after all be only an evolving thought. The distinction between the me and the not-me emerged in the earlier analysis, and the truth of things therefore presents itself as transcendent, transcending the subjectivity of the me.

Since, then, in all the content of objectivity there is absolutely nothing to distinguish a mere concept from an existent reality, it is necessary that the existent reality possess something beyond objectivity. There is a gulf between me and the not-me, and between all other existent things; but this gulf cannot be sufficiently grounded in the order of objectivity alone. If things truly transcend in my objective knowledge, then there must be a transobjective principle conjoined with objectivity. This principle may be called transobjective existence.

Transobjective existence

The object is in one way existentially neutral. In itself it may exist either in knowledge or in reality. But in another way it is by no means existentially neutral; for if it is more than mere nothingness, it must exist somehow. It is by its very nature a relation to existence, a relation still indeterminate so far as the proper line of objectivity itself is concerned, but a relation demanding further determination if the object is to be distinguished in any way from mere nothingness. The objectivity of concepts is in fact determined by the intentional existence already discovered as given in psychic phenomenality. The objectivity of reality on the other hand is determined by what must now be called real existence. But although both the intentional existence of consciousness and real existence can be regarded as properly non-objective, it seems good to call only the latter transobjective, to distinguish it as a dimension of being with its own proper mode of presentation to us as knowers. The name is suggested by the fact that such existence appears as a something more than the objectivity which is in fact first known. (On the other hand, one is reflexively aware of the intentional existence of consciousness even before he becomes aware of objectivity formulated in concepts; therefore such intentional existence is not, at least at first, manifested as a transobjective actuality.) But in any case, what will be said of transobjective existence can, at least in part, be extended to the intentional existence of consciousness as well.

The primary relation of objectivity to existence consists in the fact that objectivity would be nothing more than pure nothingness except for existence. But it is also true that the existence is precisely the existence of this objectivity and not of any other; it is an existence determined to this objectivity. Existence is said to determine an object to exist, but that object must itself in turn determine the mode or degree or intensity of existence. Such mutual causality is familiar to Thomist philosophers. It will be considered further in a later chapter.

At this point some may be asking how it is that any such transobjective or non-objective can be known at all by the intellect. By definition, such knowledge cannot be expressed in a concept. Thomists point to the judgment as the act in which existence is known, considering that the "is" of the judgment has not only the function of the copula but also an existential meaning. But it must be said that while the judgment does indeed contain a sign of existence, still it presupposes some prior cognitive union with existence. The existence of the judgment, the existence which is the affirmation itself as well as the existence of the enuntiable which is affirmed, is nothing other than an intentional existence. It is not the real existence itself but only the sign of this real existence. Real existence then is not attained primarily and directly in the act of judgment itself; the act of judgment merely formulates, in a trans-conceptual manner, the prior attainment of existence.

But then, is real existence grasped at all? This must still be insisted upon for two reasons. First, in some mysterious manner, the difference between a mere concept (mere objectivity) and reality itself is actually understood. Second, this understanding is actually signified in the judgment, which is known to have an existential significance lacking to the mere concept. It may be said that in general real existence is attained in two ways, directly and indirectly. We possess a direct understanding of our own existence as selves, as well as a direct understanding of the existence of those things which act directly upon our senses. Indirectly, we come to some understanding of existence by reasoning from the evidence of immediately given reality to the existence of other reality which is necessarily demanded by the immediately given. A further discussion of direct understanding of existence is found in chapters seven and eight.

But since existence itself is transobjective, it cannot be directly conceptualized. As a result, existence has been ignored as a factor in the majority of philosophical systems; for philosophers seeking a scientific understanding of being have tended to restrict their consideration to what can be expressed conceptually. Since existence adds no new note to the objectivity of reality, it seems unnecessary to refer to it in our attempts to discover and systematize the intelligibility of the real. From this results the essentialism of so much of philosophy, which has been so greatly deplored by Gilson in *Being and Some Philosophers*. Even more, it is this same preoccupation with conceptualization, with conceptualizable intelligibility, that has led philosophers in general to do much less than justice to the full extent of the multi-dimensionality of being which is the subject of the present chapter.

But things do not merely exist; they also act, both so as to influence each other and so as to expand their own being through knowledge and love. This is sufficiently clear in ourselves and in those beings which directly act upon us. It is also true in the case of those beings which are not immediately given but the existence of which is known precisely because their action is a necessary presupposition for the existence of beings which are immediately given. That activity and the tendency to activity are in fact attributes of all beings is seen in chapter six.

Activity is understood as a superexistence, an overflow or superabundance of existence, beyond the existence which gives reality to the primary objectivity of things even while it is possessed by this object. And this superexistence (activity) gives reality in some manner to further degrees of objectivity, the effects or products of the activity.

A special instance of this superexistence in psychic phenomenality, the phenomenality of consciousness, was considered earlier. This existence which is consciousness is also a superexistence. Yet we may persist in distinguishing psychic phenomenality from superexistential activity as well as from existence, insofar as the latter two are here regarded as transobjective dimensions of being. Psychic phenomenality manifests itself in a manner distinct from that of transobjective existence and activity, and therefore deserves to be regarded as a distinct dimension of being. This distinct mode of manifestation is itself grounded in the contrast between consciousness and "real" existence and activity.

But as has been already suggested, transobjective activity is not only distinct from psychic phenomenality but also from transobjective existence. For it is precisely a superexistence, manifested to us, not as giving reality to primary objectivity, but rather as an overflow or superabundance from an already existent objectivity. This means that transobjective activity must be added to the list of the dimensions of being.

Transobjective activity

The fact that activity does indeed occur is undeniable. To see that it is in fact a new dimension of being requires that it be distinguished very clearly from objectivity and from existence itself.

What is conceived when we conceive that-which-is in activity? We conceive that-which-acts and the result of the activity, and we conceive the dependence of this result on that-which-acts. We know (not by conception) the existence of the result over and above that-which-acts, beyond all that the mere being of that-which-acts would entail, and yet in dependence on that-which-acts. This reveals activity to us as a superexistence, an existence of that-which-acts above and beyond the existence which gives it being, a superabundance of the being of that-which-acts. Activity itself cannot be said properly to be conceived, any more than existence can be said to be conceived. Again then, activity must be completely distinguished from objectivity.

Of course, frequently a result is seen as beyond and yet dependent upon that-which-acts only because this result was not and now is, while that-which-acts both was and is. Thus the interruption of activity is a necessary aid to noting that there is an activity. If a completely uninterrupted activity is taking place, if its intensity is unvarying, it is not known as an activity at all--unless perhaps there is some means of knowing that the effect is in fact of its nature dependent and then inferring the existence of some being which has produced the effect through its activity. In this way the activity of God in creating the world and keeping it in being can be known, through the classical proofs for the existence of God (as will be seen in Part 2).

But the fact that some of the activities of beings are interrupted does not establish that every one of their activities is distinct from their being. To understand that their activity is always distinct from the being of that-which-acts requires the understanding of activity as such as a superabundance of that-which-acts. This understanding is in a way ultimately intuitive. Only in a being which was already infinite in itself, infinitely abundant and superabundant in itself, could activity be identical with that-which-acts. Thus, in every limited being, activity is an overflow of being; to act is more than to be.

But if activity cannot be conceived, just as existence cannot be conceived, then activity must, like existence, be signified in the judgment. It is signified, not in the mere existential judgment, but in the superexistential judgment in which is affirmed, not just existence, but also the superexistence of activity. Such a judgment finds expression in a sentence containing some verb of action or an equivalent construction. The structure of such a superexistential judgment is complex; but, just as in the case of the existential judgment, it can only signify, without expressing, the real superexistence which is activity. Once again then, just as with existence itself, the judgment itself must actually presuppose some prior cognitive attainment of activity. And again, some such prior knowledge of activity is in fact given. We do understand the difference between a dynamic and a static reality, between being-in-action and being-at-rest; and we do formulate this understanding in such superexistential judgments as those of which we have been speaking. The manner in which such understanding is gained is considered in more detail later (chapter seven).

As has already been seen, existence is a determination of objectivity, giving being to objectivity and at the same time being possessed by objectivity. This idea of possession of a determination is at present necessarily obscure, and must be clarified later on. But it should be easy enough to see that activity is a determination of being in which the note of possession recedes into the background. Activity is, indeed, still a determination possessed by the agent; but it is also exercised by the agent, emanating from the agent as a kind of thrust of new determinations into an already existent world. It is this note of exercise rather than that of possession which characterizes activity as a determination of the agent.

Actually, however, this same note of exercise in addition to mere possession can be discovered in existence as well as in activity. Real things are not simply sets of objective notes held in being by the existence which they happen to possess. Rather, objectively existing things assert themselves against nothingness and in the face of other being; they exert an "existential pressure." It is this active thrust against nothingness and into being that constitutes the objective existent as more than merely an objective existent, that constitutes this objective existent as an existent subject.

It is this same active thrust, this dynamic exercise, of existence that effectively establishes and guarantees the distinction of the existent thing, not just from my knowledge (this has already been guaranteed by the distinction between objectivity and real existence), but also from any knowledge, from the knowledge even of some hypothetical Transcendental Ego. It is at this point that the real difference between transcendental idealism and realism appears. For if existence were not considered as actually exercised, but only as merely possessed, the real would appear as a world of objectivity existing, possessing existence it is true, but an existence that still remains something alien to it. In this case, objectivity could still be the objectivity of someone's thought, of the thought of some Transcendental Ego. But in fact, through the actual exercise of existence, objectivity is "transfigured," becoming now a locus of subjectivity. To subjectivity existence is no longer alien; indeed, existence as exercised may even be said in a way to emanate from subjectivity, in a manner analogous to that in which activity emanates from the same subjectivity.

We have just witnessed a "transfiguration" of being. The world of existent objectivity has been transformed into a world of dynamically existent subjectivity. This has been possible only because we have discovered a new dimension of being, that of subjectivity.

Subjectivity

The notes of subjectivity and objectivity may now be contrasted in more detail. The fundamental distinction between actual exercise and mere possession of existence has several interesting consequences. Since the here and now exercise of actual existence must be unique, the subject as such is unique--its subjectivity is as such incommunicable to any other being except God, Who is the author of subjectivity and Who is closer to things than they are to themselves. On the other hand, objectivity is by its nature communicable; it is precisely what can be objectified in knowledge. Objectivity then has a note of "exteriority"; it is a "face" of being, presented to and awaiting possible knowers. But subjectivity, on the contrary, lacks exteriority; it may be regarded as a kind of metaphysical interiority or inwardness. In an intellectual subject, this interiority becomes conscious self-possession, which is the root of freedom.

The attribute of self-possession characterizes all subjects, even those that are not really selves in the proper sense of that term (which should be applied only to intellectual subjects). Objectivity cannot be said to possess itself, since it is essentially communicable. But if objectivity does not possess itself, then it must be possessed by the subject. It must be the subject which, properly speaking, possesses all that the being is, and exercises the dynamic determinations of existence and activity. Objectivity neither exists nor acts; the subject exists with a certain degree of objectivity and acts in accordance with its degree of existence and objectivity.

A more detailed consideration of subjects and subjectivity will be presented in chapter eight. Still, a few brief comments are possible now concerning the manner in which we become aware of the subjectivity of things.

Again, just as with existence and activity, subjectivity is both affirmed and signified in the judgment, insofar as the one who is judging has discerned this dimension in being. But again, just as in the cases of existence and activity, subjectivity cannot be expressed in judgment. The intellect cannot express to itself, even through conscious intentional existence, the unique and incommunicable exercise of existence that is subjectivity. Therefore again, if subjectivity is truly grasped, whether in itself (as in the case of the subjectivity of the knower himself) or in some vicarious manner (as in the case of the subjectivity of some being distinct from the knower), it is in some manner prior to the act of judgment. Judgment only signifies and affirms what is already grasped in this case in some non-judgmental as well as non-conceptual manner.

I do in fact possess consciousness of myself as subject in my own awareness of my activity, of my tendencies to activity of various kinds, and of my own exercise of my existence. This awareness is immediate and not susceptible of direct conceptual formulation. One may say that I do not so much see as feel, to speak metaphorically.

To know the subjectivity of some other being of course appears to be like a square circle. How can the incommunicable communicate itself to me? And yet, although to the intellect the subjectivity of the other remains unattainable in itself, still there is a vicarious grasp of this subjectivity when, through our affective response, we allow this subjectivity to resonate in us; and there follows a resultant tendency toward, union with, the real subjectivity of the other. This is, of course, to speak somewhat figuratively; the figure will be more fully explained in chapter eight. In interpersonal relations, in poetic intuition, in mystical experience, there does arise a union with the subjectivity of the other, always non-objective, and always founded on an at least vicarious grasp of this subjectivity. Perhaps in the case of the mystical experience of God Himself, this grasp of subjectivity is even more than vicarious, because of God's intimate presence in the soul. Gabriel Marcel, Martin Buber, Jacques Maritain, and Saint John of the Cross have all affirmed the actuality of union through love in diverse ways.

Therefore, to know the being of the not-me in its dimension of subjectivity requires awareness of the mystery of love and of the good; this dimension emerges as a result of affective response to the goodness of things. This means that in order to understand being the analysis of the mere given truth is not sufficient, unless it is prolonged to consider things as the object of our love. But if it is true, as was said in the previous section, that the final transcendence of the idealist position depends on the understanding of the dimension of subjectivity in things, then the difference between idealism and realism is more than a purely intellectual difference; all will depend on the affective relation to others, interpersonal and intersubjective relation, love, and on the extent of reflective recollection concerning these things in the very foundations of philosophical speculation.

In the analysis of being we have now come upon a universe of discrete subjects, each unique, but with which we may come into union through love, and through the knowledge arising from love, as well as through knowledge in the ordinary sense. But in fact there seems to be even more than union with other subjects; in a way there seems even to be a unity of all things, a unity transcending all differences and distinctions even of subjects themselves. Further investigation of this "unity" of which we are obscurely aware will uncover yet another distinct dimension of being.

Createdness

At this point in the analysis, there is needed, even more than before, a certain sensitivity of discernment and a silent attentiveness in the face of being. The awareness we are seeking to clarify is in itself very obscure and delicate and can easily be ignored in the face of the more obvious aspects of reality.

Yet in fact it has not been ignored in the history of philosophy. The obscure awareness of unity underlying the multiplicity of things is at the bottom of the philosophical spirit, even among the pre-Socratics. Indeed, among many, this unity has been so stressed as to destroy the true multiplicity of things, with a resultant monism or pantheism. Especially in the Upanishads is found this total absorption of multiplicity into deeper unity, with the confusion of the finite self and the Infinite Self.

But such pantheist or monist reduction of multiplicity to unity would deny the evidence that has been uncovered in the preceding analysis. Granted that there is such unity, deeper than the diversity in things, the unity cannot exist on the same level as the diversity, so as to deny the diversity. The unity must be prior to the diversity, prior in reality itself and not merely in knowledge. This unity is to be found in the Infinite Being, on which all other being depends for being. In this Infinite Being or Infinite Self is contained all the being of all other subjects, in a higher way; but these other subjects in their very subjectivity are still distinct from the Infinite

Self. From this Infinite Self flows the being of all other subjects, but these other subjects stand distinct in their own subjectivity from the Infinite Self. But such a dependence in being must be called creation, rather than emanation. Thus the obscure awareness of unity underlying all the multiplicity of things turns out to be an awareness of the createdness of things.

It should be noted that it is not a process of discursive reason, a "proof" of the existence of God, that is being here described. Rather, I am simply seeking to clarify a primitive and obscure intuition of the fundamental unity of all things, an intuition which, unclarified, would strongly suggest a pantheistic or monistic reality. There is not here a proof but rather a motivation for the construction of rational proofs of the existence of God.

But a possible objection must be faced. If this obscure awareness of unity is in fact an immediate awareness of the dependence of finite subjects on the Infinite Self, and of the supereminent presence of the being of finite subjects in the Infinite Self, then is there not required for such awareness of unity an immediate awareness of the Infinite Self? It seems that this question must be answered in the affirmative. Such an immediate awareness of the Infinite Self is given, not a vision of this Self (that would be the beatific vision, accessible only through grace and the light of glory), but an obscure presence, felt rather than seen. It seems proper to describe this, as does Maritain, as a natural mystical experience. But this experience must exist, at least in germ, in every man. That it should sometimes come to dominate the life of a poet, a Western philosopher, or an Indian sage, in diverse ways, is the result of a happy chance, an ascetical effort, or the special gift of God.

By now perhaps, many questions may have occurred concerning the manner in which this natural mystical experience takes place, or, as some might prefer, how we come to the perception of the createdness of things. Such questions will be considered in chapter nine.

Seven distinct dimensions of being have been enumerated: sensible phenomenality, psychic phenomenality, transphenomenal objectivity, transobjective existence, transobjective activity, subjectivity, and createdness. Are there perhaps more? I should at this time hesitate to deny the possibility. But, in any event, we are now in a favorable position to attempt the development of a metaphysics grounded in the awareness of the multi-dimensionality of being.

One last item remains before moving on. The analysis began at the level of sensible phenomenality. Now that we have moved so far beyond that point, it will be helpful to reconsider the true status of sensible phenomenality in the light of the understanding of the multi-dimensionality of being.

Sensible phenomenality and transphenomenal being

We have by now long since moved past the standpoint of those who maintain that the phenomena are the true being of things. And yet it is not true, as has been seen, that the phenomena are "illusion" as opposed to truth, or mere "appearance" as opposed to being. They are indeed an aspect of the real, not only the first manifestation of multi-dimensional being, but also the first aspect of this being which is manifested to us. This latter is certain from the fact of the polarization of the phenomena with reference to the me and the not-me, even on the plane of phenomenality itself. The phenomena are not mere subjective affections of me as a knower; they are real.

The sensible phenomena reveal to the knower, first themselves, but then also something of the transphenomenal objectivity of things, of the things which produce these phenomena. Since all other knowledge of objectivity depends upon that objectivity which is immediately given, it follows that the sensible phenomena are the key to an understanding of any transphenomenal object.

But this is not all. Only knowledge referring to objectivity can be formulated conceptually. This means that any attempt to formulate in a conceptual manner the knowledge of the transobjective dimensions of being depends on our ability to find some analogy of these dimensions to the domain of objectivity or to something in the domain of objectivity. But it will soon be clear that the scientific knowledge of any domain of reality, or even of being itself, must be of such a kind as to be formulable conceptually. This means that all scientific knowledge, including that of being itself, must ultimately depend upon objectivity and therefore upon sensible phenomenality.

Sensible phenomenality is in a way the humblest, most unstable, most contingent aspect of being. Yet on it, as on a necessary foundation, must be constructed the entire edifice of human scientific knowledge in every domain.

Chapter 2

THE POSSIBILITY OF METAPHYSICS

In the preceding chapter the question of whether being is more than phenomena was answered by the discovery of the multi-dimensionality of being. That multi-dimensional being does in fact exist is evident. But it may still be asked how this being is adequately distinguished from nothingness. Is being's opposition to and distinction from nothingness perhaps self-explanatory? Does the inner nature of being account for its being? Or is the being we see perhaps dependent on something else? And if so, on what?

But before we can answer the question, "Why does anything exist at all?" we must first consider in more detail what it is that exists, with regard to its inner structure. A knowledge of the general structure of the being we see before us will give the necessary clues as to where to look for its reason for being (and also for an understanding of how it is known in its multi-dimensionality).

Such an investigation of what constitutes being as being (as opposed to mere nothingness) has, since Aristotle, been called a metaphysical investigation. Scientific knowledge about this subject is metaphysics. But the possibility of a scientific knowledge of being as being at first seems rather dubious. In order to see this, consider briefly the nature of scientific knowledge.

Scientific knowledge

In general, scientific knowledge is the most perfect knowledge of whatever domain of truth is in question. But "most perfect" must not be understood as "most complete"; scientific knowledge possesses a perfection proper to its present state in a human intellect, for which the attainment of truth is never exhaustive, always increasing, essentially limited. Now, without any regard for particular subject-matters, what are the attributes of such human scientific knowledge?

Briefly, human scientific knowledge should be objective, systematic, certain, precise, and clear. Other, subsidiary attributes also appear in the analysis which follows.

It was seen in the preceding chapter that human intellectual consciousness embraces both objective and non-objective awareness. Things therefore are present both objectively and non-objectively; being reveals itself in both objective presence and non-objective presence. By presence is meant the union of some being as other with an intellectual existent.

Since consciousness is specified or determined by that of which one is conscious, objective and non-objective awareness are specified and determined by objective and non-objective presence. One difference between these two modes of presence has already been seen, namely that the content of objective presence is formulable directly in a concept while that of non-objective presence is not. This difference, however, is traceable to deeper differences in the two modes of presence.

The content of objective presence is determinate and limited to a given order of being; thus, despite the obscurity with which it is frequently known, it is still in some way a clear-cut intelligible content. This permits a sharp distinction between the knower, the known, and other things that are not known in this particular objective knowledge. But it is quite otherwise with non-objective presence. In the preceding chapter, five distinct modes of non-objective presence appeared: psychic phenomenality, existence, activity, subjectivity, and createdness. It is especially interesting that all five of these modes are closely linked with, are aspects of, existence. Now existence, unlike objective intelligibility, transcends all determinate orders and includes the knower, the act of knowledge, what is known, all that can be known--all that _is_ in any way. It is this transcendence of all determinate orders which makes existence and the other dimensions of being closely allied with existence unconceptualizable, while it is confinement within a determinate order of being that makes objectivity conceptualizable.

Since, then, the content of non-objective presence transcends all determinate orders of being, this content is in a way essentially mysterious and indeterminate to us. But the content of objective presence, while perhaps incomplete and for that reason extrinsically mysterious and indeterminate, is in fact a determinate content in itself. Now, knowledge is perfect insofar as it is more determinate. Hence, if scientific knowledge is perfect human knowledge, it must be of the more determinate, and therefore objective. (Note that we are always speaking of human knowledge; God does in fact possess a determinate knowledge of existence, but this is only because He alone is capable of comprehending in one act of knowledge all the intelligible richness of existence.)

A further contrast can be discovered between objective and non-objective presence. In objective presence, the other (or the self) is attained as other, but not in its very otherness (or selfness). In non-objective presence, the very otherness of the other (or the selfness of the self) becomes present. The first presence is _presence across a gulf_; the second is much more intimate, in some cases a true union of diverse subjectivities, intersubjectivity. In the first, the other (or self) is present only in one or other of its objective aspects or facets; but in the second, the other (or self) is present in the fullness of its being. In the first, there remains a gulf between, the sharp distinction spoken of from another point of view in the previous paragraph. But in the second, the gulf disappears; in the intimacy of non-objective presence the knower and the known are much more mutually involved in their being.

Since there is a more intimate presence and mutual involvement of being in non-objective presence than in objective presence, non-objective awareness or knowledge has less of that _transcendence of the knower as such_, which is essential to all knowledge, than does objective knowledge. Transcendence still remains, but it is not as sharp. Now part of the perfection of knowledge consists in its complete transcendence of the knower as a knower. Therefore, if scientific knowledge is perfect human knowledge, it must be of the more transcendent, and again therefore objective rather than non-objective. (But again bear in mind that we are speaking of human knowledge; God knows both the objective and the non-objective dimensions of things, but all in the same subsistent act of intelligence which is identical with Himself and utterly distinct from all other things.)

It may be objected that in fact scientific knowledge cannot be merely objective, since such knowledge requires not only conceptualization but also judgment, the affirmation of existence and activity. This is in a way true. But the affirmation of existence and activity in scientific knowledge is simply intended to declare that the concepts refer to reality; this affirmation simply asserts the validity of the objective knowledge. The non-objective awareness of existence and activity is in fact a necessary presupposition for scientific knowledge; but it is not itself what is studied in such knowledge, unless perhaps there be, in a manner yet to be seen, a scientific knowledge of being as being, a scientific metaphysics.

Scientific knowledge, then, is objective knowledge. Objective intellectual knowledge can be divided in several ways; but only one of these divisions is of special interest here--that between the objective component of common sense knowledge, the objective component of literary knowledge, and scientific knowledge. Common sense knowledge is the spontaneous, unreflective judgment of the undisciplined intellect in the presence of the real. It is obscure, global, confused, unreflective, uncritical, with a resultant mixture of truth, unfounded belief, mere opinion, and prejudice. It is necessarily a most imperfect knowledge. The truth in it needs to be extracted from the mixture by critical reflection.

Literary knowledge is an intellectual knowledge embodied in a wealth of refined sense-imagery as contrasted with the crude concomitant sense-imagery of common sense. The use of such refined imagery enables ideas themselves to be much more refined and causes a much more vivid presentation of the thing known--for the human intellect sees more easily what is embodied in the sensible, and indeed always requires some minimum of sensible embodiment. The more vivid presentation through refined imagery attracts in a special manner not only the cognitive but also the appetitive powers, this affective response bringing about a greater degree of non-objective presence. Therefore the objective component of literary knowledge is suffused with an extraordinary degree of non-objective presence as well, to constitute the total aesthetic experience. Literary knowledge may be gained from reading the great prose and poetry works of literature, but also from the experience of any other of the works of the fine arts. There even exists a literary philosophy, which I have considered elsewhere.

Yet literary knowledge is not without its imperfections. While isolated insight is deepened and strengthened, the interrelations of insights, in particular of complementary and balancing insights are frequently missed. It is easy to ignore certain truths because of fascination with others; when this tendency affects "literary philosophy," philosophy will appear as a mere succession of diverse views, or as a pendulum oscillating to and from all the diverse points of the compass. The literary knowledge of the man of culture is far beyond the crudity of common sense, but it remains imperfect in the line of objective human intellectual knowledge.

We come back then, to a further consideration of scientific knowledge, as perfect human intellectual knowledge. Besides being objective, it should also be systematic. It is a fact of human experience that the penetration of any reality in knowledge can only be accomplished in a gradual manner. It is necessary for us to piece together slowly and painfully a multiplicity of notions, little "bits," in order to acquire the very inadequate knowledge that can be gained even of the lowest beings. This fact can be understood when the position of the human intellect at the bottom of the hierarchy of intellects is considered. The higher the intellect, the more that can be grasped in one notion; the lower the intellect, the more notions that are required to know the same reality. The angels can grasp in one act of knowledge what demands from us many such acts, and the higher angels need fewer such acts than do the lower angels. And God knows everything in one act of knowledge which is Himself.

If then, we are to know any aspect or domain of reality with a perfect knowledge, perfect relative to the condition of our intellect and to the state of this intellect at this particular point in space and time, we must somehow link together our various "bits" of knowledge about this aspect or domain of reality into the unity of a system. Through such a system the knowledge of the diverse and sometimes seemingly incompatible aspects of the reality in question can be related, balanced, and understood in the light of a fundamental unity.

Since every such system must have some kind of unity, every scientific knowledge centers around certain fundamental principles, key ideas and propositions on which the rest of the system completely depends. Binding together all the fragments of the system are some logical relations, relations dependent first on the related knowledges but ultimately in some manner on the known reality itself. The logical structure makes intellectual discourse within the system relatively easy.

Since it is a defect for knowledge to be uncertain, scientific knowledge should be certain knowledge, and therefore in some way permanent. But these attributes mean that the object of scientific knowledge must be somehow necessary--not able to be other than what it is. (Even a hypothetical explanatory construction must be in its manner necessary, immutable, not subject in itself to the spatio-temporal flow.)

It is obvious that scientific knowledge has to be precise and clear as far as is possible considering the nature of its object. Precision is the sharp distinction of a given content from other contents of knowledge. Clarity is presentation of a content without concealment of anything contained in it. And this precision and clarity require a more elaborate technical terminology as a medium of expression of scientific knowledge.

Yet, although this technical terminology is somewhat more elaborate than ordinary language, from another point of view, scientific knowledge must aim at an economy of concomitant sense-imagery. The less complex the concomitant sense-imagery, the more clearly the interrelations of diverse intelligible contents can be seen. Ideally, the explicit imagery should be composed only of linguistic or "mathematical" symbols, with all other associated images left in the implicit, subconscious state.

The attributes enumerated should indicate that scientific knowledge is not a goal easy to attain. One may also suspect that it might be attained in diverse ways, because of the diversity of things studied and the diverse possible methods of systematization. One example of this diversity is in the difference between the structure of modern physical sciences and that of the philosophical knowledges.

The division and definition of scientific knowledges

Since every knowledge is determined by what is known, it follows that knowledges should be distinguished according to the diversity of what is known. Since scientific knowledge is an objective knowledge, scientific knowledge should be divided according to the object which is known. Since the same reality may be the object of more than one science (as, for example, man is an object of philosophy and of experimental psychology), one must distinguish between the object materially considered as a thing and the object formally considered as an object of knowledge, that is, the object as seen from some special point of view. Clearly, it must be this latter which governs the distinction of scientific knowledges. A given scientific knowledge can be defined by stating its object materially and then formally considered. This is sometimes also said to be giving the material and formal subject of the science. But it may happen sometimes that even this is not enough adequately to distinguish two sciences, as in fact is the case with the scholastic problem of distinguishing as scientific knowledges sacred theology and the beatific vision. These knowledges are both knowledges of God known under the aspect of His deity manifesting itself to creatures. They both have the same object materially considered (God), and the same object formally considered (His deity manifesting itself to creatures). Why then are they not one scientific knowledge?

At this point, the scholastics introduced a further subtlety into the manner of distinguishing sciences, the distinction between the formal object as an object in the knower and the formal object as in the thing. Since scientific knowledge is in the knower, it is the formal object as an object in the knower which ultimately distinguishes sciences. Thus in the case just considered, God in His deity manifesting itself to creatures through faith using reason is the object considered formally as an object in the knower, for sacred theology; but God in His deity manifesting itself to creatures through the light of glory (in the beatific vision) is the object considered formally as an object in the knower, for the beatific vision.

Thus the most complete manner of defining a scientific knowledge is to give the object first as materially considered, then as formally considered as an object in the knower. We should now like to know how the science of metaphysics is to be defined, if it exists. But no definition will be attempted until after some preliminary remarks concerning the general area of metaphysics.

Can there be a scientific
knowledge of being as being?

If there is a scientific knowledge of being as being, its formal object must be existence itself. All the terms of such a knowledge must contain an implicit or explicit reference to existence. But it has already been seen that existence is a trans-object. So also then must be all metaphysical terms, such as being, good, subject, causal efficacy, tendency, etc. Even those terms used to describe the structure of objectivity itself must contain some implicit reference to existence, insofar as they are of interest to the metaphysician.

But then it seems that a scientific knowledge of being as being is impossible. Such a science would have to be objective, yet the object of this science is necessarily transobjective. Science is expressed in concepts, but the transobjective cannot be expressed in concepts. Metaphysics, seemingly, must either be confined to the merely literary realm or be an illusion.

But do not underestimate the versatility of the human intellect. Although direct conceptualization of the transobjective is impossible for us, still there remains the possibility of an indirect conceptualization through the medium of a priori constructs. An a priori construct here means any work of the intellect other than simple concept-formation under the simply objective evidence of the immediately objective aspects of things. Such a priori constructs are found throughout the life of the intellect. Logical relations; negative entities like evil, nothingness, and privation; mathematical constructs; physical theories; any system of human knowledge in any domain--all these require at least some a priori construction by the intellect. It is a priori because it is not the result of mere imposition by reality or immediate givenness in experience (even in experience as viewed under the light of the intellect), but rather requires a further active effort on the part of the intellect itself.

Some a priori constructs are obviously grounded in the evidence of the actually real itself, such as those by which are understood blindness, nothingness, evil. Others are not so obviously grounded in such evidence, such as transfinite numbers, the idea of a unicorn, etc. And there may be more or less remote foundation of such constructs in the evidence of the actually real, as can be seen in the structure of physical science, with its diversity of concepts, laws, and theories. Clearly, a priori construction is a highly diversified activity, operating in widely diverse fields of knowledge. May a priori construction be an aid in the constitution of metaphysics as an objective science of the transobjective? Of course, if metaphysics is constituted as an objective science through the a priori construction of its content, then we are perilously close to Kant. But if this a priori construction is everywhere grounded in the evidence of the non-objective but actually real, if such constructs have as their function not to express, but only to point out and signify, what metaphysics is really after, namely the transobjective evidence of transobjective being, then we bypass Kant and come to a deeper understanding of realist metaphysics.

It was already seen in chapter one that real existence, once known, is signified in the act of judgment. But the intentional existence which constitutes the judgment as a judgment cannot be said to express the real existence, which is unique and incommunicable. The intentional existence constituting the judgment as a judgment is itself an a priori construct (though not a concept). Still, its reference to real existence is guaranteed by the reflexivity of spirit; it is the same intellect in the same soul which is aware, non-objectively, of real existence, and which signifies this real existence in the intentional existence of judgment, and which is reflexively aware of this procedure as a whole.

But this a priori construct which is the intentional existence of the act of judgment does not yet give the metaphysical knowledge of existence. For this construct is itself non-objective, while the a priori constructs of metaphysics as a science must be objective. Another a priori construct is necessary, this one founded on the first, and therefore remotely on the evidence of real existence itself, a constructed concept which should rather be called a meta-concept (since its function, unlike that of ordinary concepts, is to refer beyond the objective to transobjective existence). This constructed meta-concept must be objective; therefore, even more than does the intentional existence of the act of judgment, this meta-concept only points out and signifies real existence--it does not express it.

We come now to the most important question. How can objective elements be utilized in such a constructed meta-concept, to refer beyond the plane of objectivity? And what elements can be utilized to this purpose? These questions cannot be answered in detail at this point; they are reconsidered in chapter four, after a preliminary analysis of objectivity and its structure in chapter three. However, a few general remarks are in order at this point.

First, since the dimensions of being in existence and objectivity are quite diverse, one is unable to rely on any simple analogy of the one to the other. But perhaps it is possible to find some relations within the field of objectivity which are similar to the relations between objectivity and existence. If so, a proportionality may be conceived in the following manner:

$$\text{Given: } R_{12}(O_1O_2) \text{ and } R_{OE}(O_NE_N). \text{ Then } R_{12} \sim R_{OE}.$$

In this proportionality, O_1 and O_2 are diverse elements or levels in the field of objectivity. R_{12} is a relation of element or level (1) to element or level (2). $R_{12}(O_1O_2)$ means that O_1 has the relation R_{12} to O_2. O_N is the entire field of objectivity. E_N is the entire field of existence. R_{OE} and $R_{OE}(O_NE_N)$ have meanings analogous to those given for R_{12} and $R_{12}(O_1O_2)$. Therefore, R_{OE} is a relation of O to E, while $R_{OE}(O_NE_N)$ means that O_N has the relation R_{OE} to O_N. "$\sim$" means "is similar to." Similar symbolism, with some additions, will be employed in the detailed analysis of the meta-concept of being later on. This notation may appear unwieldy at first to those unfamiliar with the methods of symbolic logic, but I believe that in the long run some degree of simplification results.

Notice that in this proportionality the term E_N is an unknown which may be considered as defined by the other three terms and the accompanying relations. But how can such a definition be justified? How are we justified in asserting a similarity of relations in the field of objectivity (which can be understood objectively) with relations between objectivity and existence (which cannot yet be understood objectively). It is necessary here to recall that this entire construction takes place in the context of a non-objective, but nevertheless authentic, understanding of real existence. It is this understanding which can guide us to choose relations in the field of objectivity which are truly isomorphic with those between objectivity and existence, and which are seen as truly isomorphic. In this manner, E_N may be defined through one or more such proportionalities, pointing out in each case the precise point of similarity.

What are the elements to be chosen in the field of objectivity, in order to construct the proportionalities? Unfortunately, this cannot be decided at the present moment, not until we have conducted a preliminary analysis of objectivity and its structure. But in any event, the construction of a meta-concept of existence and of being as existing at least no longer appears impossible in principle.

Still, another difficulty remains to be considered. The meta-concept of existence that has just been considered will be defined only in extrinsic, together with relational, terms. Does this mean that there is no knowledge in metaphysics of the intrinsic content of existence? In a way it must mean this, if one is still looking for a conceptual expression of existence itself. However, it must always be remembered that this meta-concept is evolved in dependence upon the non-objective awareness of the real existence exercised by ourselves and by those things which act upon us, and that this meta-concept always has an essential reference to and signification of this real existence. None of the meta-concepts of metaphysics expresses the intrinsic content of existence, and yet all should be suffused with a "sense of existence."

We are now in a better position to define what metaphysics as a science will be, if the development of this science is indeed possible. Earlier it was pointed out that if metaphysics is a science, its formal object must be existence, and that all the terms of such a knowledge must contain an implicit or an explicit reference to existence. It was since seen that any "conception" of existence or of terms essentially referring to existence must be through what have been called meta-concepts. Such meta-concepts, a priori constructs under the light of the non-objective evidence of being, employing proportionalities of various kinds, do not seem to be a priori impossible. Many difficulties remain, but one is tempted at least to try to build up a metaphysical science. In the light of the method of definition of sciences seen earlier, metaphysics may be defined as the science of being as existing, known through a priori constructed meta-concepts which express the objective and merely signify the non-objective dimensions of being.

The first task of metaphysics will be to arrive at meta-concepts of existence and of being. But, as has already been shown, this presupposes some understanding of the field of objectivity. Accordingly, even before metaphysics can be begun, there is necessary a preliminary analysis of objectivity. This analysis will, however, not only provide a base for the analogical formulation of higher meta-concepts of the various dimensions of being; it will also give an appreciable understanding of what does exist and of the structure of the concrete existent. All of this objective and conceptually formulated understanding can later be assumed into the structure of metaphysics itself and reformulated in meta-conceptual terms.

One may ask whether the analysis should focus upon the phenomenal or the transphenomenal domain of objectivity. The transphenomenal dimension is of primary importance, since here can be found more of the inner structure of being. But the phenomenal is the necessary means for the manifestation of the transphenomenal; moreover, it too is part of the structure of being. And although the base for the analogical formulation of meta-concepts has historically been in the field of transphenomenal objectivity, it is quite possible that the field of phenomenal objectivity could also be of service here.

It is not necessary to make the analysis of objectivity very detailed, if that were possible. In fact, a quite general analysis of this objectivity is sufficient to enable us eventually to come to understand the general structure and reason for being. The acquaintance with phenomenal objectivity which was gained in chapter one, together with the more detailed analysis of transphenomenal objectivity in chapter three, will be enough to "get going" in metaphysics. The detailed analysis of phenomenal objectivity is the proper concern of the positive sciences, while the analysis of transphenomenal objectivity for itself, at least that analysis based on the knowledge of the physical universe, is the concern of the philosophy of nature. Thus, in the next chapter, we leave metaphysics for the time being in order to investigate <u>nature</u>, though still from a philosophical point of view.

Chapter 3

THE ANALYSIS OF OBJECTIVITY

The distinction and relations between phenomenal and transphenomenal objects have been considered in chapter one. It was seen there that the reality of the phenomenal object is a secondary and derived reality, while the primary real is the transphenomenal being with its transphenomenal objectivity. The flux of phenomenal objects is a manifestation of transphenomenal objectivity to us; the diverse groupings and patterns of phenomenal objects reveal the diversity of things and types of things in the universe of transphenomenal being. They do this by revealing the diversity of structure and of function in the physical universe. Structure refers to the organization of the diverse heterogeneous parts of the things of the physical universe and their phenomenal manifestations; function refers to the mode of dynamism or modes of dynamism characteristic of these things and manifested in their phenomena.

The actual activity itself is, as was seen in chapter one, a superexistential dimension of being which must necessarily elude the analysis of objectivity. But note that the phenomenal manifestation of structure and function is entirely dependent on the activity and interactivity of things. Moreover, the entire intelligibility of both structure and function is derived from their relations to such activity and interactivity.

But if activity as such eludes the analysis of objects, what is this dynamism to which function refers? If one is confined to the order of objects alone, what meaning can be assigned to dynamism and to function? First, it has already been seen that transphenomenal objectivity is in some manner the norm and regulator of phenomenal objectivity. It is, of course, such a norm and regulator precisely through the medium of activity; but since the analysis of objects does not consider activity as such, this analysis must simply accept the normative and regulative function of transphenomenal objectivity as a mysterious fact. So also, the influence which the transphenomenal things themselves exert on each other is due to activity but must be accepted only as a mysterious fact, as far as the mere analysis of objects is concerned. A necessity is seen underlying this fact, as will be evident when we consider the principle that "Whatever is changed is changed by another." But this necessity must remain essentially mysterious at the present level of analysis.

Function and dynamism, then, at the level of objectivity, refer to the mysteriously necessary fact of regulation of the phenomenal by the transphenomenal and of the "influence" exerted by transphenomenal things upon each other so as to change the transphenomenal objective structure of each other. At the level of phenomenal objectivity alone, function and dynamism must refer only to the mysteriously necessary correlations of one set of phenomena with another. But from this point on we shall be interested primarily in transphenomenal objectivity; phenomenal objectivity will be of interest only insofar as it manifests the transphenomenal.

Variations in objectivity

Earlier, the flux of phenomenal objects was contrasted with the relative stability of transphenomenal objects. However, this invariance is only relative; as a matter of fact there is considerable variation in the transphenomenal object. Such change is necessarily manifested only through variation in the grouping and pattern of phenomena, through a variation in the law of phenomenal manifestation for the thing.

Let us first consider a few particular cases of such variation in the transphenomenal object. Temperature variation is first of all a variation in the measurement of phenomena, but it also means some kind of variation in the thing itself. This variation may be slight or it may be great, but in some manner it affects the state of being and the dynamism of the thing. If the pattern of phenomena is altered, then the norm and regulator of the phenomena--the transphenomenal object--must also be altered in some manner. The fact that we are unable to conceive clearly the "nature of heat" means that the variation in the transphenomenal object here will remain rather obscure, but this is not to deny that it takes place.

Another example of such a transient modification appears in the case of illness. Even if the nature of the illness is not understood, the fact remains that it does modify the dynamism of the sick person in some manner; but this must mean that the transphenomenal object itself is altered. Still another example occurs in our succession of sense experiences. This succession results in a change in the dynamism of the human person who has these experiences. Some make us sad; some make us happy. Some soothe us to rest; others stir us to activity. Here again, there is variation in the transphenomenal as well as in the phenomenal object.

Besides such superficial and transient variations, there are given other variations, still superficial but no longer quite as transient. Temperature variation was considered a moment ago; sufficient variation of temperature will result in a change of state --e.g. from ice to water or from water to steam. Change of state means a considerable variation in the law of phenomenal manifestation for the thing, and therefore a considerable variation in the transphenomenal object. And this variation is somewhat more permanent than temperature variation; it requires much more heat to accomplish a change of state from ice to water at zero degrees Centigrade than it does to raise either ice or water one degree Centigrade, and the difference is even greater for a change of state from water to steam at one hundred degrees Centigrade. Yet closer observation and investigation will reveal that the change here is still relatively superficial; the substance before us is still H_20.

Another example of such a superficial, yet more permanent, modification is a chronic weakness which may have resulted from some illness, such as a weakness of the heart resulting from rheumatic fever. Still another is the transformation of the human person effected through a successful liberal education. It is still the same person, but his powers of thought and action have been enormously broadened and intensified.

There are also much more fundamental variations in the transphenomenal object. An especially evident case is the death of a living thing. What was, even in its lowest forms, a highly complicated organic structure, with the peculiar functions of one or more of the levels of life, such as nutrition, growth and development, reproduction, locomotion, sensation, intellection and volition, now gradually ceases its vital activity and finally degenerates in its structure into various non-living components. It may be difficult to tell just when the passage from life to death is made, but the two terms are finally in sharp contrast with each other. The variation in the spatio-temporal pattern of phenomena is ordinarily quite obvious, and this manifests very clearly the fundamental change at the transphenomenal level. We may not understand very clearly the differences in transphenomenal objectivity between a dog and a cat, but we can understand clearly the difference between a dog and a dead dog, between a cat and a dead cat, especially some time after death.

The reverse transition, from inanimate matter to living matter, is equally striking. Matter, the dynamism of which was formerly circumscribed by the laws of physics and chemistry, is now found to possess a new dynamism, the dynamism of the living thing. It can now perform operations by itself which it could not formerly perform even under the guidance of the intelligence of man, such as reproduction, sensation, etc.

It is more difficult to discover examples of fundamental as distinguished from merely superficial change when one considers only the inanimate world. It is difficult here to distinguish clearly between specific types of dynamism. Therefore it is difficult to say whether there is a variation in the specific type of dynamism (which would mean a fundamental change) or a relatively superficial variation in the manner in which the same basic dynamism is exercised. If all the properties of crystals, molecules, atoms, and subatomic particles can be reduced to certain properties generic to all matter and differing only in degree, such as inertia and gravitation (if these are in any way ultimately distinct), elasticity, electromagnetism, microcosmic attraction forces in the nucleus of the atom, and macrocosmic repulsion forces possibly existing between the galaxies, then it is quite possible that the only fundamental diversity in the inanimate world exists at the level of the subatomic particles or even lower, in yet undiscovered domains. On the other hand, if genuinely new properties, irreducible to the lower, appear as the degree of organization increases from sub-atoms to atoms to molecules to crystals, then fundamental diversity will exist between these various levels at least, and perhaps also within each level. Of course, in either alternative there must exist a fundamental diversity between what is ordinarily called matter and that mysterious intermatter of "empty" space, in which exist so many strange fields and vibrations. Many polemics have been made against "aether," and it has been replaced by a "space-time continuum." But this continuum has lurking behind it at least a ghost of aether. However unnecessary such aether may have become for physics (which considers the phenomenal rather than the transphenomenal) in its present state, intermatter is still a datum for philosophers.

At present, I am inclined to accept the possibility of the reduction of all diversity in the inanimate world to the diversity between subatomic particles and the diversity between matter and intermatter, since in fact modern science seems to point the way toward such reduction. But there really does not seem to be any solid basis for decision at this point in the development of human knowledge.

In the animate world, transition from one specific type of dynamism to another is difficult to observe. In fact it does occur in the gradual degneration of complex living organisms at the animal or human level, when individual cells or groups of cells may carry on vital functions for a time at the animal or vegetable level. It may also occur if some of the great leaps postulated by a general theory of evolution actually take place.

What is clear is that there are in fact at least three distinct types of dynamism in the animate world, giving rise to the distinction between plants, animals, and men. The dividing lines may be difficult to discern in many cases; but the sharp distinction between vegetative, sentient, and rational activity--or better here, dynamism and function--makes evident a fundamental diversity in transphenomenal objectivity and being. The phenomenal and transphenomenal diversity here should be more fully explained in biology and philosophical psychology, but it is beyond the scope of this metaphysical inquiry.

Are there many specific types of dynamism and consequently much transphenomenal diversity at each of these three levels of the animate world? If such diversity is widespread in the inanimate world, then it is probably widespread in the animate world as well. But I doubt that this is the case. There may yet be discovered, in the explorations of the universe, a wide variety in the bodily structure and in the intensity of the various dynamisms of rational animals, a diversity akin to that which is now found in the realm of the non-rational animals. (While any rational animal would need a fairly high degree of complexity, we might very well be the least complex ourselves.) This suggestion is, of course, rather fanciful; but it does point out that wide variety in structure and intensity of dynamism does not necessarily mean a truly fundamental transphenomenal difference.

Fundamental and superficial changes in transphenomenal objectivity have been distinguished, the former being manifested by a fundamental change in the pattern of the phenomena associated with the thing, the latter by a lesser change with the basic pattern of associated phenomena remaining the same. Such a basic pattern of phenomena is, of course, the result of a specific type of dynamism and therefore of a specific type of transphenomenal objectivity. But such basic patterns and the specific types from which they arise are difficult to distinguish, as has been pointed out. This difficulty arises from a threefold obscurity in our knowledge.

First, it is difficult to distinguish between what is basic and what is only secondary in the patterns of phenomena arising under the control of transphenomenal objectivity. We attempt to overcome this obscurity by comparing the thing in question with itself at diverse times (to see what characteristics are constant) and with other things (to detect points of similarity and difference). Elements which are invariant in the same individual and in other "similar" individuals, despite the constant variation of other elements, are said to be part of a basic pattern, which reveals a specific type. These "elements" are not so much groups and sequences of phenomena as patterns of groups and sequences, or even types of patterns of groups and sequences. For example, language and symbolization are found in many forms, as also hierarchies of means-ends relations in purposive behaviour (or rational activity); but in each specific form of language, symbolization, and purposive behaviour, there is a certain type-pattern. Combining these type-patterns (subsuming language under symbolization, as one of its special modes), there appears a basic pattern of rational activity, which serves to distinguish men from brutes in a fundamental way. This pattern reveals a dynamism, and therefore a transphenomenal objectivity, which is something new, something more, relative to the whole world of brute animals.

A similar analysis of variant and invariant characteristics reveals a fundamental distinction between brute animals, plants, and the inanimate world. But finer subdistinctions are, as has been pointed out, much more problematic. Are there merely a variety of instances of the same basic patterns, or are there a variety of basic patterns? The matter is obscure.

A second obscurity comes from the fact that it is difficult to say which similarities and differences are truly significant in the search for specific types. For example, differences in structure seem important. Certainly there are the greatest differences in structure between inanimate and animate, between most plants and most animals, and between most animals and men. Yet in some cases the differences are not so great. And even in the midst of the greatest differences among plants or among animals, it is difficult to discern true differences in basic patterns and therefore in specific types. There is much more apparent difference between an ape and an amoeba than between an ape and a man; yet there is certainly much less difference in patterns of behaviour between an ape and an amoeba than between an ape and a man.

The third obscurity and difficulty in the way of knowing how to distinguish basic patterns and specific types comes from the fact that we live in a universe of interacting things. The phenomena are always the result of interaction, not just of simple action. This means that they manifest the dynamism, not simply of the thing, but of the thing in interaction with other things. It means that it will not always be clear that the phenomenal variants and invariants are so because of the intrinsic nature of the thing or because of the particular existential context in which the thing finds itself. This difficulty is less for living things, which somehow rise above their physical environment, than it is for non-living things. Still, even with living things, one might suspect, for example, an innate tendency to vary slightly the form of some of the offspring; but now we know that such mutation can be caused by purely physical factors from the environment. An obvious way to minimize the confusion between the intrinsic dynamism and the dynamism of the existential context is to vary, as widely as possible, the environments in which observation and experimentation with the thing in question are carried out.

But there are some aspects of the physical environment which cannot be escaped, and there the obscurity remains.

However, granting the difficulty in distinguishing basic patterns of phenomena and the diverse types of transphenomenal objectivity which give rise to these basic patterns, it is still possible to state a few general rules for deciding whether a variation is fundamental or only superficial.

When common patterns of phenomena, characteristic of certain kinds of reality, are found now as parts of a larger pattern, more diversified and with some new "higher" type of pattern dominating over all, we have found a new level of the real, a new level of transphenomenal objectivity. Such is the case when one moves from the inanimate world to the vegetative world; the same physical and chemical laws are followed, but they are followed inside a larger pattern not found in the merely inanimate world, the pattern of vegetative activity and phenomena. So also, new and larger patterns, inclusive of but also transcending the lower patterns, are found as one turns to sentient and rational life. But it is difficult to discern a hierarchy of patterns <u>within</u> these four levels; perhaps there is no hierarchy here, but only a variety of the same fundamental patterns and therefore of the same specific type of transphenomenal objectivity. In view of the foregoing remarks, certain variations, such as the death of a living organism, are evidently fundamental; others, such as a mere slight change of temperature, are obviously superficial; still others must remain doubtful, though it seems more likely that they are only superficial.

When the basic type of dynamism does not vary, but its intensity and mode of exercise do vary somewhat, as is often clearly the case within each of the four levels here considered, the difference seems to be only superficial; consequently, change from one such state to the other also seems to be only superficial.

Similarly, mere change of place does not of itself result in any fundamental variation in the thing. Some superficial variation must, however, occur in order to account for the transition from one state of motion to another.

Variations in structure may be signs of fundamental differences and fundamental changes if they are great enough; but the key again must be variation in the basic patterns of phenomena in which the dynamism of the thing is manifested. Mere structural difference of itself, difference in size, shape, density, arrangement of parts, and even type of parts, does not necessarily indicate anything more than superficial difference and change, apart from the aforesaid differences in the basic patterns of dynamism.

General analysis of variations in objectivity: intrinsic structure

Two kinds of variation in objectivity have been distinguished: phenomenal and transphenomenal. But in fact both kinds have much in common. In both cases, the variation takes place against a background of something more permanent. What varies is a characteristic of something; a common subject, in which the variation takes place, persists throughout the variation; there is a continuity between the old state of things and the new. Mere appearance and disappearance of characteristics could be interpreted as a mysterious substitution (through instantaneous creation and annihilation), but this is not what we observe to take place. This means that the variation described is some type of change.

A reconsideration of some of the examples given earlier should suffice to make this clear. First, the variation of phenomena themselves is clearly manifested as a variation of the phenomena of things. Phenomena are attributes of the transphenomenal thing; they are in this thing and of it. It is really impossible even to know the phenomena without knowing them, however obscurely, as special aspects of the transphenomenal being. Accordingly, the flux of phenomena is seen to be a continual superficial change of the transphenomenal being. Temperature variation not only indicates variation in the transphenomenal object; such variation is already of itself a change in the thing in its phenomenal aspect.

But variations in the pattern of phenomena are an indication of variations in the transphenomenal object. Here too, these variations turn out to be genuine change of something into something else, rather than simple substitution. For example, illness affects a man in one way or another; but it is still a man who passes from one state to another. So also the flux of sense experience affects us in diverse ways, and indeed is itself already a series of diverse affections; but it is the same man who persists throughout the flux. Water may change from solid to liquid, but it is still H_2O.

Even in fundamental variations in the transphenomenal object, there is not mere substitution but genuine change. When a living thing dies, one body is not replaced by another. In some way yet to be seen it remains the same, even while becoming other than it was. It is the same in the reverse process, where inanimate matter is assimilated into the living substance. Thus, all the variations observed in the physical world are changes of one kind or another.

As has been pointed out, in every change there is continuity throughout; something endures throughout the change, which, for reasons which will be apparent later, is called the common subject of the change. On the other hand, there is also something new as a result of the change; and of course there must have been an original lack of this "something new" at the beginning of the change. If one objects that change is continuous, so there is no beginning of the change, it may be answered that even in such continuous change earlier stages may be distinguished from later (if any change is really taking place at all). Now the earlier stage must lack what the later stage has, if there is any change at all. This earlier stage then is quite satisfactory as a substitute for our "beginning" (although in fact not all change is as continuous as the objection suggests).

Intrinsic to change then (set aside the extrinsic presuppositions of change for the time being), there are at least three components: a common subject, something new, and an original lack of something new. The transition from the original lack to the something new may be either gradual or instantaneous. If it is gradual, there is something new at every moment of the transition itself. The distinction between gradual and instantaneous change may be ignored in the general analysis of the structure of change. Besides the three components already mentioned, there may have been some other characteristic which has been lost as a result of the change, as in the change from one color to another, or in the physical change to which corresponds an increase of "entropy." In such "negative change" the same basic components are involved as in positive change (although in a reverse manner). Negative change may even occur without an accompanying positive change, as when we forget something we once knew. But the discussion here of the intrinsic structure of change concentrates upon positive change and leaves for the reader the application to negative change.

The original lack is not a mere nothingness; it is precisely a lack of the "something new," a nothingness relative to this "new." But what is it that lacks the "something new"? It is that common subject which endures throughout the change, the man whose temperature changes, the thing which changes its phenomenal appearance. But if the lack is in the common subject, then so also the "something new" eventually is in the common subject and of the common subject--the man has the temperature; the thing has its phenomenal appearance. And if the common subject eventually has the new characteristic, then it must have originally had (and must still have) some capacity to receive this new characteristic. The common subject is capable of acquiring this new degree of determinate objectivity, of being further determined in its objective being by this new characteristic.

It is time now to assign some technical names for the structural components which have been described. The capability of the common subject to receive new characteristics is called potentiality or potency, and this common subject is said to be in potency for or to have a potency for such characteristics. Note that the potency is present not only before the acquisition of the new characteristic but also during its possession--nothing has a given characteristic unless it is at the same time capable of having this characteristic. The characteristic or determination itself is called an act. Potency and act are correlative terms. Later on, the possibility of act without potency will be seen; but in the objective structure of the physical world, just as potency is essentially a capacity for act, so also act is essentially a determination and fulfillment of potency. Thus potency and act in the objective structure of the universe are elements, not in the sense of diverse things, but rather as diverse co-principles of things.

Act was called a determination of potency. In what way does it determine? First, potency in the physical world is a potency for many diverse acts or for many diverse intensities of act. In itself it is in a way indifferent and indeterminate, getting further determination from act. Second, potency of itself lacks the act, has a "nothingness" relative to act. From this point of view, the objective being of potency is not as determinate as it might be; act fills the void with a determinate degree of being.

This void or lack in the common subject having potency for some act is called privation. Again recall that this lack is not anything positive at all. And yet it cannot be described merely as a nothingness. It is a nothingness; but it is a nothingness in the subject, a nothingness where there could be act. This nothingness is of course not really distinct from the potency itself; it is the potency precisely as not having an act which it could have.

It should be fairly clear by now why what endures throughout the change has been called the common subject. It is common to both the initial and the terminal stages of the change, as well as to whatever intervenes. And it is that in which acts exist as in a kind of substratum or subject.

Also, it is evident that the distinction between potency and act in real things is a real distinction, a distinction which is "there" independently of intellectual analysis. For the change is real; the original lack is real; the new determination is real; the common subject is real; its capacity for new determinations must also be real, and distinct from the new determinations themselves. Potency and act, as elements in the structure of real change, are real and really distinct.

In view of the distinction between superficial and fundamental change, potency and act will be found on more than one level in the structure of objectivity. Some distinction of such levels is attempted in the next section; it will be seen that potency and act are found in diverse modes, so that the potency-act relation is not everywhere the same but rather analogical. But it may be said in general that act is in the potential subject (not as water is in a vessel, but as temperature is considered to be in a body or as ideas are in a mind) and of this same potential subject (not as material property is of some owner, but as temperature is of some body or ideas of some mind). In the course of this investigation of being, many diverse instances of the potency-act relation will appear; we shall even come to consider the possibility of act being found apart from any potency for that act.

Finally, if potency and act are necessary components of change, then they are also necessary components of the changeable thing. The objective structure of the changeable thing, no less than the objective structure of change itself, includes both act and potency.

The intrinsic structure of superficial changes in objectivity

In the consideration of superficial change, it is possible to begin by a simple application of our knowledge concerning the general structure of change. There must be potency, act, and privation. In superficial change, the fundamental transphenomenal objectivity of the thing endures as a common subject (and in this common subject also endure the various superficial characteristics which do not enter into this particular change), the subject in which the potency for the superficial act is located. Such superficial act is more technically known as accidental form or an accident. (As the analysis proceeds, it will become evident that there are in fact some accidental forms which are not so superficial in the constitution of reality as are others.) The fundamental transphenomenal objectivity of the thing has already been called the subject of the accidents; in a later chapter this idea will be penetrated more deeply. For the present, a subject is that to which belong in some manner various characteristics or attributes, as the superficial objectivity belongs to the primary or fundamental objectivity of the thing. More commonly, this fundamental transphenomenal objectivity of the thing is called a substance, insofar as it is that which "stands under" its various accidental determinations. Substance, then, has the potency for further accidental determinations. Superficial change, and therefore also the superficially changeable thing, is composed of substance and accidental form, related as potency and act. Since superficial change is a change of accidental form, it is called accidental change.

The phenomenal flux, variations in the state of local motion, changes in size, shape, internal arrangement of parts, transient or permanent modifications of disposition which modify the dynamism of the thing in its intensity or secondary pattern without changing the fundamental dynamism of the thing--these are all accidental changes in themselves.

A few more remarks may be made concerning the nature of substance and accident as principles of objective being. Substance is in a way imperfect, relative to accidental form; such form supplies to substance something which it does not have in itself. Therefore accidental form is a perfection of substance, fulfilling the possibilities of substance, in a way completing it. But note that the substance stands on its own, independently of the accidental forms, while the reverse is by no means true. Accidental forms, by their very nature, demand substance in which to inhere, to which to belong; one does not naturally find phenomena, etc., unless they are in and of some substance. Substance and accidental form are indeed co-principles of things, but they are by no means on an equal plane as principles.

The intrinsic structure of fundamental changes in objectivity

In fundamental change, the fundamental transphenomenal objectivity of the thing changes. What makes the thing to be this specific type of thing is replaced by what makes the thing to be of another specific type. This act is called substantial form, the act by which a material substance is constituted as this kind of substance. The common subject, in this instance, is called prime matter, a subject which remains through the most fundamental changes.

Since everything in the physical universe is capable of undergoing fundamental or substantial change, as it is called, every material substance is composed of prime matter and substantial form. If one objects that it is impossible to assert that everything in the physical universe is capable of substantial change, since it is impossible to distinguish with sufficient clarity between the various specific types of substances, it may be answered that in fact such clear distinction is not really necessary in order to make the universal assertion. For suppose that the entire inanimate world is of one specific type. Then, since some parts of this world can in fact be assimilated into living substances, they must be composed of prime matter and substantial form. Now if some are so composed, then all are so composed, since they are all of the same specific type. But suppose, on the contrary, that there are many specific types in the inanimate world. It still follows that even those types which are not directly assimilable into the substance of living things are composed of prime matter and substantial form, since even those types may be changed into other specific types of inanimate matter by nuclear and chemical transmutations. There still remains the problem of intermatter. Its matter-form structure cannot be established from an analysis of change, since no change of matter to intermatter or vice versa seems clearly given. However, the matter-form structure of intermatter can be shown in other ways, as will be seen later.

Two important questions may now be asked. Is prime matter different in some way in diverse things or is it merely diverse? Can there simultaneously be more than one substantial form in one thing? These two questions are closely interrelated, and will be considered together.

In the first question, it is asked whether prime matter can have different characteristics in different things, or whether it has the same characteristics in all things, or whether perhaps it has no determinate characteristics at all, as the Thomists and Aristotelians maintain. If it should have determinate characteristics, whether the same in all things or different in different things, then prime matter has of itself some substantial determination. But if this is so, then either all modifications of the thing will be accidental (which has already been seen not to be the case) or there is a possibility of more than one substantial form in the one thing. On the other hand, if there can be only one substantial form in each thing, giving all the substantial characteristics of the thing, then prime matter must necessarily lack all determinate characteristics in itself and therefore be merely diverse instead of different in all material things. The question of the indeterminacy of prime matter, then, is reduced to the question of the possibility of a simultaneous plurality of substantial forms in the same one thing, a question much agitated among medieval and later scholastics.

Certainly the plurality of forms is a tempting idea. After all, are not certain physico-chemical laws followed by all material things, regardless of the diversity of specific type in these things? Does this not seem to indicate that there is some basic substantial determination common to all material things, either identical with prime matter or distinct from it as a "form of corporeity" received before the reception of any further substantial determination? Or perhaps this "form of corporeity" is received simultaneously with other forms. And is it not possible that a further substantial form is added at each step up the scale of being, a form of vegetativity, a form of sensitivity, and a form of rationality, at the very least?

But in fact, a simultaneous plurality of substantial forms in the same thing is impossible; and as a result, prime matter can be seen to be completely indeterminate in itself, needing some determination by form. For suppose that there is a simultaneous plurality of really distinct substantial determinations in some material thing. The various determinations come either in an ordered hierarchy (in at least some logical, if not temporal, order) or in simple simultaneity without any order. If they come in an ordered hierarchy, then only the first is substantial and all the others are accidental relative to this first. For the first already constitutes the thing as a determinate substance with a fundamental intelligibility of its own. But on the other hand, if all the determinations come simultaneously without any hierarchy, either they are all identical with prime matter and consequently identical with each other, or they are all distinct from prime matter. But in this latter case, prime matter must be completely indeterminate in itself. But if prime matter is considered to be completely indeterminate in itself, then it is impossible to distinguish between the individual forms in the supposed plurality of forms. For if these forms are in diverse prime matter, then they are the forms of diverse things, as shall be seen later; but if they are in the same matter, then there are several simultaneous actuations of one potency in diverse ways. But there cannot be several simultaneous actuations of the same prime matter in diverse ways, since this same one prime matter, entirely indeterminate, is in no way differentiable in itself into more than one potency. Thus a plurality of substantial determinations in one thing is impossible, and as a consequence prime matter must be in itself completely indeterminate, as opposed to the one substantial determination of each thing. These same two points will be seen even more clearly in a later chapter.

The discovery of the complete indeterminacy of prime matter and the oneness of substantial form sheds some interesting light on the potency-act relation between prime matter and substantial form. This potency-act relation is not the same as the substance-accident relation. Substance is already something determinate to which some further determination is added. This further determination is of substance and inheres in substance. But since prime matter is not anything determinate, but rather a pure potency for act, even though substantial form is in a way of prime matter and in prime matter, still it is better to say that substantial form adheres to prime matter rather than that it inheres in prime matter (as accidents inhere in substance). "Adherence" focuses upon the quasi-equality of the two substantial principles (they are at the same general level of objectivity), while "inherence" focuses upon the inequality of substance and accidental form (as two diverse levels in the structure of objectivity).

But just as substance and accidental form are co-principles of the one thing, so also are prime matter and substantial form. Just as accidental form is a perfection of substance fulfilling its possibilities, so also substantial form is a perfection of prime matter. Here again there is the same basic relation of determinable to determining, of capacity to fulfillment, which is the heart of the potency-act relation in every instance.

One further question suggests itself. As has been seen, accidental form is by its nature a determination of substance and needs a substance in which to inhere, while substance is in a way independent of its accidental forms. One may wonder whether there is a parallel situation with prime matter and accidental form. Could substantial form ever exist apart from prime matter, or prime matter apart from substantial form?

At present, the answer to this question must be rather limited and qualified. We can speak only from the limited point of view of the analysis of the objective structure of the material universe. From this perspective, substantial form is always seen as a determination of prime matter. Furthermore, the dynamism consequent upon each substantial form of the physical universe demands that the substance itself be spread-out in space and time, "extended." It will be seen soon that the root of spatial and temporal extension is found in prime matter. But this means that the substantial form needs prime matter as a subject to which to adhere. (One exception must be noted to this rule, namely, the human soul, which in some of its dynamism transcends the spatio-temporal world. But even the human soul should be unified with prime matter, in order that the full dynamism of the human being be exercised.) Are there perhaps other forms which are complete substances by themselves, outside the spatio-temporal world? To philosophers this is an interesting question, to which divine faith concerning the existence of angels (and perhaps mere historical experience as well) gives an answer.

Again, prime matter is always seen as determined by some substantial form. This is, of course, necessary; for since prime matter is of itself entirely indeterminate, it could never manifest itself phenomenally without substantial form. Phenomenal manifestation requires dynamism, and dynamism requires some degree of substantial determination. Furthermore, nothing can be known at all except insofar as it is somehow determinate--potency is known through its act. Therefore, prime matter could never be known except as determined by substantial form.

One might go even further and ask whether any completely indeterminate principle of being could ever be by itself. Must not everything that exists have some determinate degree of existence? But clearly this question can be better answered after the analysis of objectivity, when all is considered in relation to transobjective existence.

General analysis of the one and the many in objectivity

A specific type of object, such as rationality or some particular shade of phenomenal red, is of itself one perfection containing the fullness of itself. Therefore, when the philosopher finds that this one perfection is in fact found in many diverse instances (no one of which, obviously, contains the fullness of this perfection), he must be mystified at such an apparent contradiction. And yet the contradiction must be only apparent, if human knowledge and objective presence are in any way distinguishable from utter nothingness.

Now the resolution of this apparent contradiction in the order of objectivity must be accomplished on the plane of objectivity itself; for unless a thing is identical with its existence (and the things here analyzed are not thus identical with their existence, since they come into being and pass away), its possibility is distinct from its existence and located in the order of objectivity alone. Moreover, no appeal to anything outside the given instance of limited perfection in some individual thing can suffice to ground the possibility of such an instance. Granted that such an extrinsic cause may be necessary (as indeed it is, as will be seen later), still such an extrinsic cause can only produce an objectively possible effect. Therefore in summary, there must be an objective possibility for such a limited perfection; and this objective possibility must have some ground or reason intrinsic to the thing which has the limited perfection. The apparent intrinsic contradiction involved in the existence of things with limited perfection must be resolved by an analysis of the intrinsic objective structure of these things.

It was seen earlier that this objective structure is composed of two levels of act and potency: substantial form and prime matter compose substance, and substance receives various accidental forms. Every aspect of objectivity can be located in this framework, even including phenomenality. At this point, the way to the resolution of the apparent contradiction between the one and the many at the objective level becomes evident. If the perfection of a given accidental form is in fact found in many diverse instances, this cannot be because of the form itself but only because of its reception in diverse substances or in diverse parts of the same substance. The diverse instances of the perfection, then, are not distinguished as perfection, but rather by their relation to this or that diverse substance or part of substance. Similarly, if the perfection of a given substantial form is in fact found in many diverse instances, this cannot be because of the substantial form itself, but only because of its reception in diverse prime matter. Certainly it could not be due to any accidental forms, since they are only received in the already constituted individual substance with its given limited instance of a given substantial form; their being is a secondary being, which cannot contribute to the constitution of the fundamental being.

But here a serious difficulty arises. It is true that once the existence of distinct individual substances is presupposed, the possibility of individual limited instances of the perfection of accidental forms (the individuation of accidental forms) is accounted for. But in the individuation of substantial forms a special difficulty occurs. If this individuation is accounted for through reception in diverse matter (as it ultimately must be), some way must be found to explain how prime matter is itself diversified. This is the well-known scholastic problem of the principle of individuation in material substances.

The principle of individuation in material substances

Concerning this principle of individuation in material substances there has been a long controversy among scholastics. However, in keeping with the method indicated in the Preface, we shall not enter into the details of this controversy but proceed immediately to our own analysis.

In material substance there is at once a substantial unity and a substantial multiplicity; each substance is one substance and yet it is extended so as to be at the same time multiple in some manner. This multiplicity is not simply accidental; it is the substance itself which is so extended as to have a multiplicity of substantial parts. Some accidental form or forms may play a role in this extension, but these cannot by themselves account for the multiplicity of substantial parts.

On the plane of objectivity it is substantial form that dominates the thing, that makes its parts to be parts of this one thing, that makes this thing to be truly one thing as opposed to many things. The parts are said to be parts of one substance insofar as they all have the same substantial form. Prime matter cannot have such a unifying function, since of its very nature it is common, found in the many distinct things of the physical universe. Therefore, substantial form is the ultimate principle of unity in material substance.

On the other hand, it was pointed out in the preceding section that prime matter must be in some manner a principle of divisiveness between things even while it is common to the many things in the physical universe. It makes it own contribution to the unity of the individual insofar as it divides it from other things, and in particular from other members of the same species; but it does this only insofar as it is a principle of divisiveness in things. But it is not only a principle of divisiveness between things. It is also a principle of divisiveness within each thing, insofar as it is the ultimate root of the multiplicity of parts in any extended material substance. Later, this multiplicity of parts in the extended substance will be considered in more detail.

Prime matter is the ultimate root of individuation, dividing even things having the same specific form from each other, precisely because it is the ultimate principle of multiplicity in material substances. Prime matter of itself has no unity at all; what unity it has in a concrete thing must come from the form; of itself it is not only pure potency but also pure multiplicity. Thus there is really no problem about how to divide prime matter so that diverse prime matter can receive individually distinct substantial forms. Prime matter is already utterly divided, purely multiple in itself. If, then, it be asked how one substantial form can have many prime matters in which to be individualized and multiplied, it may be answered that prime matter is always other than itself, always a many. The only way that something of this pure manifold becomes gathered into one is insofar as it is determined by some substantial form.

But prime matter is in no way actual by itself. It has no determinate characteristics and can only be found with substantial form. From this point of view, the pure multiplicity of prime matter is not a determinate, actual multiplicity in itself. And since this is so, the pure multiplicity must also be a confused multiplicity; the parts of the prime matter must exist in a kind of confusion with each other--they lack an order among themselves. If they had an orderly arrangement, prime matter would not be a pure potency but would have in itself at least this determination which is the ordered arrangement of itself.

Thomists, however, have always said that the principle of individuation is not simply prime matter, but prime matter "signed with quantity." Some meaning will be assigned to this phrase in a later section.

Material substance and quantity

The unity of an individual material substance proceeds from its form, while the multiplicity of this substance proceeds from its matter. This leads to conceiving prime matter as a pure multiplicity. But this multiplicity must be a confused multiplicity in prime matter, since any order in it would remove the indeterminacy essential to prime matter. Now in fact, the multiplicity of any individual material substance is not confused but ordered --parts are outside of parts in a determinate order or sequence.

How does this determinate order of parts outside of parts arise? First, it is impossible that substantial form should suffice to order the confused multiplicity; the union of prime matter and substantial form alone can give only one substance with confused multiplicity of parts. The multiplicity of parts will now be in a way actual, in that the substance with an intrinsic multiplicity now actually is; but this actuality of multiplicity is not yet an ordered actuality. (Note that this is not to say that the parts of the substantial continuum are contained actually and not just potentially in the continuum. This consideration is at altogether another level.) For if this were an ordered actuality of multiplicity conferred by the substantial form, then the actual ordering of parts in the extended substance would be in some manner essential. But in fact this ordering is only contingent; the substance could still be this substance and this kind of substance without this determinate ordering of parts. There could be many possible orderings of parts outside of parts for the same substance, as for example, according to a mirror-image of the actual ordering, or such as is found in diverse members of the same species. Therefore the determinate actual order of parts outside of parts in a material substance must be due to an accidental form distinct from the substance itself, even while the parts themselves are substantial parts and result from the very union of prime matter and substantial form. This accident which confers a determinate order upon the parts outside of parts of material substance, removing the prior confusion of parts, is what is here called quantity.

The nature and formal effect of quantity

Because quantity is an accidental form, it has some immediate formal effect in substance. This formal effect arises in virtue of the very presence of quantity, and it is so immediately consequent upon quantity that if it were not present quantity itself could not be said to be present. This effect, as has been seen, is not the plurality of substantial parts (no mere accidental form could produce this) but rather the dispersion of these parts outside of each other in a determinate ordering.

This ordering is not a new reality in the parts taken as parts; the only new reality is in the whole considered in its parts, and this reality is the accidental form of quantity. The whole was composed of a multiplicity coexisting in a concentrated but confused manner; but the accidental form of quantity makes this multiplicity in the whole to be dispersed so as to coexist in an ordered continuum, that is, a continuum in which each part occupies a determinate position in relation to each other part.

Prime matter, quantity, and spatio-temporal extension

Since prime matter is the ultimate root of the intrinsic multiplicity of material substance, and since quantity has as its formal effect the ordering of this intrinsic multiplicity, it follows that every substance with ordered extension (every "material" substance) contains prime matter. From this, incidentally, it follows that intermatter must also possess prime matter, since intermatter is an extended substance.

If the above consideration is inverted, one can see that prime matter, as pure confused multiplicity and the root of the intrinsic multiplicity of material substance, is the ultimate root of the demand of material substance for quantitative extension, for the spatial extension without which the dynamism of material substance could not be exercised, without which the heterogeneous structure of material substances could not exist, and without which the spatially spread-out world of sensible phenomenality could not be produced.

Prime matter is also at the root of the temporal extension of processes of change in the physical universe. Substantial changes cannot take place without a preparation through accidental changes, which bring about the conditions for and even necessitate the substantial changes. If there are accidental changes which take place as instantaneously as do substantial changes, these too require a gradual process of preparation. For changes to occur, ultimately there must be the action and interaction of material things upon each other; and this can take place only gradually in a universe of spatially extended things. For the required physical contact (whether immediate or mediate) in order that action and interaction may take place cannot be made simultaneously in every part of spatially extended things--unless there were complete compenetration of substances, which does not appear to be given, and which itself could not be brought about instantaneously. Thus spatial extension is at the root of the temporality of physical process and natural process generally. Now since the root of spatial extension has been traced back to prime matter, it follows that prime matter is also the root of the temporality of things in the physical universe. Therefore prime matter is the ultimate root of the spatio-temporal extension of the physical universe in both the transphenomenal and phenomenal domains.

When prime matter is viewed as a pure confused multiplicity, then, it has a certain exigency for quantitative extension; it thus is "signed with quantity." Now since prime matter is the principle of substantial individuation, not merely as pure potency but rather also as pure confused multiplicity, the principle of such individuation is said to be prime matter "signed with quantity."

Material substance, quantity, and quality

Material substance and quantity together account for a homogeneously extended substance, but they do not account for the diversities of structure in things, the varying dispositions of things, the varying dynamism in the diverse parts of the same thing (as in the diverse organs of the living body). The principle of differentiation and heterogeneity within the one homogeneous extended substance is a new accidental form--quality. The heterogeneity is due to the reception of diverse qualities at the diverse points of space and time. Note that such reception of diverse qualities at diverse points of space and time presupposes in fact that the substance is extended through quantity; the qualitative structure of the thing presupposes quantity. But it is not proper to say that the qualities are in the quantity as in a potency; rather, they are in and of the extended substance, inhering directly in the substantial parts themselves, and extended in virtue of the extension of substance.

Quantity, quality, and sensible phenomenality

Sensible phenomenality has an aspect of the quantitative, insofar as it is extended in space and time; and it also has an aspect of the qualitative, insofar as it is diversified in the diverse points of space and time. Nevertheless, sensible phenomenality as phenomenality does not have an intrinsic potency-act structure. This phenomenality is simply the superficial and sensible face of extended and qualitatively diverse transphenomenal being. It stands, then, as an "extrinsic synthesis" of quantity and quality, as a new type of accidental form, not simply reducible to quantity or quality or even to both together, in its intrinsic being, but emanating in its being as an extended heterogeneous flux from the transphenomenal quantity and quality and the substance in which they inhere.

It should now be possible to reflect upon the fundamental role of quantity in all physical process, both transphenomenal and phenomenal. Because of the quantitative, extended character of the things in the physical universe, all qualitative interaction and process in this universe is in fact conditioned by spatio-temporal factors. This conditioning affects not only the trans-phenomenal level of physical process but the phenomenal level as well. What this means is that qualitative variation at both levels is always subject to determinate quantitative conditions and has determinate quantitative results and takes place according to determinate quantitative laws, all in a determinate spatio-temporal context.

This does not, however, imply that the laws of natural science must always follow the pattern of the laws of classical physics with their determinism. It may well be that, owing to our radical inability to gain precise knowledge in the domain of the infinitesimally small or in the domain of exceedingly large aggregates, we must be frequently content only with statistical laws and apparent indeterminism, as in quantum physics or in statistical thermodynamics. But here there is question, not of the nature of physical theory and experimentation, but rather of the nature of being itself; being is always determinate, even if our knowledge of it fails to be so determinate. Therefore one need not hesitate to posit strict and determinate quantitative conditioning, results, and laws for the qualitative process in our world. All this, of course, in no way denies the possibility that such determinate patterns of process may be assimilated into still more embracing patterns, such as those of freely directed human activity. Nor does it deny the fact that there is contingency and chance in the universe. It only asserts that when physical process does take place, it takes place with determinate quantitative as well as qualitative characteristics, and that the quantitative and qualitative aspects of such process are closely correlated.

And while the qualitative is difficult to deal with directly, to establish precise laws of process according to variations in qualitative intensities, the concomitant quantitative conditions and results of such variations are in fact accessible to precise measurement in many ways. This is the ground for the existence of mathematical sciences of the physical world. Such mathematical science could be ordered toward a fuller understanding of the universe in its physical (transphenomenal) nature, as were, for the most part, the ancient and medieval mathematical sciences of nature. Or such mathematical science could focus exclusively upon the laws of quantitative variation in sensible phenomenality itself, and their theoretical correlation, as is the case with modern natural science. The history of the evolution of mathematical science of nature from the former standpoint to the latter, its gradual disengagement from the philosophical inquiry about trans-phenomenal natures, the long period of confusions and mistakes about the relations between these two types of knowing, all this makes a most interesting story. But it is beyond the scope of the present essay.

The reality of relations

Without doubt there are real accidental relations between the things of the physical universe. That these relations have some reality distinct from the reality of substance, quantity, quality, and phenomenality has been a common teaching of Thomists. However, some modern Thomists have questioned this teaching, and rightly so.

First, every relation presupposes relata (related things); in these relata, the subject, term, and foundation of the relation are distinguished from each other. The subject is that which has the relation; the term is that to which the subject has the relation; and the foundation is the reason why the subject has such a relation to the term. If relation has a distinct reality of its own, this reality must be distinct from that of the subject, the term, and the foundation. In fact, proofs have been given which show adequately that the relation cannot be identified with any one of these three; but they fail to show that the relation is something more than all three taken together. As a matter of fact, the notion of a relation really distinct from the absolute being of the thing seems to be inherently unintelligible; it can have no intrinsic intelligible content, since this would reduce it to a mode of absolute being. If its total intelligibility is extrinsic, then so is its total being extrinsic and reducible to the being of the subject, term, and foundation. Moreover, the reality of relations is not eliminated by denying their distinction from their subject, term, and foundation; they are real with the reality of the subject, term, and foundation. For example, by the very fact that A and B are interacting they are interrelated; there is no need of any new reality distinct from the interaction itself to relate A and B; and this interaction is a pair of transobjective activities, not an objectively intelligible relation. Or, to take another example, by the mere fact that A came into being in dependence on B and C,

A can be said to be related to B and C. No added relation, distinct from the being of A, is necessary; for this being of A is, or was, intrinsically dependent in some manner upon B and C. This intrinsic dependence is quite sufficient as the reality of the relation of A to B and C.

Thus the reality of all accidental relations can be reduced to the reality of absolute accidental forms. (So in fact also can the reality of all so-called "transcendental" or essential relations be reduced to the being of the relata, which from this point of view are relations: e.g., potency and act do not merely have relations to each other; they are relations to each other.) Accidental relations are the relative aspects of absolutes. Because of the weakness of human conceptualization, such relative aspects of absolute being are known in separate concepts; such relative aspects are isolated in constructed "relation-fictions," which are not objective forms of reality but rather objective formalizations of the mind.

One may object that if all relations as distinct from the relata are "relation-fictions," then a distinction can no longer be drawn between "real" and "logical" relations. In fact this is not so; for relation-fictions founded upon real subjects, terms, and foundations can still be distinguished from relation-fictions which are not founded upon real subjects, terms, and foundations. The former are "real relations" and the latter are "logical relations."

The generic types of objectivity

Four irreducible types of objectivity have been distinguished in the given objective real: substance, quantity, quality, and phenomenality. Prime matter cannot be regarded as a distinct type of objectivity, since it cannot of itself be an object at all. Relations do not comprise a new type of objectivity in the objective real; for, as distinct from absolute objectivity, they are only formalizations or constructs of the mind.

These four irreducible types of real objectivity are akin to the supreme genera of Aristotle; indeed, the first three correspond to the first three enumerated by Aristotle himself. However, Aristotle's categories are primarily categories of logical classification, as is shown by his inclusion of relation and six other categories arising out of our manner of conceptualizing reality rather than out of immediately given objective reality itself. When such categories of logical classification are uncritically transposed onto the metaphysical plane, there is considerable confusion, as is evidenced in the case of relation.

At this time there is no need of being concerned with the question of the categories of logical classification (which, it seems, will have to be considerably different from those of Aristotle). The four generic types of objectivity here are types of real objectivity.

Extrinsic presuppositions of variations
in objectivity: the agent

The mutual influence and interdependence, the interaction, of the things of the physical universe is an evident fact of experience. If one toys with some iron filings on a piece of paper by moving a magnet about under the paper, soon there will be no doubt that the magnet does in fact exercise some influence upon the iron filings, even through the paper. If a plate of food is set out for the pet that has not eaten all day, there is no doubt that the food somehow stimulates the animal. If the explosion of a stick of dynamite is observed, there is no doubt that it brought about the ensuing destruction. If a bottle has fallen from a shelf on the head of a mischievous child, there is no doubt that both the broken bottle and the injured head are the results of some physical interaction between the two.

Such obvious facts of experience prompt the general observation that every change has a reason in some factor outside the change itself, that every change presupposes an agent to produce the change. However, this observation meets with certain challenges. Radioactivity and the dynamism of life seem to be spontaneous, not needing any outside influence. If Newton's first law of motion, that a body continues in its state of rest or of motion in a straight line unless acted upon by some external force, retains any validity (and it does, since the property of inertia remains even in the later developments of physics), then it seems that this change (local motion) does not necessarily need an extrinsic influence to keep it going. These difficulties do not mean that the general observation must be denied, but they do suggest the need for a deeper investigation of the relation of change and its producing agent.

A sufficient analysis of change has already been made; now it is necessary to make a few remarks about the agent. The agent is characterized by a certain dynamism, which up to now has been linked with the form of the agent, but which can be understood properly only after a detailed consideration of existence and activity. It is this dynamism, this mysterious influence of activity flowing from a deeper tendency toward activity, that actually produces the change. At this point it is helpful to distinguish the agent which actually produces the change from an agent which merely removes the impediment to the influence of another agent. The agent which merely removes an impediment is called an active condition for the change in question. Similarly, the agent must be distinguished from the mere occasion which provides the agent with an opportunity to act, as an accidental meeting may be the occasion for changing one's plans for the day. In some manner, the change produced is similar to the agent which actually produces the change, since the change is produced in accordance with the dynamism of the agent, which dynamism itself is determined by the form of the agent. But this will be considered further in the later chapter on activity. Also, there are many diverse types of agent and therefore of activity; but these too can be left for later treatment.

Now consider the general assertion that whatever is changed is changed by some distinct agent. "Distinct" here means "outside the structure of the change itself." Positive change is the acquisition by some common subject of an act to which the subject was previously only in potency. But if the act was previously absent, then the subject could not confer this act upon itself. To deny this would be to abolish the distinction between objective being and nothingness, since the act would in effect be coming out of nothingness. But if objective being is not distinct from nothingness, then there is nothing to know and knowledge loses all determinate meaning. Since the act cannot simply emerge from nothingness by itself, it follows that its actual coming-to-be-present must be due to some influence from outside the change itself. This influence must proceed from some being rather than from nothingness, for the same reason as above. It therefore proceeds from the dynamism of an agent, an agent outside the structure of the change itself. Similarly, spontaneous negative change (loss of act) would also imply the abolishing of the distinction between objective being and nothingness.

Both accidental and substantial change depend on the dynamism of an extrinsic agent: accidental change is traceable to the dynamism of some accidental form of the agent, while substantial change must somehow be traceable to the dynamism of the substantial form of the agent. But in fact this dynamism of the agent and activity itself are rather mysterious. So also are the coming and going of form, whether substantial or accidental. No adequate account can be given of these things at the level of objectivity alone. Therefore, a fuller treatment of these matters is reserved for later chapters, when they will be considered in the broader perspective of transobjectivity.

The three difficulties raised earlier can now be briefly discussed. From the analysis it is clear that no real change can be entirely spontaneous in fact. Radioactivity can be traceable to the inherently unstable combinations of particles in interaction. In the living thing, the diverse parts act upon each other; and the living thing itself interacts with its environment. In local motion, if there is genuine change going on in the motion itself, then there must be some extrinsic agent, whether it is known what this agent is or not. It must be remembered that laws of physics are not philosophical explanations, and that the concepts of physics do not attain to the natures and real dynamism of transphenomenal being.

In the light of the analysis thus far, it may be wondered whether or not every material agent must itself be changed in some way in order that it produce a change in anything else, in order to "trigger" the dynamism of this agent. In any event, because of the resistance to change inherent in every material thing, such change always exacts a certain toll from the agent itself--there is a "reaction" upon the agent. The question of a possible "trigger" change in the agent itself and all that this would imply is better discussed later, from a broader perspective than that of mere objectivity.

Extrinsic presuppositions of variations in objectivity: the end

When we consider the uniformity of the course of interaction in the physical universe, how the same things tend to produce the same effects in the same circumstances, such as the effect of the magnet upon iron filings, or of food upon living things deprived of food for some time, or of exploding dynamite upon the immediate vicinity, we observe that things have definite tendencies to act in one way rather than another. One cannot get any result from any thing, but only certain results from certain things. This observation is confirmed when the complex patterns of behaviour evident in certain cases, such as in the life of the ant or the bee, are considered. Just as rationally directed life tends toward certain definite goals or ends, rather than toward others, so all non-intelligent agents as well are thought to tend toward such definite ends in their activity.

However, this belief is somewhat shaken when the role of chance in the physical universe is considered. Chance events do occur, such as lightning striking a man dead, which do not seem to be in any way intended. If agents do always tend toward determinate results or ends in their activity, how is it possible that such unintended events can occur? Chance events force a reexamination of the spontaneous conviction of the finality of all agents.

But in fact there is not only a tendency toward an end in every agent, whether intelligent or non-intelligent, but also in every activity of every agent. Whenever an agent acts, it always acts in this manner rather than in any other manner; it cannot act at all except in some determinate manner or other. But this means that there is a tendency in the agent toward this activity rather than toward any other, and toward the natural result of this activity rather than toward any other result. And this result in turn finds its place in the order of the universe and is therefore subordinate to this order. Now all these objects of tendency represent a hierarchy of ends. Therefore every agent in each of its acts tends toward an end or hierarchy of ends. Therefore, if change cannot take place without an agent, a second presupposition of change is the end of the agent.

Before the problem of the chance event can be attacked, it is necessary to consider the difference between the influence of the end in the action of intelligent beings and the influence of the end in the action of non-intelligent beings. In an intelligent agent acting according to his intelligence, the end influences action precisely insofar as the end is known. The agent sees that certain action is a means toward a desired end and therefore acts in accordance with this knowledge. Such action subordinate to known means-ends relations is a property of intelligent agents alone; sense knowledge could not perceive such relations, since they are not given in sensible phenomena. (Incidentally, we have just now entered for a moment the field of psychic phenomenality and the world of logical objectivity which the existence of consciousness brings into being. This logical objectivity does not fit into our list of the dimensions of being, but it is not itself a distinct dimension of real being. For it is not revealed entitatively but only representatively, not as reality but as representation of reality.)

At this point it is helpful to distinguish between the end and still another influence which is operative in intelligent agents. Like the end, it too influences action insofar as it is known; but while the end influences action by being the object of desire, the exemplar influences action by being the model or idea which is the plan of action or the design of the product, present in the intellect of the intelligent agent. While there are, of course, concrete exemplars and concrete ends even at the level of mere sense knowledge and desire, they are not known as ends or exemplars at this level.

But even the non-intelligent agent is in fact influenced by ends. How is this possible? The end does not exist in reality yet, and it does not exist as such in the sense knowledge of those things which have sense knowledge. How then can the end actually influence or determine the action of such non-intelligent agents? It is possible to go even further. Even the intelligent agents of our experience have tendencies toward ends which are presupposed for the very first activities of such intelligent agents, for example, the general tendency to know and the general tendency to desire what is good. These ends do not arise from the activity of such intelligent agents; rather, they are presupposed for such activity. They actually influence action and the tendency to action in the transphenomenal natures of things, but they do not yet exist in reality or in the knowledge of the agent. Where then are they?

Such an end must exist in the knowledge of some higher agent, higher because it is the reason for the tendency toward such an end in the lower agent. But this means that the tendencies toward action (and therefore the entire transphenomenal objective intelligibility of things, which is here called their nature) of all the things in the physical universe are determined to be such by some higher intellect. This higher intellect must be identical with its activity of knowing, or it will have its own tendency toward its activity of knowing, which tendency itself would be traceable to some still higher intellect. In coming to acknowledge the necessity for such a higher intelligence or intelligences, we are approaching the problems of the existence and nature of God. But these can be treated more properly later.

It is now possible to resolve the problem posed by the occurrence of chance events. First, it must be said that the occurrence of chance events does not deny that there is a tendency toward some determinate end in every agent and in every activity of every agent. As a matter of fact, the occurrence of chance events even presupposes that every agent acts for an end, since determinate actions of some sort must occur if there is to be even the possibility of a chance event.

But if activity is in fact intended, how can a chance event occur? Such an event does not occur simply as the result of the action of any one agent but only as the result of the interaction of a plurality of agents. As a result of the crossing of the lines of intended action, something happens which was unintended by any of the individual agents involved. Lightning did not "intend" to strike the man dead; the man did not intend to be struck dead by lightning. But the two agents, each pursuing an intended line of activity, crossed paths, with the unexpected result.

But the unintended event did actually occur. Therefore it too must have been intended somehow; if there were no tendency anywhere toward this event rather than any other, this event would not have occurred rather than any other. Sometimes, this tendency can be found within the physical universe itself, in the order of the universe, in the case of so-called "chance" events that take place too frequently, or even as a matter of course. The periodic spring floods of various rivers could not be called chance events. Sometimes the tendency can be found in some intelligent agent in the physical universe, as when one person plans the chance meeting of two others. But sometimes the chance event is not simply traceable to the order of the universe or to the plans of the intelligent agents in the physical universe, as, perhaps, if two stars were to collide. Such a chance event may well be, absolutely speaking, a true chance event in the physical universe. But even this event must have been intended somewhere, since it did in fact occur. This intention must be located in some higher intellect.

The existence of chance events does not deny, but rather presupposes, the tendency of every agent toward some determinate end. But such chance events do point out in a new way the necessity for that higher intelligence which is already demanded by the tendencies toward determinate ends in all the things in the world.

*　　*　　*　　*

This completes the preliminary analysis of objectivity. This analysis has by no means been very detailed, but it will be enough to begin the attempt to formulate metaphysical knowledge in meta-concepts. Later on in the course of the metaphysical investigation, it will be possible to enter into much greater detail, from a properly metaphysical perspective, concerning some of the points touched upon here.

Chapter 4

THE PRELIMINARY META-CONCEPT OF BEING AS BEING

Before beginning the investigation of the meta-concept of being as being, several preliminary distinctions and notes must be made. First, there are three levels at which being can be considered, and consequently three levels of meta-conception. There is first the primitive knowledge of being, the being of common sense, "vague being," as it has been called by Maritain. Then there is the knowledge of being required for the start of metaphysical science, the preliminary meta-concept of being as being. Finally, there is a developed knowledge of being, which presupposes considerable progress in metaphysics. This knowledge is never complete, for being is a mystery which can be understood ever more fully. The meta-concept of being as being at this level is more complex, but it is open to even greater complexity as insight into being deepens. This chapter will attend briefly to the "vague being" of common sense, but its primary interest is in the preliminary metaphysical meta-concept of being as being.

Two possible approaches to an understanding of this meta-concept suggest themselves. One might examine the process of its formation in the intellect--this would be a genetic analysis. Or one might analyze the achieved meta-concept by a structural analysis. Here both possibilities are pursued.

What is to be the scope of the meta-concept of being as being? There is not only actual being but also possible being, not only real being but also logical being. But still the primary meaning of being must be actual being. Possible being is called being only because it could be actual; logical being is called being only because it either reflects actual or possible being in some way or because it is somehow like this being. Therefore in the evolution and analysis of the meta-concept of being, one need attend directly only to actual being, the being which actually exists in independence of knowledge of it.

But does this actually existing being include every actual existent? We do not know every actual existent. In particular, it is difficult to take into account whatever being is given in that obscure intuition of createdness that was spoken of toward the end of chapter one. After some metaphysical analysis and development, it may be possible to understand this createdness of things better, along with the being of the creator. But at the start of metaphysics it is best to attend only to that being which is given in some clearer manner. It is true that in the vague being of common sense no such limitation is made, since all is present only in confusion anyway. But at the outset of metaphysics, the preliminary meta-concept of being as being must suffer such limitation in its extension, in the interest of the clarity that is demanded for scientific knowledge. However, this meta-concept must be somehow open to a broader extension, in the event that other actually existent reality is discovered. Otherwise we shall end in the position of the neo-Platonists such as Plotinus, who affirmed some reality beyond being itself.

In fact, the analysis of the dimensions of being in chapter one was all made within the domain of what has been called "proportionate being." This proportionate being is the being that first manifests itself through sensible phenomena, that is understood through objective insight into, and direct conceptualization of, phenomenal and transphenomenal objectivity, and the existence of which is affirmed through the act of judgment. In such being, existence is always a transobjective dimension, really distinct from the domain of objectivity, and therefore demanding that the act of judgment follow upon the acts of objective insight and conceptualization. It is in this proportionate being that metaphysical analysis and meta-conceptualization must begin, since this is the only being that can be known with sufficient clarity at the beginning of metaphysics. The preliminary meta-concept of being as being is a meta-concept of proportionate being as being. We already know vaguely that being is more than this, so this meta-concept must be kept open to further extension; but the price of achieving clear and firm scientific knowledge is to proceed only step by step and not to attempt "leaps" across obscurity.

But if objectivity and existence are really distinct in the domain of proportionate being, then the metaphysical meta-conceptualization of being as being in this domain will require two prior meta-concepts: of being and of existence. The meta-concept of being will be a bi-polar structure, since it must include in some manner both objectivity and existence, as well as the distinction between them. This bi-polarity will, however, still be asymmetrical, since existence is primary in being. On the other hand, the meta-concept of existence will be uni-polar in its primary focus, though it will of course have to include some reference to that of which it is the existence. The meta-concept of being as being is formed by some conjunction of these two prior meta-concepts, since that which makes being actually to be being is its actual existence.

It is necessary then to investigate these two prior meta-concepts before it is possible properly to understand the meta-concept of being as being. It might seem best to focus first of all on existence itself, since it is an element in the meta-concept of being. But it is better to begin with a consideration of being rather than of existence, for existence is not given apart from being but precisely as a constituent of being. Composite being is first and better known than is existence, both in pre-scientific and in scientific knowledge.

The meta-concept of being must refer to both objectivity and existence. But it may be objected that in fact this only takes into account three of the seven dimensions of being which were enumerated in chapter one. What of the others? Just as the preliminary meta-concept of being suffers a limitation in its extension, so also it suffers a limitation in its comprehension. It does not include an explicit reference to the other dimensions of being. But still the other dimensions may be said to be referred to implicitly, insofar as the existence which is explicitly referred to does in fact in some manner implicitly include all the others, as will be seen in the course of the metaphysical analysis of being. Indeed, existence is the ultimate ground for all the dimensions of being, both objective and non-objective.

The meta-concept of proportionate being is an all-inclusive meta-concept, that is to say, a transcendental meta-concept. It refers to the being of any and all of the irreducible genera: substance, quantity, quality, and phenomenality. It refers to the being of every species within each genus, and to the differences between these species as well. It refers not only to the specific natures of things but even to all their individuality in its tiniest details. It refers to anything that is, in the domain of proportionate being, in any way at all. By its recognition of existence as primary and quasi-formal in being, it is open to a still further extension of its transcendentality, supposing that other being is found to exist outside the domain of proportionate being.

But if the meta-concept of being is transcendental, so also must be the meta-concept of existence, since existence is quasi-formal in being. From this follow later a whole host of other transcendental aspects of being, which flow in one way or another from existence.

Now existence, despite the multiplicity of its modes spread out all through the diversity of being, still possesses a certain intrinsic unity as a certain "thrust" into and against nothingness, an affirmation of each being in itself which constitutes this being as distinct from and, in a way, opposed to nothingness. But this "thrust" and "affirmation" is never the same in any two instances; each being affirms itself in its own way--its existence is unique. This means that the intrinsic unity of existence is at the same time intrinsic diversity. The transcendentality of existence and of being means that neither existence nor being can be conceived (in a meta-concept) as having simply one meaning, to which extraneous differences could be added. The only possible difference could be non-being, which would add precisely nothing. But if the meaning of being and of existence is one, but not simply one, then the meta-concepts of being and of existence cannot be univocal but only analogical.

Genesis and structure of univocal concepts

In order the better to understand the analogical meta-conception of being and of existence, it will be helpful first to make a few remarks about univocal and analogical conception. From a genetic viewpoint, a univocal concept is formed through a process of abstraction, a leaving out of differences or otherness in order to achieve a better understanding of some sameness in the objects to be understood. Presupposed to the actual conceptualization is the act of intellectual insight, of which the concept is only the formulation; but here attention is focused upon the concept itself.

It was seen in the previous chapter that the determinate sameness of several things is to be traced to their possession of similar forms, whether substantial or accidental. The fact that these forms are only similar and not identical is due to the potency in which the forms are received; potency, whether it be substance or prime matter, thus stands as an ultimate principle of otherness in things. Prime matter is, of course, the ultimate principle of otherness in things, and is itself pure otherness as well as pure potency. But potency, and especially prime matter, is a principle of otherness not only in grounding the possibility for many instances of the same form but also in that it can receive, not just the particular formal determination in question, but a whole hierarchy of formal determinations, whether identified in the one substantial form of the thing or distinguished among its various accidental forms. What happens in the conception of the determinate sameness of several diverse things is that the twofold role of potency as a principle of otherness is ignored, and the potency is considered simply as a potency for the determination in question. Sometimes abstraction will proceed even further, so that the potency is ignored altogether (and consequently also both of its roles as a principle of otherness); here is what Saint Thomas Aquinas calls an "abstraction of the form" as opposed to the prior "abstraction of the whole" (of the potency-form composite). Through both of these types of abstraction one is left with a concept of some determinate sameness in distinction from any otherness, that is to say, with a univocal concept. For example, I may form a concept of "man," apart from any of the differences of individual men, or even a concept of "humanity," as the substantial form of man apart from any potency in which to be received. Such univocal concepts are called universals, since they each express one intelligible content which can be found realized in each of many diverse individuals.

From a structural point of view, such a univocal concept can be considered at two moments: the moment of conception and the moment of predication. It is possible also to distinguish between the content of the concept and its mode of conception. It is not the mode of conception which is of interest here but only the content. But of great interest is the distinction between the moment of conception and the moment of predication, for here are found important differences between univocal and analogical concepts.

But before the content of concepts is analyzed, some preliminary distinctions are necessary. Actual content is distinguished from potential content, according as the content is actually found in the concept or the actual content is such that the further (up to now only potential) content could be added. For example, the actual content of the concept of animality includes such notes as "having an organized body," "life," and "sensitivity." The potential content of animality includes the various characteristics by which one kind of animal, or even one individual animal, is distinguished from another.

Explicit content is distinguished from implicit content, according as it is directly seen through the concept or is really identical with what is directly seen but is itself not directly seen through the concept. For example, the clear and explicit content of "animal" includes "having an organized body," "living," "sensitive." But there can be no animal without some difference making it to be this kind of animal rather than that kind and without these individual characteristics rather than those; therefore such differences and individual characteristics must pertain in some manner to the implicit content of "animal." It may seem at first that this distinction between explicit and implicit content is the same as that between actual and potential content, but there is a difference. The actual content need not be all explicit, for this actual content may be known in an obscure manner. A special instance of this will be seen in the meta-concept of being. Potential content in fact is itself always implicit, but in order to understand this assertion properly it is necessary to distinguish two types of implicit content.

Implicit content may be determinate or indeterminate. Determinate content is this definite content, or this <u>and</u> that definite content; indeterminate content is this <u>or</u> that definite content, without further clarification. For example, if the animality-of-man is conceived, rationality is included implicitly and determinately; but if mere animality is conceived, rationality (and all other specific differences of animality) is included implicitly and indeterminately.

These distinctions are, of course, burdensome. But they will permit considerable clarification of the differences between the structures of univocal and analogical concepts and meta-concepts. Now, what can be said of the structure of univocal concepts in the light of the above distinctions?

First, the explicit content of a univocal concept is a pure sameness of meaning. Every difference and individual characteristic of the diverse things in which this content is realized or capable of realization is set aside, even though in the diverse things themselves these differences and individual characteristics are in some manner unified with that one same content or meaning (which therefore is only similar and not identical in the diverse things). This is why Thomists say that in the intelligible content as in the thing itself there is an analogy (a unity and diversity at once), while in the univocal conception of this intelligible content there is no analogy but only sameness of meaning.

Second, the univocal concept must be said to include potentially all this diversity of differences and individual characteristics with which the actual content is in fact associated in actual or possible reality. Otherwise such a concept would be impossible to predicate of any real thing.

But the univocal concept can at best include all these differences and individual characteristics only implicitly and indeterminately, not implicitly and determinately. Univocal concepts gained by abstraction of form do not include such diversity even implicitly; univocal concepts gained by abstraction of the whole include such diversity implicitly but only indeterminately. For example, the concept of animality obtained by an abstraction of form is a concept of a form as distinct from its matter, and consequently from all further formal determination which could be associated with this formal determination in matter; it therefore does not include any other formal determination even implicitly. On the other hand, abstraction of the whole gives a concept of form in matter, which therefore is associated with other formal determinations in the thing; therefore in this concept must be included this possible diversity of associated formal determinations implicitly but indeterminately. In such a concept of animal are included the possible differences and individual characteristics of animals, and therefore whole individual animals, implicitly but indeterminately. It is only because of this implicit, indeterminate content in addition to the explicit determinate content, which together comprise the total actual content, that the content of the concept can be predicated of individual things without a part being said of a whole. If the total actual content of the concept did not include in some implicit and indeterminate manner the total intelligibility of the thing, then the affirmation of this content about the thing would amount to an affirmation that the thing is only a part of its total intelligibility, which is absurd.

Earlier, two moments were distinguished at which to consider the structure of a concept: the moment of conception and the moment of predication. With respect to its content, the structure of the univocal concept must be said to be identical at both moments of consideration. No matter how many individuals it be said of, the content of the univocal concept is always the same. For it concerns precisely that element of sameness which would even be identity if it were not for the diversity with which it is in fact also unified in the real things themselves. As will be seen, however, it is quite otherwise with the analogical concept.

Genesis and structure of analogical concepts

Before beginning a description of the genesis and structure of analogical concepts, it is necessary to distinguish between properly and non-properly analogical concepts. In non-proper analogy there is really not just one but a plurality of concepts, to which the same name is applied because of some similarity in the diverse concepts. In proper analogy there is one concept which focuses upon what is similar in the content as found in diverse things, without losing sight at the same time of what is diverse in this same content. Non-proper analogy will not present special difficulty since it is in fact reducible to univocity, but proper analogy is not thus reducible.

Since non-properly analogical concepts are themselves each univocal, they are generated by the type of abstraction already described. But in order that the point of similarity between the diverse univocal concepts be itself seen, there is need of a further consideration; non-proper analogy between concepts presupposes insight into the similarity-in-diversity of these concepts. If this insight were to be conceptually formulated, there would result a properly analogical concept of the similarity-in-diversity of the diverse univocal concepts. But such conceptual formulation is ordinarily omitted in the case of non-proper analogy.

One of the most common examples of non-proper analogy and consequent transfer of names is metaphor. In metaphor, we consider one thing in relation to its phenomena and note a similarity between this relation and that of another thing to its own phenomena. Because of this perceived similarity of relations, we take the name of one and transfer it to the other as well. For example, when the sea has an extremely turbulent appearance, it might be described as "angry," being here compared with men, who, when angry, ordinarily show it in a turbulent appearance. Or a man's behaviour and appearance might be characterized as "leonine," because of some comparison to the behaviour and appearance of a lion. Metaphor can even be employed beyond mere comparisons of phenomenally manifested things and their phenomena, though one of the terms of comparison should always be such a phenomenally manifested thing. An example of such extension of metaphor as a means of comparison can be found in the Scriptural uses of metaphor to describe God, as when it speaks of God's arm, His anger, jealousy, etc. In general, any attempt to describe the action, effect, or impression of what is not in itself sensible in any way by a direct comparison to the phenomena of what is sensible can be called a metaphor. The comparison in this case is suggested by the transfer of the name of the sensible thing or its appearance to the non-sensible thing or its action, effect, or impression. But metaphor always requires diverse realities diversely conceptualized, with a transfer of the name of one to the other because of some noted similarity of the kind described.

Another example of non-proper analogy is found in the analogy of attribution. In the analogy of attribution, a name which is applied to some thing because of one of its notes is also applied to other things which do not themselves have this note but nevertheless have some relation to it. For example, a man is called healthy because of his general activity and appearance. This same name "healthy" is also applied to medicine of some kind because it tends to produce health, or to some food. It is also applied to the man's appearance, which is a sign of his health, and to various activities which tend either to promote or to manifest his health. Underlying the same name is a wide diversity of realities and of concepts; but the concepts do have some point of similarity in that they all contain, despite their diversity, some reference to the health of the man. It is this perceived similarity which is the reason for the transfer of the name.

Unlike non-properly analogical (really univocal) concepts, properly analogical concepts are not achieved through the simple process of abstraction described above, the mere leaving out of differences or otherness in order to achieve a better understanding of the sameness in the objects to be understood. In a properly analogical concept, both the sameness and the otherness must be somehow grasped at once; such a concept aims at expressing both the unity in diversity and the diversity in unity of the content. But although the diversity cannot be simply left out, still it must somehow recede into the background in order that the concept may preserve enough unity to remain one concept. This is achieved by a special type of abstraction, which may be called "abstraction by induced ambiguity." We deliberately allow a degree of obscurity in the formulation of the concept, where the removal of the obscurity would destroy the unity of the concept. We deliberately refuse to clarify this ambiguity at the moment of conception; it becomes clarified only at the moment of predication, clarified in a diverse manner in each diverse predication of the content of the concept about diverse things. But these diverse clarifications at the moment of predication are all seen now against the prior unity at the moment of conception, and thus do not destroy the basic unity of the concept.

There is then a difference in the structure of the properly analogical concept at the moment of conception and at each individual moment of predication; a certain internal readjustment of meaning takes place with each predication. There is need to consider in more detail the structure of such concepts, first at the moment of conception and then at the moment of predication, setting aside all possible potential content and considering only the actual content of such concepts.

The actual explicit content at the moment of conception is the point of similarity in the similarity-in-diversity. Such a point of similarity must in fact be present if there is any proper analogy at all rather than mere equivocity. It is true that this point of similarity is in fact identical with the points of diversity in the content; but "induced ambiguity" in formulation yields a concept which in its explicit content is inadequate as an expression of that which is known, focusing on the point of similarity and leaving the rest in obscurity.

The points of diversity in the content comprise the actual implicit content of the concept. This diversity is included in the concept implicitly, but not just indeterminately (as the diversity is included in a univocal concept achieved through abstraction of the whole); rather, here the diversity is included implicitly and determinately. The properly analogical concept must in this manner embrace the full amplitude of all its diverse modes of realization. These cannot be expressly enumerated (they are only implicit); but they must be remotely enumerable (if they become known, they should be able to be recognized as realizations of this concept).

This structure of a properly analogical concept at the moment of conception can be represented by the diagram below, in which the unshaded area represents the explicit content, while the shaded area represents implicit content. The same relation is also represented by the arrow, its area of origin being implicit in the area in which it terminates. The diverse points of diversity are all represented by little x's (all located in the shaded area, since they are only implicit). Note that they are all present in the implicit content, since they are included determinately.

PROPERLY ANALOGICAL CONCEPT
AT THE MOMENT OF CONCEPTION

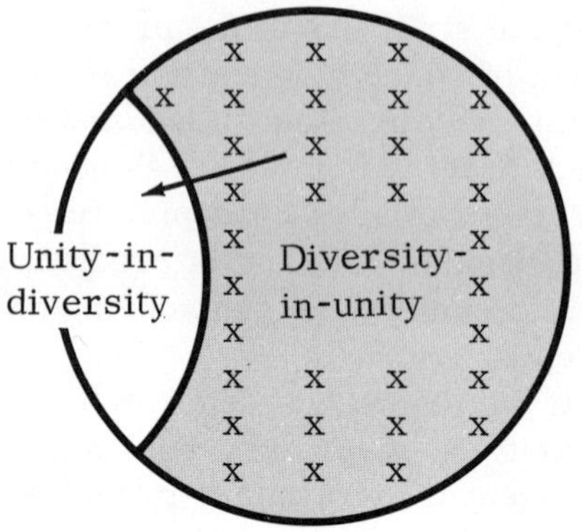

At the moment of predication, this structure changes. Since predication is saying the content of the analogical concept of some definite individual instance or instances of realization, it no longer is possible to continue in the same manner to include determinately all the diverse modes of realization (except in the case in which the predicate is said precisely of all the possible instances). This means that some of the original implicit content is ordinarily dropped from the concept considered in its primary reference (though it reappears in the secondary reference of the concept, as will be seen in a moment). In predication, the primary reference of a concept is to the subject of which it is being predicated; but the concept retains a secondary reference to all other possible subjects of predication, and this secondary reference cannot be simply ignored in outlining the structure of the concept. When I actually say that the content of the concept is realized in some instance or instances, I also understand implicitly that it could be realized in other instances as well. In a univocal concept, this secondary reference is achieved through indeterminate inclusion of diversity; in an analogical concept this secondary reference is achieved through determinate inclusion of diversity. But in both cases the diversity is only implicit.

But, as was said, at the moment of predication some of the original implicit content is ordinarily dropped from the concept in its primary reference. One of two things may happen to the remainder of the explicit and implicit actual content of the concept. First, one may continue to focus attention upon the point of similarity. In this case: the original actual explicit content remains the same; the actual implicit content in the primary reference of the concept is diminished so as to include only the necessary diversity in the present subject of predication; the actual implicit content in the secondary reference of the concept is all the diversity-in-unity taken determinately again. Second, one may focus no longer on the point of similarity but precisely on the particular mode of its realization in this one individual instance diverse from all others. In this case: the original actual explicit content now becomes implicitly actual, though still included in the primary reference of the concept; one of the points of diversity included in the original actual implicit content now becomes explicitly actual; all the other points of diversity are dropped from the primary reference, even implicit, of the concept; but they are all included implicitly and determinately in the now implicit content of unity-in-diversity, as themselves pertaining to the secondary reference of the concept.

This description of the internal readjustments in the content of the concept at the moment of predication has been rather intricate; but emerging from the analysis is the fact that at all times the sum total of actual implicit and actual explicit content of the properly analogical concept is the same, whatever be the adjustment made. This means that the properly analogical concept preserves some kind of unity (an analogical unity) throughout its diverse predications.

The structure of the properly analogical concept at the moment of predication, in the cases considered in the preceding paragraph, can be represented by diagrams similar to the earlier diagram representing the properly analogical concept at the moment of conception. However, somewhat greater complexity is necessary here. Again the shaded areas represent implicit content, while the unshaded areas represent explicit content. Again the same relation of implicitness is also represented by an arrow, its area of origin being implicit in the area in which it terminates. The ordinary arrow is used for content implicit in the concept in its primary reference, while a broken arrow is used for content implicit in the concept in its secondary reference. The diverse points of diversity are all represented by x's.

PROPERLY ANALOGICAL CONCEPT
AT THE MOMENT OF PREDICATION

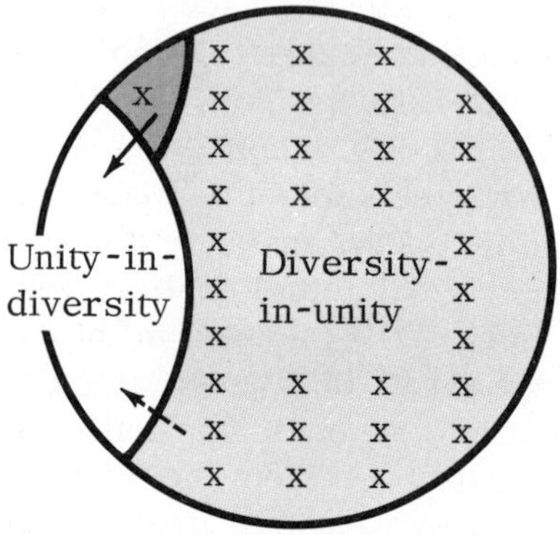

Predication of one subject with focus on point of similarity in diversity

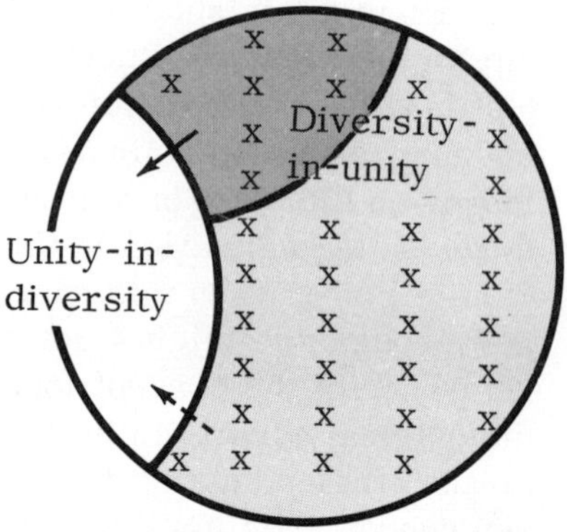

Predication of several subjects with focus on point of similarity in diversity

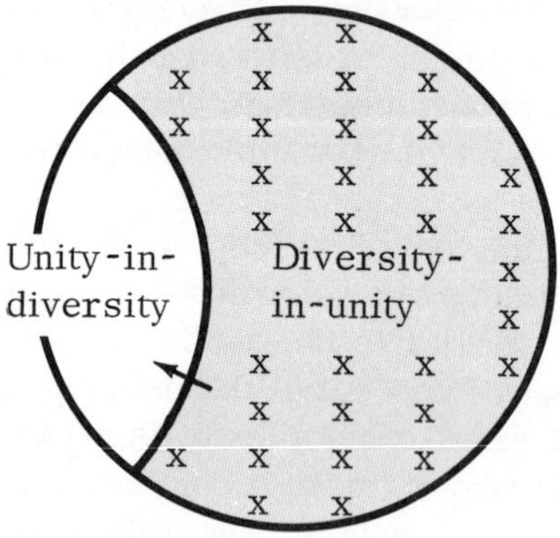

Predication of all possible subjects with focus on point of similarity in diversity

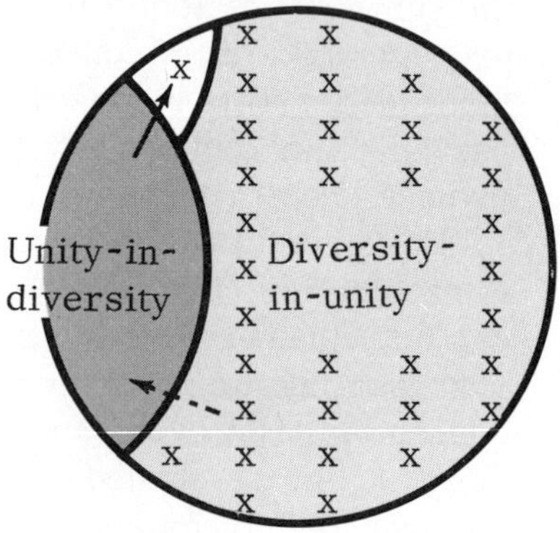

Predication of one subject with focus on its particular mode of diversity in unity

One type of proper analogy has some resemblance to the non-proper analogy of attribution. Here again, the several analogates have relations to one common term (one intelligibility or one reality). But there are two differences between this proper analogy of several in relation to a common term and the non-proper analogy of attribution. First, in this type of proper analogy the common term itself is not one of the analogates at all. Second, the point of similarity here is not merely that all have some relation to the common term but that all have similar relations to this common term. This means that there is similarity in the diverse subjects of the relations themselves, intrinsic similarity which permits them all to be known under one analogical concept. One instance of this is the analogical concept of objectivity in general, which applies to all the diverse levels and types of objectivity. The common term here is the possibility of conceptualization; every level and type of objectivity is conceptualizable in principle, even if we are unable to achieve the conceptualization. This conceptualizability is not itself one of the analogates, but all the analogates have similar relations to the possibility of conceptualization. And this similarity of relations itself presupposes some prior characteristics of every level and type of objectivity, such as the communicability and determinateness which ground the possibility of conceptualization. (Even prime matter is conceptualizable not in itself but in virtue of the form which it has--and prior to its conceptualizability is its communicability and determinateness, which it has, again, not in itself but in virtue of the form which it has.) Another example of this proper analogy of similarity of relations to a common term is found in the analogical concept of accidental form in general. The common term here is substance; every accidental form needs to be in and of substance, to inhere in the substance as a secondary form of the substance. This similarity of relations to a common term means that there is an intrinsic similarity in all accidental forms, despite their diversity. Other instances of this kind of proper analogy have already been seen, in the concepts of substantial form, dynamism, transphenomenal objectivity, etc.

Another kind of proper analogy is the analogy of complementarity, such as is used when both act and potency are called principles of the objective thing. Each relatum is quite diverse; the relation of act to potency is one of determination, while the relation of potency to act is one of determinability. And yet despite this diversity the relations are relations of mutual complementarity--this is the point of similarity which is focused upon when act and potency are considered together as principles of things. Note that this analogy of complementarity presupposes that act and potency have been already defined in concepts which are themselves each analogical by a proper analogy of similarity of relations to a common term. Moreover, since the common term here in the case of act will have to be potency, while the common term in the case of potency will have to be act, both common terms are themselves analogical. This means that here in the case of potency and act these proper analogies of similarity of relations to a common term become proper analogies of proportionality.

In the proper analogy of proportionality, there are not only diverse subjects but diverse terms, but nevertheless with a similarity between the diverse relations of diverse subjects to diverse terms. Of course this is impossible unless there is already some kind of similarity between the diverse terms themselves; for relations here are distinguished according to their terms, and the similarity of relations must proceed from a prior similarity of terms. Whence proceeds this prior similarity of diverse terms? Clearly, there must be some other analogy somehow prior (at least ontologically if not conceptually) to the proper analogy of proportionality.

Considering the properly analogical conceptions of act and potency in the light of the preceding paragraph, the following conclusions may be drawn. The diversity of act can be unified in one analogical concept through an analogy of proportionality between the diverse instances of act and the diverse instances of potency, and the diversity of potency can be unified in one analogical concept through an analogy of proportionality between the diverse instances of potency and the diverse instances of act. But the former conceptualization ultimately depends on the latter. For the similarity and diversity of potencies is in fact known only through the similarity and diversity of acts; potency is known through act. Therefore, potency is ultimately to be defined through its proportionality to act.

But how then is act ultimately (and not merely correlatively) to be defined? At present an adequate discussion of this question is not possible. Nevertheless to anticipate the solution to the problem, formal act will be seen to have a proportionality to existential act, while this existential act itself eventually will be seen to be all similarly related to a common term, which is the pure act of existence. But this must wait until later.

The primitive being of common sense

Before trying to explain the analogical meta-conception of being and of existence by the metaphysician, it seems desirable to make a few observations about being as it is primitively known to common sense. The common sense knowledge of being is obscure, global, and confused. The various dimensions of being are all given in a confused total experience. In particular, this being is not at all disengaged from sensible phenomenality and may be said to be "immersed in sensibility."

If an attempt is made, at the level of common sense, to formulate conceptually the evidence of being, not of this or that being but of common being, the being of all things, this attempt will proceed by way of ordinary abstraction; for the intricacies of analogical conception are inaccessible to uncultivated common sense. If each thing that is can be affirmed in a judgment by which I simply say, "It is," then the obvious way to achieve a conceptual understanding of the being of all things is to remove all determinate attributes from the objects of possible affirmation, so as to leave only this "it." All the diversity of things is removed in order to consider the simple unity of affirmability in judgment. What is left then is a quasi-univocal concept: "univocal," since all the diversity of things has been removed; "quasi-univocal," since this diversity reappears the moment one tries to give the concept any real reference at all. In itself this common sense being is a logical construct of the general class of what is affirmable in true judgment. The transcendentality and analogicity of real being remain hidden behind the univocity of the most general logical category. In such a knowledge of being there is no awareness of the transobjective dynamic act of existence as such.

It is interesting to note, however, the contribution of vital religious faith, giving a special knowledge of God and of spiritual reality, to the common sense knowledge of being. If God and spiritual realities are known in any way whatsoever, then the slightest amount of reflection begins to suggest the analogicity of being and to open in a special way, still long and arduous to be sure, to what Maritain has called the "intuition of being."

The intuition of being

Preceding every conception there is insight, and preceding the analogical meta-conception of being there is an intuition of being. This preliminary intuition of being must not be confused with the much deeper intuition of being which is the result of prolonged metaphysical study, or even with the more analytic knowledge which is gained in the process of formulation of the meta-concept at the outset of metaphysics, which can also be called an intuition of being. This pre-meta-conceptual knowledge is still obscure, but in comparison with the knowledge of common sense it appears as a sudden clarification. It is still not scientific metaphysical knowledge, but it opens the way to such knowledge.

It is fundamentally an awareness, provoked by some profound experience or other, that to be is not simply the most common characteristic of things but their very reality itself. It is an awareness that being is consequently more than thought, more than phenomena, more than all the world of mere objectivity. It is necessarily also an awareness that being reveals itself in the activity of dynamic subjects, and that these subjects, despite their diversity and independence, must be understood against a background of pervasive unity. Implicit in all this is the understanding of the multi-dimensionality, the analogicity, and the transcendentality of being. Here is revealed the fact that being as such has its own special mystery beyond that of all the particular domains of being which are studied in the diverse particular sciences of things. This is the invitation which draws one to become a metaphysician despite the never-ending succession of critics and would-be undertakers of metaphysics. But now it is necessary to formulate meta-conceptually the fundamental content of this intuition, and thus to begin scientific metaphysics.

The genesis and structure of the analogical meta-concepts of being and existence

Before setting about the work of achieving meta-concepts of being and of existence, recall briefly a few points previously noted. First, actually existing being is being through its existence; without existence there would be only nothingness. But neither existence nor its related dimensions (psychic phenomenality, activity, subjectivity, and createdness) are objective. Therefore, being cannot be known in a mere concept, however analogical, but only in a meta-concept (a concept which includes an explicit reference to transobjectivity) constructed a priori out of various univocal and analogical elements (themselves obtained by ordinary abstraction or by induced ambiguity), under the guidance of, by reflection upon, our total objective and non-objective encounter with being (and in particular the intuition of being that was spoken of in the preceding section). The primary focus of this meta-concept must be upon objectivity-in-relation-to-existence; the other non-objective dimensions of being can be tied to, or incorporated into, this meta-concept later on in the development of metaphysical science. Finally, the meta-concept to be developed at this point is a meta-concept of proportionate being, the being that is known through its phenomenality, transphenomenal objectivity, and existence, through the medium of sense experience, intellectual understanding and conceptualization, and judgment grounded upon insight. In this being, as was seen earlier, objectivity and existence are really distinct from each other. We may be aware of other being besides proportionate being; but the consideration is at this time limited to proportionate being, until we are in a more favorable position to extend the scope of the meta-concept of being. However, the possibility of such an extension is assured by the fact that only existence itself is primary and normative in the meta-concept, as it is in being and in every possible instance of being.

The construction of the meta-concept of being begins by a consideration of the relation of objectivity to existence. The objectivity considered is primarily substance, but secondarily it includes accidental forms as well. On the plane of objectivity existence stands as an unknown x, although it is known non-objectively. Since existence is itself known only non-objectively at this point, the relation of objectivity to existence cannot itself be directly conceptualized. But it is possible to note isomorphisms between the relation of objectivity to existence and other relations between various elements, types, or levels of mere objectivity. Since these latter relations are entirely closed within the domain of objectivity, they are directly conceptualizable. To find the isomorphisms is not easy, but still it is possible to detect them by reflecting simultaneously and comparatively on the diverse modes and objects of intellectual awareness.

When such an isomorphism is discovered, a proportionality can be constructed within the field of objectivity according to the following pattern, where O means objectivity, X signifies the existence which is as such an unknown on the plane of objectivity, Y and Z are diverse elements, types, or levels of objectivity, and the rest proceeds in accordance with the rules already set down on page 45 in chapter two.

Given: $R_{YZ}(Y, Z)$ and $R_{OX}(O, X)$. Then: $R_{OX} \sim R_{YZ}$.

The meta-concept (a meta-concept since it includes X) of this proportionality can be said to be a meta-concept of objectivity-in-relation-to-existence, constructed out of objective elements in an a priori manner, under the guidance of our total objective and non-objective encounter with being. This is to say that there is here a grounded meta-concept of being. Now the problem is to fill in the proper objective components for Y and Z. Reflection reveals that the proper components in general are: for Y, potency; for Z, act. Potency and act here are the principles of objectivity which were discovered in the previous chapter. The relation of objectivity to existence is similar to the relation between objective potency and objective act.

Just as objective potency is a capacity, awaiting fulfillment through objective act, so also objectivity in general is only a possibility for actual existence, a capacity to be fulfilled by actual existence itself. Just as objective potency is a determinable, awaiting determination through objective act, so also objectivity in general is in a way indifferent to actual being and nothingness (it can exist, but it need not), a determinable awaiting determination by actual existence. In fact, this similarity of the relation of objectivity to existence to the relation of potency to act within the domain of objectivity justifies the analogical extension of the potency-act relation, so that the relation of objectivity to existence may now be described as a relation of potency to act (and not merely like the relation of potency to act).

And because of certain relations of Latin roots, what has been called objectivity by reason of its relation to the possibility of conceptualization can now be called essence by reason of its relation to the act of existence. Objectivity and essence are the same domain of being, considered from diverse aspects; and the divisions made of objectivity in the preceding chapter can now be understood as divisions of essence. Essence is the potency for existence, and the act of existence is fulfillment of this capacity which is essence.

But even as the essence-existence relation is considered as an instance of a more generalized potency-act relation, it should be realized that, since the potency-act relation is analogical even within the plane of objectivity, a fortiori the similarity of essence-existence to other instances of potency-act may at the same time be accompanied by very important diversity. In fact, existence is an act of essence in quite a different manner from that in which substantial form is an act of prime matter or accidental form of substance. This means that the meta-concept of being in terms of essence and existence needs refinement beyond the mere assertion that essence and existence are related as potency and act. This refinement can be achieved by a comparison of the essence-existence relation to other relations of potency and act, and even to other relations (as will be seen in this and in a later chapter). This necessitates a somewhat more complex meta-concept of being, which is to be defined, not by the simple general formula (where P and A are potency and act in the domain of objectivity),

$$\text{Given: } R_{PA}(P, A) \text{ and } R_{OX}(O, X). \text{ Then: } R_{OX} \sim R_{PA}.$$

but by a whole sequence of similar formulae, to be listed as more determinate qualifications of the general formula.

First, the relation of essence to existence is like the relation of prime matter to substantial form, since existence confers determinate being where otherwise there would be mere nothingness, while substantial form confers determinate being where otherwise there would be the pure indetermination of prime matter. Therefore:

$$\text{Given: } R_{MF}(M, F) \text{ and } R_{OX}(O, X). \text{ Then: } R_{OX} \sim R_{MF}.$$

Second, the relation of essence to existence is like the relation of substance to accidental form, since existence comes to that which is in a way already determined (in the line of objectivity), while accidental form comes to an already determinate substance. Therefore:

$$\text{Given: } R_{SA}(S, A) \text{ and } R_{OX}(O, X). \text{ Then: } R_{OX} \sim R_{SA}.$$

Third, the relation of essence to existence is like the reverse relation of accidental form to substance, since existence gives being to essence, while substance in a way gives being to accidental form.

$$\text{Given: } R_{AS}(A, S) \text{ and } R_{OX}(O, X). \text{ Then: } R_{OX} \sim R_{AS}.$$

Fourth, the relation of essence to existence is like the relation of objectivity to the dynamism of objectivity, since existence is an assertion of the thing against other being and against nothingness, while the dynamism of objectivity is an assertion of objectivity against other objectivity and against nothingness in the order of objectivity. Therefore:

Given: $R_{OD}(O, D)$ and $R_{OX}(O, X)$. Then: $R_{OX} \sim R_{OD}$.

Fifth, the relation of essence to essence-plus-existence is like the relation of the absence of objectivity to the presence of objectivity, since without existence there would be only nothingness. Therefore (using -O to signify the absence of objectivity):

Given: $R_{-OO}(-O, O)$ and $R_{O(O+X)}(O, O+X)$.

Then: $R_{O(O+X)} \sim R_{-OO}$.

The meta-concept of proportionate being, then may be considered as being defined by the general formula and the sequence of five sub-formulae, as follows.

$$R_{OX} \sim R_{PA} \quad \left[\begin{array}{l} R_{OX} \sim R_{MF} \\ R_{OX} \sim R_{SA} \\ R_{OX} \sim R_{AS} \\ R_{OX} \sim R_{OD} \\ R_{O(O+X)} \sim R_{-OO} \end{array} \right.$$

It must again be emphasized that this meta-concept constructed on the plane of objectivity cannot be said to express the reality of being, since it cannot express the reality of existence itself. Rather, this meta-concept only serves to designate and signify the being which has revealed itself as more than mere objectivity.

All that was said earlier concerning the explicit and implicit actual content of properly analogical concepts can now be applied to the properly analogical meta-concept of being as well. Only one qualification must be made: the meta-concept of being cannot be said to have any potential content at all, since it must apply to all the diverse modes of reality, primarily to every mode of actual reality, but also to every mode of possible reality and even to every mode of logical being. The implicit actual content of being as meta-conceived includes determinately every mode of being. The explicit actual content of being is the point of similarity of every proportionate being, namely the essence-existence pair in relation, which is signified by the sequence of formulae given above.

If it should seem that the meta-concept focuses so much upon the point of similarity of the diverse beings that it has a certain appearance of univocity, it should be remembered that the essence-existence pair and relation is in fact diversified in every diverse being. Every such being has its own unique existence, and also its own individuality even in the order of objectivity. This means that the essence-existence pair and relation are at best a unity-in-diversity, rather than a simple unity. The meta-concept of being is properly analogical by an analogy of proportionality.

The analyses made earlier of the structure of the properly analogical concept at the moment of conception and at the moment of predication may be taken to refer to the structure of the properly analogical meta-concept as well, at the moment of meta-conception and of meta-predication.

So much for the meta-concept of being. But it is time to make some brief remarks concerning the meta-concept of existence itself. This meta-concept of existence is contained implicitly in the set of proportionalities used to define the meta-concept of being. The X which signifies and designates existence in those proportionalities can be considered as defined extrinsically (which is as close to a definition of transobjective existence as we can come) by the other three terms of each of the proportionalities and the isomorphism of relations (total isomorphism in the general proportionality, and partial isomorphism in the secondary qualifying proportionalities). Therefore, replacing X by E (for existence), and reversing the relations, the following set of proportionalities may be considered as a definition of E, the first being the general proportionality and the others more determinate qualifications.

$$R_{EO} \sim R_{AP} \; - \left[\begin{array}{l} R_{EO} \sim R_{FM} \\ R_{EO} \sim R_{AS} \\ R_{EO} \sim R_{SA} \\ R_{EO} \sim R_{DO} \\ R_{(E+O)O} \sim R_{O(-O)} \end{array} \right.$$

Being as being

The preliminary metaphysical meta-concept of being as being is formed by combining the meta-concepts of being and of existence, since being as being is being as existing. The proper concern of the metaphysician is to understand the fact of existence in all of its principles that are accessible to the light of reason, both the intrinsic principles within the structure of the existent thing and the extrinsic principles, whatever they may be.

The affirmation of meta-conceived being: the principle of identity

After the meta-conception of being follows its affirmation (or, more properly, meta-affirmation). This affirmation is the principle of identity. It has been variously formulated: "Being is;" "What is, is;" "Being is being." Sometimes it is formulated with a conjugate negation: "Being is; non-being is not;" "Being is being; non-being is non-being;" "What is, is; what is not, is not." But the fundamental meaning of every one of these formulations is the same: Being positively exists as opposed to mere nothingness. Being, known through the meta-concept, is affirmed to possess actual existence and thereby to be positively and sharply and irreducibly distinguished from mere nothingness. The principle of identity is thus no mere tautology. Even when it is formulated in the sentence, "Being is being," the first being refers to that which is known through the meta-concept of being while the second being is a participle referring to the act of existence itself. If this second being were conceptualized, it would be through the meta-concept of existence itself.

The principle of identity should be distinguished from the principle of non-contradiction. The principle of non-contradiction is an affirmation about logical being, being insofar as it is known, insofar as it exists in the intellect in knowledge. The principle of non-contradiction may be formulated as follows: "It is not possible simultaneously to affirm and to deny the same of the same." Clearly this is a principle concerning the judgment and not concerning the thing as really existing.

And yet there is a close dependence of the principle of non-contradiction upon the principle of identity, since its truth presupposes the truth of the principle of identity. It is only because of the sharp and irreducible opposition between being and nothingness (affirmed in the principle of identity) that it is impossible simultaneously to affirm and to deny the same of the same. Affirmation is the affirmation of being; denial is the denial of being. If then, being is irreducibly opposed to nothingness, affirmation must be irreducibly opposed to denial. If the principle of non-contradiction were to be denied, not only would all rational thought become impossible, but the very distinction between being and nothingness would be destroyed with the destruction of the principle of identity. The principle of non-contradiction is in fact nothing but the logical counterpart of the principle of identity.

An immediate consequence of the principle of identity: the principle of sufficient reason

If being as being can be understood as opposed to nothingness, then every being should be in principle knowable as adequately opposed to nothingness. I say "in principle," since we are here dealing with human knowledge and understanding, which is limited and which runs against the fact of mystery in things at every turn. But to say that every being is in principle knowable as adequately opposed to nothingness is to say that every being is intelligible. This intelligibility of being is also called its sufficient reason (for being distinguished from mere nothingness). If the being is distinguished from nothingness in its own right, by virtue of itself alone, then this being has, or is, its own sufficient reason in itself. If it is not adequately distinguished from nothingness in its own right, in virtue of itself alone, its sufficient reason must be sought in some other being (and not in mere nothingness, since this would destroy the fundamental distinction between being and nothingness). But in any case, it is an immediate consequence of the principle of identity that "Every being has a sufficient reason for its being, either in itself or in some other being or beings." This principle of sufficient reason assures us that the metaphysical quest for the reason for existence as opposed to nothingness is in itself justified, whatever obstacles may arise in the way of the movement toward such understanding.

Chapter 5

EXISTENCE AND OBJECTIVITY

Now that the possibility of a scientific discussion of being and existence has been firmly established, the relation between objectivity and existence may be considered in more detail. Since objectivity and essence have already been equated, we will henceforth speak of essence instead of objectivity. Essence is a capacity for existence, but without some kind of existence essence is not distinguished from mere nothingness. The formal perfection of essence, its formal act, determines what its capacity for existence is, the possibility of existence, and therefore the degree of existence which the thing has. And yet there is no formal perfection, no essence at all, except through the act of existence. Existence and the formal perfection of essence are therefore covariant. This kind of mutual influence or causality is peculiar to the essence-existence relation; other acts suppose the reality of the potency they inform, but existence confers reality upon the potency it informs.

At once the whole domain of essence is seen to be in some manner secondary in being; what is primary is the act of existence of each thing. But why then is there the domain of essence or objectivity? Why cannot being be nothing more than a spot of existential actuality, as some of the existentialist philosophers seemingly would have us believe? In what manner is the objective structure of essence necessary in the constitution of existing being? Essence is necessary, as will be seen below, as a principle of limitation of existence; it is the principle grounding the possibility of the multiplicity of beings, both the variety of types and the diversity of individuals of the same type.

The limitation of existential act by essential potency

In chapter three was seen the necessity for potency in order to limit essential act: prime matter to limit and thereby ground the multiplicity of substantial form, substance to limit and thereby ground the multiplicity of accidental form. But the problem of the one and the many in the order of essence has its parallel in the order of existential act. It has already been seen that existential act has a certain unity--of itself it is one act, containing all the perfection of itself. But in fact there is found, not one plenitude of existence, but a vast multiplicity and diversity of acts of existence, none of which contains the fullness of the perfection of existence (at least none in the domain of proportionate being here considered), and every one of which is consequently a limited existential act. How is a limited existential act possible?

Any act is the same with itself; by itself it is one. As one, it would contain all the perfection of itself and thus be infinite in its own order (that is, unlimited in its own line as act, lacking nothing for its own proper completeness). Thus any act which is found to be limited in its own order is so, not in virtue of itself, but in virtue of something other than itself.

There are only two possible factors which could bring about the limitation of the act. One is some other intrinsic element or principle of the being which has the act; the other is an extrinsic element or principle, which will later be called an efficient cause, a cause which gives being through its activity. Clearly, all the possibilities reduce to these two: the act is limited either from within the being of which it is the act or from outside the being of which it is the act. Consider the second possibility.

Can the limitation of act be due solely to the activity of the extrinsic efficient cause? This efficient cause can only produce a limited effect insofar as the effect is in itself limitable. Not even the most powerful efficient cause could produce a limited act that is limited in itself, since it is the very being of an act to be itself one and the same, to contain all the perfection of itself--to be unlimited. Even granting the necessity for some efficient cause (its necessity will be seen in the next chapter) for the production of the limited act, the being of the act as limited remains to be explained. The limitation of an act depends not only on an extrinsic factor but also on something else intrinsic to the being which has the act.

There are three possible intrinsic factors: some potency for the given act, some other act of the potency for the given act, or some act of the given act (to which the given act is itself in potency). The second possibility is reducible to the first, since such an "other act" could only influence the given act through the potency in which both acts are. Therefore there remain only the first and third possibilities.

First, consider the third. Could the given act be limited by some other act to which it is itself in potency? If this were the case, the same difficulty of limitation would again arise with the new act, which is certainly not limited by its nature and which therefore needs a principle of limitation in the thing, ... and so to infinity. Even supposing that this new act were in itself limited or that it did not have to be limited, it would be difficult in most cases to see just how it could have any function in the limitation of the first act. For the radical constitution of a potency as such is presupposed to, and not determined by, its act, except in a way in the case of essence and the act of existence. Therefore, the radical limitation of a potency, except in a way the potency to existence, cannot be traced to its act. With respect to existence itself, it is true in a way to say the potency to existence will only be limited if the existence is limited, since existence gives being to the potency for existence. But existence itself is not limited in itself; moreover, as the act of all other actuality, it is not itself in potency to any further actuality, and hence could not be limited by any further act. Therefore the potency to existence cannot be limited simply by existence itself; rather, this limited potency is itself absolutely required for the limitation of existence.

With the second and third alternatives rejected, there remains only the first, namely that any act (including the act of existence) is limited only insofar as it is received in some potency (which, in the case of existence, is essence). The potency must of course itself be somehow limited already, which means that the limitation of existential act necessarily presupposes prior limitation in the essential order, whether it be the limitation of this type of form as opposed to that type of form, or the limitation of accidental form as being received in this substance rather than that substance, or the limitation of substantial form by prime matter as the ultimate principle of individuation in material substances. All the diversity, limitation, and multiplication of acts of existence is thus traceable to the reception of the act of existence in diverse essential potencies, already themselves limited in one way or another.

The manner of limitation of act in general, then, may be explained as follows. An act, one in itself and therefore in itself unlimited in its own proper line, but now received in some given potency, is in that potency as the act of that potency--as act in relation to that particular potency. In the composite, this relation is not really distinct from the act itself. Therefore this act stands as distinct from any other possible similar acts of other potencies, since these other acts would be identical with their own relations to their own particular potencies. Since other such similar acts are indeed really possible, the given act must be said to be limited in the instance in question.

From the theorem just established, that any act is limited only insofar as it is received in some potency, it follows that every limited being must be composed of essential potency and existential act, and that every limited instance of some essential type must itself be composed of some potency and form (this latter point was already seen in chapter three). This means that even if there are limited beings outside the domain of proportionate being, the definition of being (the meta-concept) can be extended to include them, since they too are composed of essence and existence in real distinction from each other. Moreover, if there is some unlimited act of existence, it must be unique; for if it were not unique, it would not contain all the perfection of itself and would therefore be a limited act. This means that there is at most only one being which utterly transcends meta-conceptualization. But it will be seen in Part 2 that even this being is known in such a way as to allow the extension of the scope of the meta-concept of being to include it in some manner.

Redefinition of the principles of objectivity

Since objectivity or essence receives its meaning from the existence to which it is in potency, it is desirable to redefine the principles of objectivity or essence (substantial form, prime matter, substance, accidental form) in relation to existence. Substantial form is that formal determination which confers some determinate degree of fundamental or substantial existence. Prime matter is a pure potency, without formal determination of any kind, and therefore undetermined in itself to any particular degree of existence, but to be determined by substantial form so as to constitute the substantial existent. Substance, in proportionate being, is the composite of prime matter and substantial form which is the immediate potency for substantial existence. Accidental form is a formal determination which confers some determinate degree of superficial or accidental existence on the existent substance.

Reconsideration of the plurality of substantial forms and the indeterminacy of prime matter

At this point it is possible to reinforce the conclusion in chapter three that a plurality of substantial forms simultaneously existing in the same prime matter is impossible, and that prime matter has no determination in itself but receives all substantial determination from substantial form. If it is the function of substantial form to constitute a determinate substantial potency for substantial existence and to confer a determinate degree of substantial existence corresponding to this potency, then once the substantial potency is constituted and the corresponding existence conferred, the only further potency and existence in this thing will be accidental. This means that a hierarchy of simultaneously existing and really distinct substantial determinations in the same thing is impossible. Nor is a non-hierarchical set of distinct substantial determinations any more possible. First, some kind of hierarchy would seem necessary, since the more specific substantial determinations presuppose the more generic. Second, even if, per impossibile, the plurality of determinations were found simultaneously and in distinction from each other, but in a non-hierarchical manner, each distinct determination would confer a distinct substantial existence; but a plurality of substantial existences in one substance seems to destroy the existential unity of substance.

Now if prime matter had any substantial determination of itself, it would also have substantial existence of itself. But this would mean that any further determination would have to be merely accidental, which would destroy the whole meaning of prime matter as a potency for substantial form conferring substantial existence on the composite thing. Therefore prime matter must be purely indeterminate in itself.

The question of whether prime matter could ever exist by itself apart from substantial form may now be answered. Since the degree of existence is determined by the potency for existence and its intrinsic formal determination, prime matter cannot be in itself an immediate potency for existence; for it is not in itself determined to any particular degree of existence.

Primary and secondary existence

The substantial and accidental existence of the thing have already been distinguished. Some Thomists have denied this distinction and asserted that there is only one substantial existence in the thing, giving reality to both the substance and its accidental forms. The reason for denying this distinction is the desire to preserve the unity of the substance-accident composite, which seems endangered by the distinction between the primary substantial existence and secondary accidental existences.

In fact, however, the unity of the substance-accident composite can be sufficiently safeguarded without removing the distinction between substantial and accidental existence, as will be seen in a later chapter. But more directly to the point at this moment is the impossibility of substantial existence giving being to accidents; this would destroy the meaning of substantial existence or of accident or of both. Rather, as a substance is related to its existence, so an accident is related to its existence. There is a proportional similarity between these two modes of being; but substance is being in the primary sense (and has existence in the primary sense) and accident is being in a secondary sense (and has existence in a secondary sense). For accidents are still only <u>beings of substance,</u> needing to inhere in substance. But a more complete understanding of the relation of substance and accident to existence will be possible in a later chapter, from the perspective of subjectivity.

The dynamism of objectivity

In chapter three the presence of a mysterious dynamism of objectivity or essence was noted. This dynamism cannot be adequately understood from the restricted perspective of the analysis of objectivity. It is clear that it is somehow related to actual existence, since only actually existent things exercise such dynamism. At the same time it is something more than simple existence, since through it things seem to transcend their own being. Here again activity appears as a superabundance of being.

Another related motive forces a deeper consideration of activity. It was already seen in chapter three that change of objectivity or essence presupposes the influence of some extrinsic factor, an agent. Now this change of essence is also change of existence, since formal determination and existence are covariant. Therefore, the metaphysician as a philosopher of existence must feel compelled to investigate the nature of the agent and of the influence exercised by the agent through its activity. This is the concern of the next chapter.

A note on being and the principles of being

The term being is used sometimes for existence, sometimes for essence, and sometimes for the principles of essence; later it shall be used also for the subject which has existence. At present, however, only the first three usages are of interest. Since things are beings only through their possession of the act of existence, being in its participial sense, as meaning the act of existing, is primary. Being in a secondary, nominal sense, is applied to essence, as to the immediate potency which receives existence as its act. But the term being can also be applied to the diverse principles of essence (and therefore of existence as well). Here being is used as a noun, and is applied by an analogy of several (the diverse principles) to a common term (immediately, essence, and remotely, existence). Among the diverse principles there is a certain order. Being is said primarily of substance, then of substantial form, then of accidental form, then of prime matter. But it must be understood that being as a noun in these cases signifies that by which an essence is constituted, rather than essence itself. Indeed, even when being is applied to essence, it signifies that by which the thing has existence, rather than that which is. This latter is not simply essence, as will be seen in a later chapter, but the <u>subject</u>. At present essence is spoken of as having existence; but as one penetrates more deeply into the meaning of "having existence," he comes to see more clearly that the essence does not, properly speaking, <u>have existence</u>. Essence is only the immediate potency for existence in the concrete subject, which is somehow more than essence alone.

Chapter 6

THE DYNAMISM OF EXISTENCE

The reality of activity and its distinction from the agent have already been discussed in chapter one. However, many further questions occur to the metaphysician concerning activity. Since every being of our experience seems to have its own proper activity, it may be asked whether activity or the tendency to activity is not a property of being as such. This in turn leads on to other questions. But before any of these questions can be considered there is the problem of the meta-conceptualization of activity, analogous to the problem of the meta-conceptualization of existence.

The meta-concept of activity and of the agent

The basic technique to be employed in achieving meta-concepts of activity and of the agent in proportionate being is similar to that employed in achieving meta-concepts of existence and being. This time, however, it is possible to use the meta-concepts of existence and being as well as the ordinary concepts of objectivity, substance, accident, and objective dynamism in order to construct the new meta-concepts. Again the definitions of these meta-concepts can be formulated in proportionalities, with activity as the unknown X this time. Using the same type of symbolism as in the definitions of being and existence (with E_S and E_A for substantial and accidental existence), the agent (OEX) may be defined by the following formulae. The first pair are the general formulae; the third and fourth are qualifications of the first.

(1) $R_{(OE)X} \sim R_{PA}$ (2) $R_{(OE)X} \sim R_{OD}$

(3) $R_{(OE)X} \sim R_{SA}$

(4) $R_{EX} \sim R_{E_S E_A}$

Activity itself (X) may be defined simply by reversing relations, as was done in the case of existence and being.

(1) $R_{X(OE)} \sim R_{AP}$ (2) $R_{X(OE)} \sim R_{DO}$

(3) $R_{X(OE)} \sim R_{AS}$

(4) $R_{XE} \sim R_{E_A E_S}$

Since these proportionalities all contain as a term either OE (being) or E (existence), which are both essentially analogous terms, it follows that OEX and X are both analogous. The analogy here again is a proper analogy of proportionality. If it can be shown that in fact activity or the tendency to activity is a property of being as such, the analogy of agent and of activity will be isomorphic with that of being and existence.

The above formulae and their implications will be examined more closely later on in this chapter. Now that the possibility of a metaphysical meta-conceptualization of the agent and of activity has been indicated, it may be asked whether or not every being insofar as it is a being is essentially dynamic (that is, either in activity or tending toward activity).

The dynamism of being

In approaching the question of the dynamism of being, it is helpful to begin with a brief survey of the diverse types and levels of activity which are found in the universe of proportionate being. In chapter three, diverse levels of transphenomenal objectivity were seen as revealed through diverse patterns of phenomena. And if the diversity of basic patterns of phenomena reveals the diversity of transphenomenal natures, the diverse degrees of nature and of being, it is only because this same diversity of phenomena reveals the diverse degrees of activity in things. The survey of the degrees of activity, then, proceeds through an examination of phenomena, an examination parallel to that of chapter three.

The phenomena of symbolization and of varied purposive behaviour reveal the activity of intelligence and free will in the human existent. The phenomena of animal behaviour reveal the presence of sense knowledge, sense appetities (with some instinctive responses to certain types of stimuli), and self-locomotion. Vegetative life is observed with its power of regeneration of worn-out cells, and of growth, through the assimilation of foreign matter into the living thing; living things are seen to bring forth other living things in the mysterious process of reproduction. Even in the non-living universe things are not simply inert, but rather exercise certain determinate influences on each other by way of action and reaction. Yet these non-living things do not possess any power, as do living things, to produce others of their kind, to modify their structure or to rebuild it, to modify patterns of activity in themselves in accordance with knowledge and desire. Inanimate things have only outward-directed activity, while living things also have inward-directed activity. The degree of inwardness increases as one ascends through plants and animals to men, reaching a summit in the spiritual life of intelligence and will. At the same time, the possibilities of communication to others do not decrease but increase, from the varied influences of plants and animals upon the natural environment, and the possibility of reproduction, all the way to the self-giving of human love.

In fact, then, every being that we know in the domain of proportionate being does act. Those which are known through sense experience manifest themselves through their direct or indirect operations on our senses; those which are not known through immediate sense experience but rather by some kind of inference are known only insofar as the immediately known is found to be dependent upon the activity of such beings.

But just as it was necessary to inquire why the existents in the domain of proportionate being all have essences, to see why essence is demanded by existence, so also here it may be asked why all these beings act, and whether or not the tendency to activity is somehow a metaphysical consequence of existence itself. Metaphysics cannot rest content with the mere evidence of fact; it must seek for some intrinsic necessity in the connection of the properties of being with the act of existence.

It is most interesting to note that when existence is not seen as the primary root of being, when things are viewed in an essentialist light, activity is by no means seen as a necessary consequence of being. For if being is merely essence, then each being is complete by being what it is, or by the addition of new forms to it. Activity here cannot be understood as anything real beyond the order of form. If this is so, then finite being appears as open to being acted upon, but without any intrinsic drive to act itself. But here occasionalism remains as a metaphysical possibility--God can act alone, while creatures are all merely acted upon. The only way of avoiding occasionalism here is by recourse to the simple factuality of activity, of which we are aware through our intellectualized sense experience. And the moment that sense experience itself is undermined through philosophical criticism, occasionalism puts in an appearance, just as Malebranche followed Descartes. Metaphysically then, essentialism simply fails to account for the activity of finite beings; the fact that they act is a mystery, and it will be called an illusion as soon as possible.

Yet this very fact that activity and the tendency to activity remain unintelligible from the viewpoint of mere essence provides the clue to the adequate ground of their intelligibility. Consider the relation of essence to activity in the light of the Thomist distinction between essence and existence. As Saint Thomas pointed out in the _De Ente et Essentia_, one can know all of what a thing is (its essence) without knowing that it is (its existence). He might have said the very same about what a thing is and that it acts. Mere essences of themselves have no efficacity in the concrete universe; mere ideals do not make the world any better by themselves. We may heap up formal degrees of perfection as high as we please, and the real world will be influenced not a bit by it. What is it then that constitutes the precise point of difference between the merely possible agent and the dynamically actual? There is only one answer to this question--the immediate presupposition, the proper cause, of the tendency to activity (and hence also of the activity itself, so far as the being in question is the cause of its activity) is actual existence.

To say it in another way, no amount of formal perfection, no perfection in the line of essence alone, can constitute being as dynamic; on the other hand, there is nothing more in being than essence and existence. Hence the tendency to activity must be rooted in existence.

Now if the tendency to activity is grounded in existence, if existence is radically one act (not numerically but "formally"), if every being is being through its existence, then it follows that every being insofar as it is a being must tend toward activity, that every being is essentially dynamic.

Note that the analysis just made can be extended beyond the domain of proportionate being to whatever other being there may be, since every being is being insofar as it has existence. It will apply in an eminent manner to the pure act of existence, if this pure act is shown to exist.

In every limited being this dynamism is a tendency to superabound in existence, a tendency to a superexistence, which is activity itself, as was seen in chapter one. From this point of view, activity is a fulfillment of the tendency and capacity of the agent, a perfection of the agent, related to it as act is to potency. This is what is expressed in the first formula in the definition of the agent and of activity, at the beginning of this chapter.

Union and communion

Considered as merely existent, every limited being is isolated from every other limited being. But, as has been seen, no such being is merely existent; each tends to superexist in activity. And it is through activity that isolation is surmounted in union.

But what is this union? Diverse degrees of union are discovered in the activity of things. If we consider the lowest degrees of being and activity--those of inanimate nature--we find that the union of activity consists in the imposition of a certain likeness of the agent upon the other being which is acted upon, which is called the patient. This likeness is considered in more detail later on in this chapter. With the imposition of the likeness, the union ceases; for the being on which this new form has been imposed remains an <u>other</u>. This is the union of outward-directed, or transitive, activity.

When the next higher degree is considered--that of vegetative life--one finds, in addition to the lower type of activity, some inward-directed activities (immanent activities) and a higher degree of union. Here, the vegetative being strives to assimilate the other, as far as possible, to itself in the processes of nutrition and growth. Here there is a certain triumph over isolation, but it is achieved only at the price of the destruction of the otherness of the other. Yet, at this vegetative level of activity, there is more than the mere drawing of the other into the being of vegetative life. There is also an "outgoing," as the vegetative being seeks to bestow itself upon the other as far as possible, through the generation of another vegetative being. Reproduction is, of course, for the good of the species; but it is also a manifestation of the tendency of the individual vegetative being to transcend its isolation.

At the level of sensitive activity, two new forms of union appear, namely sense knowledge and sense desire. In sense knowledge the other becomes present even while remaining other; there is in addition a tendency to retain this other in memory. And yet, despite the superiority of this new mode of union, it has certain deficiencies. So long as the other is possessed in knowledge while remaining apart from physical union, the knower still remains in relative isolation. For the being of the other is in no way affected by this mere knowledge; it stands there in indifference to the knower. Indeed, if the knower is considered only as a knower, there is even a kind of indifference of the knower to the known. Moreover, the union of sense knowledge is very limited in that it is restricted to particular things existing here and now.

The first deficiency, the indifference of the known to the knower, is not surmounted on the level of mere sensitive life at all, but only in human knowledge and love of person and person. But the second, the indifference of the knower to the known, is surmounted in the act of the sense appetite. The third deficiency, the limitation of sense knowledge to the here and now particular is surmounted only in man with his intellectual knowledge.

By intellectual knowledge, man can achieve a cognitive union with all being, even the being of God, as will be seen in Part 2. (But while the principal object of the intellect is in fact God, still in this life the human intellect has no vision of the intrinsic being of God. The modes of natural cognitive and affective union with God in this life will be considered in Part 2.) But there is a most important deficiency in this intellectual knowledge, considered as a mode of union with things. By itself, it can only attain to the other in its "thereness," although it does this by living again the being of the other in the intellect; but it can never attain by itself the very "here-and-nowness" of the other, its subjectivity.

But although the intellect cannot of itself attain the subjectivity of the other, it can do so through the medium of the act of love of the will (see chapter eight). The intellectual attainment of the other is properly called union, but the attainment of the other by the intellect through the medium of the act of love of the will is more properly called communion. For though the intellect receives the other into its presence on an unequal plane as an object or quasi-object present to the subject which is the human existent, through the medium of love the other is present on an equal plane, as another subject. Moreover, in this act of communion, the human existent not only embraces the subjectivity of the other but also in a way totally gives himself to the other, especially if the other is a person. (This total self-giving, however, is always relative and conditional, or should be so, unless the other is God.)

There is also another manner in which the isolation of the human existent is surpassed in union--the way of communication and dialogue. Communication and dialogue take place through the medium of language or a variety of other symbolic forms. They are the natural consequence of intellectual knowledge and love, and they necessarily presuppose knowledge and that minimum of love which prompts one person to try to communicate and another person to be willing to listen.

In general then, the tendency to superexistence or superabundance in every being is at the same time a tendency to union or communion with others in some manner. But in this union or communion may be discerned still another aspect of activity, namely, the diffusion of being. Being is diffusive of itself. This is the dynamic generosity of being.

The diffusion of being

In considering the diverse modes of activity and the resulting union of beings, one finds that, while some of these modes do not immediately physically diffuse or communicate being to other beings, still there is always a tendency toward some diffusion of being. Knowledge is not in itself a physical diffusion of being to the known; but knowledge is the preliminary to love--in which being is given in one way or another to the loved thing, whether it be, for example, by the simple assimilation of food or by the spiritual self-giving of human friendship or by the offering of oneself for disposal at the hands of God. Reproduction is a diffusion of being. Mere transitive activity is a diffusion of being. The language and art of man are diffusions of being. The creative activity of God and His movement of His creatures to their diverse ends, which will be seen in Part 2, are diffusions of being. Even when there is not an immediate physical diffusion of being to some other being, the superabundance of being within the same being can be regarded as diffusion of being in a certain sense, as when the knower becomes the known in the very act of knowledge, or when the living organism modifies its own state in some manner.

Activity is always diffusion of being in some manner or other. This fact is recognized in the second formula in the definition of activity, in which activity is compared to the dynamism of objectivity--which is known through the diffusion of objectivity.

The relation of activity to the agent

Several aspects of activity have appeared. It is a superexistential act, a superabundance emanating from the agent, a mode of union between the agent and what is distinct from the agent. And activity is in some manner really distinct from the essence and existence of the agent, as was seen in chapter one. But more still remains to be said about this mysterious actuality.

Since activity is distinct from the essence and existence of the agent, and yet somehow in and of the agent (though it is even more than this, as will be seen), it must be compared to the agent as act to potency, and indeed as a quasi-accident to substance. This was pointed out in the third formula of the definition of activity. But it is only a quasi-accident, since it is not as such a form but a superexistence. This was pointed out in the fourth formula of the definition.

But to say that activity is a superexistence raises other problems. Of what is it the existence? The agent already has its existence. If the agent is in potency for a further perfection in the line of existence itself (such as is activity itself), this potency must have a peculiar structure unlike any seen so far. If there is a new existential act in activity, then there must be something new in the line of objectivity too, to limit and in some manner receive this act. It may well seem just about impossible to understand activity in the framework of the metaphysics of act and potency, of existence and essence.

At this point it is useful to make explicit a distinction which has been implicitly assumed all along in the discussion of activity. Activity is somehow of (and therefore in some manner also in) the agent, and it is at the same time in that which is being acted upon. At this point activity is considered insofar as it is of the agent. Later it will be considered insofar as it is in that which is being acted upon, insofar as it is in the product of the activity. Then it will be evident that in fact activity involves two superexistences of the agent, one in the agent and one in the thing acted upon, except in the case of perfectly immanent activity in which there is no product outside the agent as such.

The superexistence in the agent is necessarily itself directed toward the result to be produced. It is therefore in some manner an intentional superexistence, and the formal objectivity correlative with this intentional superexistence is an intentional form. An intention is simply a tendency toward, grounded in a certain likeness and relation. The intention is like and somehow related to that which is intended or tended toward. Since the intention is a tendency toward, it results in a certain union between what has the intention and the intended. It has already been seen that intentionality is fundamental in knowledge and love. Now, the importance of intentionality for an understanding of all activity becomes evident.

That the agent act, two requirements must be met. First, the agent must be determined to act precisely in this way at this point in space and time. This determination does not result merely from the agent's being an agent; the agent might act in many possible ways at many diverse points in space and time, but in fact it does act in this way at this point. This means that there must be a tendency toward this activity in this way at this point. This ultimate tendency determining the agent to act is the intentional form of activity, and its intentional existence is the superexistence of activity insofar as it is of and in the agent.

The second requirement for the activity of the agent is that the agent be actually in a dynamic union with what is being acted upon. But the unifying function of intentionality has already been pointed out. The intentional form and superexistence in the agent unify the agent with what is being acted upon.

And correlative with this intentional form and superexistence in the agent is the form and existence of the result produced in the activity. During the activity, this form and existence are dependent upon the intentional form and superexistence in the agent; they are the being of the agent as diffused. The existence of the result in activity can be called a second superexistence of the agent, this time in the thing acted upon. It is a superexistence of the agent, not only because it is dependent upon the agent, but also because it is referred to the agent through the intentionality of the form and superexistence in the agent itself. This intentionality in the agent not only unifies the agent with what is being acted upon but also unifies what is being acted upon, precisely insofar as it is being acted upon, with the agent. This point will become clearer when the necessary likeness between the agent as agent and the result as result is considered.

But at the moment the problem is still to understand the relation of activity to the agent. There is still the problem of understanding more precisely how activity can be a superexistence of the agent. It would seem that this superexistence is nothing more than an ordinary accidental existence, the accidental existence of the accidental intentional form which determines the agent to act in this way rather than that, at this point in space and time. But this would only be a further determination of the absolute existence of the thing, while activity is in fact not the absolute existence of the thing but precisely an overflow of this existence toward another, or at least beyond the absolute being of the thing itself.

It is necessary to say that this superexistence which is activity in the agent is not so much an accidental existence of an accidental intentional form as a simple accidental superexistence. This is to say that the intentional form is indeed necessary in order to limit this superexistence, since formal objectivity is always required as a limiting principle of existential, and therefore of superexistential, act. But it is also to say that this superexistence should be seen primarily, not as giving being to the accidental intentional form (though it does do this), but rather as an overflow or superabundance of the existence of the agent itself. The intentional form serves as the ultimate determinant of the direction and degree of this overflow and superabundance (as a modulator), but it remains primarily the overflow of being of and from the agent. If it be asked, then, what it is that properly can be said to possess this superexistential act, one must say that it is not so much the intentional form as the agent which has the intentional form as the modulator of its superabundance. This means that the immediate potency which is informed by the superexistential act (both the potency and the act being modulated by the intentional form) is not the intentional form but the power of acting, which is either the agent or some part of the agent.

This immediately raises the question of this power of the agent. How is this power related to the agent? Is it perhaps identical with the very substance of the agent? Or is it necessary to posit certain accidental determinations of the agent as its active powers? Certainly, the second alternative is at least suggested by the plurality of powers in the same agent that is observed in complex living organisms. The diversity of function in accordance with the diversity of systems and organs seems quite unintelligible without a plurality of active powers in the diverse parts of the organism. If all things exhibited the same heterogeneity of structure and function that is exhibited by the complex living organism, the case might be considered closed. But in fact the case is not so simple. Do the subatomic particles exhibit such heterogeneity of structure and function? And even if they do, may there not be some one power in such cases which in fact is identical with the substance itself even while the other powers are accidents distinct from the substance? And, to go in the other direction, how is one to be certain of the relation of intellect and will, as active powers, to the incorporeal, and therefore non-organic, substantial principle which possesses them?

It seems clear that mere empirical analysis and introspection cannot suffice to settle the general question of whether the active power is identical with the substance of the agent or an accident distinct from the substance of the agent. However, a metaphysical analysis in terms of potency and act brings more definite results.

Every limited existential act requires a potency of the same genus: substantial existence demands substantial potency; accidental existence demands accidental potency. So also, accidental superexistence requires an accidental potency. Now although it is true that the intentional form correlative with the accidental superexistence of activity is itself accidental and limits this superexistence, it has been seen that it does so only as a modulator of the more fundamental potency for superexistence, which is the active power itself. Now, if the active power itself is the potency for the accidental superexistence which is activity, then this active power must be accidental rather than substantial, and therefore distinct from the substance of the agent.

The power of activity, then, is an accident, a specific tendency of the substance toward a specific type of activity. It has been assumed all along that in fact in many things there is a plurality of such powers. It seems worthwhile to attempt to clarify this point by setting down a metaphysical criterion for the diversity and distinction of powers.

Active powers are essentially tendencies toward activity; and activity itself is always a tendency toward the communication of perfection through the superabundance of being. Since a tendency receives its meaning from that toward which it tends (its object), activity and active powers will be diversified according to the diverse objects which they have. An individual here-and-now activity can be understood by pointing to its individual here-and-now object. Where there are specific types of object, there are specific types of activity, and consequently specifically distinct active powers. But how are the diverse types of object of activity and of active powers to be distinguished?

If activity and active powers tend toward the communication of perfection through the superabundance of being, it is clear that the diversity of objects can be discovered in the diversity of types of perfection to be communicated through the superabundance of being, or even more formally, in the diversity of modes of communication. Some of these modes have already been seen, such as substantial assimilation (in nutrition and growth), substantial separation (in reproduction), the diverse modes of intentional assimilation in sense and intellectual knowledge and love, and the diverse modes of physical accidental assimilation in transitive activity. Without entering further at present into the details of the distinction of active powers, it is clear that a wide diversity of active powers is in fact found in things.

Two final observations may close the account of activity in relation to the agent. First, activity and the active power both presuppose the existent thing. There can be no superabundance, no overflow, without the prior existence of the spring in the substantial existent. Second, the degree of activity and power is in direct proportion to the degree of being in the thing. The activity flows from the thing; the tendency to the activity in the power is a tendency of the thing. Therefore, as a thing acts, so it must be--from the degree of activity is understood the degree of existence. This principle is correlative with the principle discussed earlier in this chapter, that every being insofar as it is a being tends toward activity. Now, since the degree of existence is also covariant with the degree of objectivity or essence (as determined by its formal content), in every being there are three covariants--essence, existence, and the tendency to activity (except in the case of pure existence, which will be considered in Part 2).

The relation of activity to the result of activity

That which is called an agent when it is considered as the source of activity is also called the agent or efficient cause, when it is considered in relation to the result of the activity. The activity of the agent cause is the means of agent or efficient causality. When the agent is considered, not merely as an agent, but as an agent cause, some new problems come into view.

First, when is an efficient cause required? The statement of conditions which demand an efficient cause is a principle of efficient causality. Certain philosophers who are in general rather oblivious of metaphysical evidence have denied that any principle of efficient causality can be stated at all. However, against the background of metaphysical evidence gathered so far in this inquiry, a principle of efficient causality going even much deeper than Aristotle did is seen to be absolutely necessary.

Consider first a more restricted form of the principle: Whatever comes to be has an efficient cause. This can be seen by considering the meaning of coming-to-be. In coming-to-be, either a potency receives an act which it did not have before or (in the special case of creation, which will be considered in Part 2) there is now something where there was simply nothing before. The need for an efficient cause in the second case, supposing that the case is given in fact, is evident; otherwise the distinction between being and nothingness would be denied, since something would come from mere nothing. The need for an efficient cause in the first case is likewise evident, by an extension of the analysis made on the level of pure objectivity in chapter three to the level of existence and being in the proper sense. The act, simply speaking, did not exist in the potency before the coming-to-be; there was with respect to this act a nothingness in the potency, a mere lack. Thus, to maintain that the act could by itself come to be in the potency would be to deny either the distinction between potency and act or the distinction between being and non-being. Therefore, this act must come to be in the potency only in virtue of the activity of some extrinsic agent (extrinsic to the changing being in transitive activity, extrinsic to this particular aspect of the changing being in immanent activity). Therefore, whatever comes to be has an efficient cause.

But the principle of efficient causality can be more general and more profound. Now it will be formulated as: Every contingent being has an efficient cause. To call a being contingent is to say that of its nature it is able either to exist or not to exist; the opposite of contingent is necessary--a necessary being by its very nature must exist. This formulation of the principle of efficient causality is more general than the first, since a being could well be contingent even if it had always existed; this formulation of the principle does not introduce the notion of temporal origin.

Now, every limited being is a contingent being. In every limited being, the act of existence is limited by a potency which receives it, namely the essence or nature of the being. Therefore in such a being the existence and essence are really distinct from each other. And in this case, the existence cannot be said ultimately to flow from the essence as from an adequate source; for nothing can flow from the essence unless this essence first exist. Therefore, this existence is possessed only contingently by the essence.

But not only is every limited being a contingent being; every contingent being is also a limited being. If the being is contingent, its nature or essence cannot be identical with existence; for identity of essence and existence mean a necessary being. But if essence and existence are distinct, then the essence is a potency which limits the act of existence. But if the existence is limited, then the being is limited; for the being is being only insofar as it has existence.

Now limited being cannot stand in being by itself, since limited existence cannot stand by itself but is "essentially" dependent on some other being. If this existence stood by itself, it would be one and infinite, just like any other act that stands by itself apart from potency. But this act of existence is not one and infinite; therefore it is dependent. But despite the fact that it is the existence of an essence, it cannot depend for its being on the essence; for it was just seen that existence cannot be said to flow from the distinct essence as from an adequate source. Therefore, this limited existence must depend on some other being in some manner. But the necessary influence of this other being on the being in question must take place through the superabundance of being which is activity, and therefore this other being is an agent or efficient cause. Therefore every limited being has an efficient cause, and therefore every contingent being has an efficient cause.

Any change, and in general the being of any contingent being, demands an efficient cause. The fundamental reason for this is that anything that is essentially dependent demands the existence of that on which it depends; otherwise the distinction between being and nothingness would disappear. But even more precisely, anything that is essentially dependent must be here and now depending; otherwise it would be here and now independent and therefore not essentially dependent. This is to say that the effect precisely as an effect must be simultaneous with the cause precisely as a cause. If change requires an extrinsic agent, then it requires the extrinsic agent at every moment of the change. If contingent being requires an extrinsic agent, then it requires this extrinsic agent at every moment that the contingent being is.

At the moment of activity, then, the produced act of form or existence in the thing acted upon has an essential relation of immediate dependence to the agent as agent. This immediate dependence introduces an element of intentionality in the effect as an effect; the produced form is in this respect an intentional form referring back to the agent as agent, and its existence is in this respect an intentional existence. This is a physical intentionality in every effect-to-agent relation, and not especially the spiritual intentionality of knowledge and love, which will be considered in the next chapter. This physical intentionality in the effect is the complement of the physical intentionality in the agent; and just as the intentionality in the agent unifies the agent dynamically with the thing acted upon, so also the intentionality in the thing acted upon unifies this thing with the agent at the moment of activity. Thus the existence of the effect as an effect may be regarded as a second superexistence of the agent, not a superexistence in the agent, but a superexistence of the agent outside the agent in the effect.

Still another aspect of the intentionality in the effect as an effect appears in considering that the dependence of the effect as an effect on the cause as a cause implies the similarity of effect to cause. For if dependence means a genuine "influx received," then the effect must have already existed in some manner in the agent itself. For from nothing comes nothing, and being only from being, and a given perfection only from what has this perfection itself. But it is possible to locate even more precisely the point of similarity between the agent as an agent and the effect as an effect. This similarity does not necessarily involve the whole being of the agent or the whole being in which the result is produced. It does not even mean that the effect is simply similar to the power of activity. Rather, that determination which is produced through the activity must be most formally similar to the ultimate intentional determination of the power, the intentionality which modulates the activity of this power. For the power may produce many diverse effects; but this particular effect is due, not to the power considered simply in itself, but rather to the power considered as ultimately informed by the intentional form correlative with the activity itself. This means that there is a true assimilation of the agent precisely as agent to the effect precisely as effect. With this ground of likeness and dependence in physical intentionality, it may be said that the agent as an agent becomes the thing acted upon, precisely insofar as it is acted upon, and that the thing acted upon, insofar as it is acted upon, is the superabundance of the agent as an agent.

One may perhaps ask whether this similarity between the agent and the thing acted upon is a similarity of analogy or of univocity. In the things themselves, this similarity must be one of analogy, since in reality diverse instances of a perfection are always only analogically alike. But in the knowledge of the things, this similarity may be either one of analogy or one of univocity, depending on the type of perfection which is being communicated, since some perfections can be conceived univocally while others can be conceived only analogically.

Activity and permanent changes

It may be objected that while the account just given of activity in relation to that which is acted upon is satisfactory for the production of superficial and transient determination, it seems to fail to account for the loss of determination of any kind, or for the production of deeper and more permanent accidental determination, or for the communication of substantial determination. This latter is especially difficult to see. If active powers and their intentionalities and their superexistences must all be accidental, it seems that no limited being can ever communicate a substantial perfection. For as has been seen, the determination communicated must be similar to the determination in the active power of the agent. How then is substantial determination communicated?

First, it does indeed seem necessary to rule out the direct communication of substantial perfection by limited beings. The most that can be done directly by the activity of a limited being is to modify the existential state of a given substance in such a manner that it is no longer suited for the same substantial determination--at which point one substantial determination disappears and another appears. The same observation applies in understanding the loss of given accidental forms, and the supplanting of more permanent, deeper-rooted accidental forms with others. What is done by the agent is to modify the existential state of the thing acted upon by the production of various superficial accidental dispositions in it. If the presence of these new accidental dispositions is incompatible with the continued presence of certain former accidental dispositions, then these former dispositions disappear. If the new accidental dispositions are such as to render the position even of deeper-rooted accidental forms untenable, and even that of the substantial form itself, then these disappear and are replaced by appropriate new determinations.

In order to understand more clearly this strange replacement of determination by other determination, it is necessary to examine more closely this just mentioned "existential state." The state of some thing or principle of being is determined, not by its mere absolute being but by the context in which it is. However, there is no such thing as an "essential state"; for essences simply are what they are, without anything new being added to them by reason of their contexts. But when essences are informed by actual existence, the context can make a great deal of difference in the "existential state" of the thing or of some principle of the thing. For example, the capacity of a potency to receive a given act may be greatly affected by the coexistence of other acts in the concrete thing which has this potency. More specifically, the capacity of prime matter to receive a given substantial form is not everywhere the same, but is affected by the presence of diverse accidental forms in the thing which has this prime matter. The prime matter of a stone is not as apt to take on the form of a living thing as is the prime matter of some carbohydrates; the former would require a series of intermediate modifications, accidental or substantial, in the thing in which it is, while the latter are readily assimilated into the living substance. This strange modification of the capacity of a potency for act, by reason of its context, seems unintelligible from the point of view of essence alone, and arises in virtue of a change in the existential state of the potency. The essence of the potency has remained the same, but its conditions of existence have changed; the essential potency has remained the same, but the existential potency is not the same any more--and the difference is a difference of existential state.

Another example of this influence of existential state may be offered from quite a different field. The capacity of the human mind for learning a given branch of knowledge, for studying some particular aspect of things, is greatly influenced by the kind of knowledge which is actually already possessed, and by the ideals of the learner in his whole life, etc. All these things contribute to constitute the existential state of the learner, to influence in the concrete the capacity of the individual intellect. They are not taken into account in any abstract discussion of the intelligence of the learner and the nature of the subject-matter.

The production of various accidental dispositions, then, so modifies the existential state of the thing acted upon that various determinations, both substantial and accidental, may be lost and replaced by other determinations. At this point, a new difficulty occurs. We see a continuing ingression of new determinations and a loss of old ones. True, this is partially accounted for by modifications of existential state. But surely such modifications cannot give an adequate account of the being of the new determinations. Certainly they provide the opportunity for the ingression of these new determinations; but to leave matters at this point would be in effect to allow act to come forth from potency, or being from nothingness, both of which were ruled out long ago. And yet at present matters must be left at this point. On the plane of proportionate being, or even of limited being in general, the ingression of such determinations and the loss of old determinations must appear radically mysterious. These data have given rise to various untenable theories in the history of philosophy, such as that of the ideas of Plato. But light can be shed on the mystery only from beyond the perspective of proportionate and limited being.

Types of efficient cause

Certain efficient causes seem to exercise their activity under the direction of some other efficient causes, as when man uses machines to do his work. This gives rise to the distinction between principal and instrumental causes. A principal cause acts in accordance with the power of its own nature in order to produce an effect within the power of this nature. An instrumental cause acts in accordance with the power of its nature (all questions concerning the miraculous or the supernatural are here set aside), but under the direction of some other agent, so as to produce an effect which is in a way within the power of this given instrumental agent but, simply speaking, beyond it. For example, the product of the machine is produced in accordance with the physical laws of the components of the machine; but that these components should be arranged in this pattern so as to produce this special order in the result cannot be traced to the physical laws alone but demands the directing intelligence as well. Therefore, in the instrumental cause two powers may be distinguished: the natural power and the instrumental power. The natural power is possessed by the instrumental cause in virtue of itself, while the instrumental power is possessed in virtue of the higher agent. But this distinction between the two powers is a partially artificial one. In fact, there is only one activity, flowing from the natural power of the instrument. However, the instrument also has a certain intentionality produced in it by the principal cause, which moves and applies the instrument in its own ways.

The distinction between principal and instrumental cause should not be confused with the distinction between first and secondary cause. Both first and secondary causes act in accordance with the power of their nature, but the first cause can pass over into activity without the help of any other agent while the secondary cause cannot pass over into activity without the help of some other agent. Since there is a relation of potency to act in the relation of any limited being to its activity, it is clear that no limited being can be a first cause, but only a secondary cause. Some obvious conclusions suggested by this fact are left to Part 2.

To make clearer the distinction between an instrumental and a secondary cause, it may be pointed out that the instrumental causality of an instrument as such is only the transmission in an intentional manner of the activity of the principal cause; but secondary causality is the proper activity of the secondary cause. It is possible for the same cause to be both instrumental and secondary, but these are not the same thing.

A note on activity and sensible phenomenality

At this point it is possible to gain a deeper insight into the nature of sensible phenomenality. The relativity of sensible phenomena in relation to the position and state of the observer has led some to deny that these phenomena possess any objectivity which transcends the sense powers themselves. In particular, it is frequently denied that these phenomena are any direct manifestation of the active powers themselves in such a manner that color would be in the colored thing as it is seen by us, or that sound would exist in reality as it is heard by us. This view is confirmed by the fact that the same thing may exhibit quite diverse phenomena (e.g. differences of color) under diverse circumstances.

First, it is necessary to point out that sensible phenomena are observed as a consequence of the activity of sensible things upon the organs of sense. The manner in which this activity produces a change in the organ of sense so as to produce sensation will be considered briefly in the next chapter.

Second, this activity requires and is modulated by the ultimate formal intentional determination of the active power in the thing, or in the medium between the thing and the organ of sense. Moreover, the determination produced in the organ of sense by this activity is similar, not to the active power of the thing or medium taken simply as the active power, but rather to the active power precisely as determined by the ultimate formal intentional determination.

Third, the same active power may in fact be determined by any one of various ultimate formal intentional determinations, depending upon the variety of other agents which may act upon this power to produce the intentional determination to act or to dispose it for its intentional determination to act.

Fourth, corresponding to this diversity of ultimate formal intentional determinations in the active power of the thing there will necessarily be a diversity of ultimate formal determinations produced by the activity of the thing upon the sense organ, since these determinations are similar and correlative.

Fifth, as a result of this diversity the same thing with the same active power will be manifested in sensation through diverse phenomena, in accordance with the diversity of circumstances in which the thing is placed.

Therefore the qualitative relativity of phenomena is not an insurmountable objection to the objectivity of phenomena as transcending the sense powers, but it does mean that the attempt to regard these phenomena as a direct manifestation of the active powers themselves must be qualified by the realization that what is thus attained is not simply the active power but the active power as modified by some ultimate formal intentional determination. The color is in the colored thing, but only in the sense that the thing shows this color under these circumstances.

Sensible phenomenality then is not in itself a revelation of transphenomenal absolute being, although it is the necessary means to the understanding of such being. Rather, sensible phenomenality in itself is the revelation of the being precisely in its activity relative to the organs of sense, whether this activity takes place through immediate contact or indirectly through a medium.

Finally, none of this is meant to deny the existence of other sources affecting the relativity of phenomena, both qualitative and quantitative relativity. Certainly, the state of the sense organ itself is a factor; and certainly too, differences of perspective are an important factor in both quantitative and qualitative relativity. But it does not seem necessary here to enter into such details. Rather, the focus here is upon what seems to constitute the essential relativity of phenomena in their qualitative aspect. This relativity results from the fact that sensible phenomenality is essentially a revelation of things in their activity relative to the organs of sense.

The goal of activity and tendency

The principle that every agent acts for an end has already been established in chapter three with reference to variations in objectivity. The general extension of this principle to the plane of existence as well, to the plane of existent and not merely objective agents, presents no special difficulty. If every agent acts in a determinate manner, then every agent has some determinate tendency (in each one of its activities) to <u>this</u> activity and to the object of <u>this</u> activity and to the natural result of <u>this</u> activity, and not just to the immediate natural result but even to more remote natural results, which will occur unless chance intervenes. But all of this is only saying that every agent acts for an end.

In every case where the end and the tendency to the end are really distinct--and this is the case everywhere in the domains of proportionate and limited being--the end can be regarded as a cause of the tendency. "Cause" here is not used in the sense of efficient cause, but rather by a certain analogy with the efficient cause. Just as the efficient cause in some manner constitutes a dependent being as a being through its influence by way of activity, so also the end here constitutes the tendency as a tendency through its influence by way of "attraction." From this point of view, the end is here called the final cause, and its influence final causality.

The mysterious "attractive" influence of the end cannot be considered more closely at this point. It will be necessary first to find out where the end exercises this attraction. Now in fact the end of activity cannot physically cause the tendency to activity, as would an efficient cause, for the very good reason that this end does not yet exist, but rather is to be brought into existence through the activity. But if the end does not yet exist, how can it exert any influence at all in any manner? And if the end is as yet a mere nothingness, in no way influencing the tendency, then the tendency as such is a tendency to nothingness and not to anything determinate. But the tendency is in fact more than this; it is always a determinate tendency. The tendency receives its meaning from the end; its intelligibility is constituted by the intelligibility of the end. And therefore the existence of the tendency presupposes the existence of the end.

More generally, even if the end does in fact actually and physically exist, as in the case of the agent which is already here and now in activity, still the tendency to the end cannot be constituted by this physical existence of the end; for the tendency, precisely in its being as a tendency, is even in this case really distinct from and presupposed to the end toward which it tends.

Since the tendency toward the end is in some manner constituted as a tendency by the end, but not by the physical existence of the end, therefore this tendency must be constituted as tendency in some directive knowledge, in which both the tendency and the end exist as known, and known in relation to each other. This knowledge must be intellectual and not sensible, since such relations do not appear in sensible phenomenality. Therefore the final causality of the end must be exercised in some intellect. Therefore, wherever there is tendency toward an end distinct from the tendency itself, as there is in all the activity of proportionate and limited being, there is dependence upon some intellect. Again, some obvious lines of further inquiry will be left for Part 2.

The question again arises, How does the end exercise its "attractive" influence in intellectual knowledge? But before attempting to answer, we must first, in the next chapter, examine more closely the nature of intellectual knowledge and desire.

To return now to the immediate context of agents acting for ends, an interesting correlation may be noted between the principle "Every agent acts for an end," and the principle, which was established earlier in this chapter, "Every being tends toward activity." The first principle sees the tendency toward activity as coming from the final cause, and may be called the principle of the finalization of the agent. The second sees the tendency toward activity as in the agent, and may be called the principle of the finality of the agent.

But in fact, tendency and the object of tendency are found in things at an even deeper level than that of agent and end. For even deeper than and prior to the dynamism of activity in things is the dynamism of existing. Underlying the finality and finalization of the agent is the prior finality and finalization of the existent. Since the intelligibility of essence is in its relation to and capacity for existence, since an existent being tends to remain in being, "every being and principle of being tends toward existence." This is the principle of the finality of the existent. Turned around and viewed from the perspective of finalization, it becomes, "Existence is the good of all things," where "good" is simply the object of tendency.

Activity and subjectivity

Activity is in the agent, not merely as a form is in matter, but as a dynamic overflow or emanation arising from a being already in act and as a superabundance of this act. There is a potency-act relation in the agent-in-activity; but the mere relation of possession, characteristic of the relation of potency to act, is found together with this relation of dynamic exercise. Activity is not merely a possessed act but an exercised act. Later, existence also will appear as an exercised act, which will considerably modify the idea of being.

The exercise of the superexistence which is activity means that the agent cannot be thought of as a mere existent objectivity, to which other objective determinations are simply added so as to be further possessions of the primary existent. The fact that activity in some manner emanates from the depths of the agent means that this agent has some depth beyond mere objectivity. This depth in the agent is its subjectivity. Objectivity is a set of potencies determined by completely extrinsic acts; but an act exercised by a subject somehow emanates from the mysterious depth of the subject. Activity presupposes subjectivity; and the subjectivity of the agent necessarily presupposes the subjectivity of the existent itself, since nothing acts except insofar as it is. This subjectivity of the agent and of the existent is considered in more detail in a later chapter.

More immediately, however, we turn our attention to certain special modes of activity, that is to say, those which constitute or are the necessary presuppositions of psychic phenomenality.

Chapter 7

PSYCHIC PHENOMENALITY--THE PHENOMENALITY OF SPIRITUAL INTENTIONALITY

We now turn our attention to what would seem to be only a special mode of being and therefore inappropriate in a general inquiry into being, namely the dimension of psychic phenomenality. Although it is not a dimension of all being, nevertheless it is of fundamental importance in the inquiry for four reasons.

First, the phenomenality of intellectual knowledge and love, which is psychic phenomenality, is in a way a reflection in man of all being, a new mode of existence for all being. Second, an understanding of psychic phenomenality will lead to a clearer understanding of the diverse dimensions of being, since all of them must be somehow manifested in or through psychic phenomenality. Third, in the union of knower and known which is knowledge, there is a component contributed by the thing and a component contributed by the knower; an analysis of psychic phenomenality should contribute to the clearer distinction of these two components from each other. Fourth, in the course of this inquiry there will be seen the fundamental place of intellectual consciousness in knowledge and love in the finality of all existence.

Just as with the other dimensions of being, no attempt is made to give any thorough account of psychic phenomenality here, but simply to clarify its nature and types. A detailed account of the structure and genesis of psychic phenomenality should be the concern of another book. And it would only be after such a detailed account that one could properly engage in the critical analysis of the contributions of the knower as such in the act of knowledge. In this light, the present work is really only the barest beginning of an inquiry into being; but any properly scientific analysis of psychic phenomenality in fact presupposes the beginnings of a scientific analysis of being itself, for psychic phenomenality is essentially relative to being.

This is a difficult situation: no adequate account of being without a detailed analysis of psychic phenomenality, but no detailed analysis of psychic phenomenality without some degree of scientific knowledge of being. One possible way to avoid this difficulty might have been to begin the analysis with psychic phenomenality *as relative to being* and then to move outward to focus more directly on *real being*. Such a manner of approaching being may well be possible, but attempts to follow this path ordinarily lead to idealism of one kind or other. Too frequently, psychic phenomenality is equated with the phenomenality of objective intellectual knowledge and its affective correlate; when this is done, being must be finally conceived as mere objectivity, as it is in some varieties of idealism. In any event, when being is considered only in relation to psychic phenomenality, all its dimensions appear as simply correlative with psychic phenomenality; but here the transcendence of being over human knowledge is lost, and real existence with its proper dynamism disappears from view. It is therefore necessary to begin with being in itself, and only then to move to the consideration of psychic phenomenality and its relation to being, or more properly, of psychic phenomenality as a special mode of being and of its relation to all being. At this point then, a few observations may be made concerning the nature and types of psychic phenomenality, observations which will be further elaborated in the next two chapters as still other aspects of being itself are uncovered, and consequently still other modes of psychic phenomenality relative to these aspects.

The nature of psychic phenomenality

Psychic phenomenality was seen in chapter one to be nothing but the phenomenality of consciousness that is simultaneously reflexive and intentional. This consciousness is itself a special mode of existence, or rather superexistence, of the conscious being. It is a mode of activity, but of activity with a special kind of intentionality beyond that mere physical intentionality that has been seen to be associated with any physical activity. This intentionality is spiritual, and refers to the other precisely as other.

But psychic phenomenality must be sharply distinguished from another semi-spiritual intentional superexistence, namely, sense knowledge and appetition. Psychic phenomenality is the phenomenality of intellectual knowledge and appetition. There are some notable differences between this life of the intellect and the life of the senses. First, psychic phenomenality is indeed a phenomenality precisely because intellectual knowledge is reflexive. But sense knowledge is non-reflexive; and therefore if there is any knowledge of sense knowledge on the sense level (by a "higher" sense), this can be reduced to a knowledge of sensible phenomenality, now transposed to the conditions of existence within the sentient being. The intentional superexistence in the life of the senses is not an object of direct sensible consciousness and is only known as such by intellectual reflection, while the intentional superexistence in the life of the intellect is immediately and reflexively (even though obscurely, in the ordinary case) known as such.

So also, the intentional form which determines the sense power to its intentional activity or superexistence is not itself known but is simply a medium of knowledge in the act of sensation, or a medium of appetition in the act of sensual appetition. It is possible for this form to become known by some higher sense in the organism, but the thus known form is known simply as the form of some sensible phenomenality transposed to the conditions of existence within the sentient being.

But in intellectual activity, the intentional form, itself unknown, which determines the intellect to insight, tends to fructify into a further intentional form, itself known as such, at least in its representational function if not in its entity. This is the concept (pertaining as a representation to the domain of logical objectivity). Something analogous occurs in the will after an initial affective complacency.

Other differences also exist between psychic phenomenality and the life of the senses. One of the most commonly noted differences is in the object of each. In the life of the senses the object is always something extended (and so also in some manner is the intentional form by which this object is attained), while in the intellect the object--however much immersed in the extended being in reality--as an object of intellectual activity is inextended.

Also, the formal object of the life of the senses is always the objective phenomenality of things. But the formal object of the intellect is the being of things, which includes both the phenomenal and the transphenomenal, but primarily the transphenomenal. In fact, the intellect never sees pure phenomenality divorced from every reference to transphenomenal being; it sees phenomenality precisely as an aspect of being, a "face" of being, a manifestation of being. It is only by a kind of intellectual asceticism that the positive sciences are able to confine their attention to the phenomenal surface of things, without using this knowledge as a means to probe below the surface.

By now the distinction between psychic phenomenality and sensible awareness and appetition should be fairly clear. It is possible to look more closely at this world of psychic phenomenality, so as to distinguish its various parts, levels, and types.

Modes of psychic phenomenality

The fundamental distinction in psychic phenomenality between the phenomenality of knowledge and the phenomenality of love has already been seen. First to be considered is the phenomenality of knowledge. A distinction has been made between objective and non-objective knowledge. Consider first objective knowledge, the knowledge that is expressible in the concept.

Before the expression in the concept must come the initial insight. This insight itself requires an intentional form as a determining cause, but this intentional form is part of the subconscious life of the intellect. This form cannot be seen because of its spiritual nature in an existent made to understand things through the medium of the senses. However, we are reflexively aware of the intentional existence correlative with this form; this existence, or rather superexistence, is the very act of conscious insight.

Since there is question here of knowledge immediately expressible in a concept, it is a knowledge of objectivity. When the concept is expressed, some objectivity is "transposed" from the real to the domain of logical objectivity, or to speak properly, the objectivity which was seen in the real is now expressed logically. Once this objectivity has been logically expressed, the original insight is in some manner stabilized; henceforth, things can be viewed under the light of this concept so that the original insight is easily recalled.

Next to be considered is non-objective knowledge, knowledge that is not immediately expressible in a concept. How such knowledge can in fact be designated or signified by constructed concepts or meta-concepts has already been discussed in earlier chapters. Therefore there is no need to enter into that now. But it is still necessary to point out the locus of original insight in these domains.

Our non-objective grasp of the existence and activity of ourselves can be easily understood. Since consciousness is by its nature reflexive, it reveals the knower at the same time as it reveals the known; and it reveals this knower precisely as an agent, and therefore also as an existent, since activity is necessarily a superabundance of existence. There is also a further special mode of self-knowledge which will be considered in chapter nine.

But it is more difficult to understand the non-objective grasp of the existence and activity of other things. Here, just as in objective knowledge, there is a necessary dependence upon the evidence of the senses. No detailed account was given of how the evidence of the senses is used by the intellect in order to arrive at objective knowledge; this has been discussed frequently enough elsewhere. However, it seems worthwhile to say a few words about how the evidence of the senses is used by the intellect in coming to a non-objective grasp of or insight into the existence and activity of other things.

It is necessary first to understand that when the sensible thing acts upon the sense organ and power so as to produce the intentional form through which sensation takes place, the intentional existence itself, which is sensation, also is in some manner produced by and immediately dependent upon the activity of the thing. In fact, this intentional existence is the very superexistence of the active sensible thing in the sense itself. At the instant of activity, therefore, there is a dynamic immediate union between the sense organ and power and the active sensible thing. And the immediate reference of this intentional existence to the active sensible thing is not merely a physical intentionality but also a spiritual intentionality, though only semi-spiritual by comparison with the intentionality of intellectual knowledge. This means that in the datum of the senses is contained in some obscure manner the activity of the sensible thing exercised upon the faculty of sense; to put it another way, the very act of sensation <u>is</u> in a way the activity of the sensible thing itself upon us.

Now of course this act of sensation is not a reflexive act; therefore it does not of itself convey to us an awareness of the activity *as such* of the sensible thing upon us. Nor is this awareness conveyed by the higher internal senses, since they too, just as the external senses, focus upon objective sensible phenomenality.

However, all that occurs in the life of the senses occurs in the immediate presence of the intellect; sensible awareness is suffused with intellectual consciousness. Concomitantly with sensible awareness occurs not only the intellectual insight into objectivity but also the non-objective intellectual insight into the activity upon us by the sensible thing. While the medium for the insight into objectivity is an intentional form in the intellect, the medium for the non-objective insight into activity itself is the intentional existence of this same intentional form. The psychic phenomenality of intellectual insight into the objectivity of sensible things is then the very medium through which the activity of these sensible things upon us is intellectually attained.

But it is possible to go still further. The intentional existence in the sense organ and power, which was also the superexistence of the sensible thing, is also the medium through which is attained in some manner the very existence of the sensible thing; for the superexistence of the thing in the sense organ and power must be in immediate union with and dependence upon the superexistence of the thing in the thing itself, and this in turn refers back immediately to the thing precisely as existent. However, the existence of the sensible thing is here attained not in itself but only "from outside," through its superexistence *in another*, in the sense organ and power. Hence, implicit in the sensible awareness and concomitant intellectual consciousness (through psychic phenomenality) of the activity of the sensible thing upon the sense organ and power is also the awareness and consciousness that the sensible thing is, not through any awareness or consciousness of this existence in itself apart from us.

Besides the phenomenality of knowledge, there is also the psychic phenomenality of love. While love is not itself consciousness of the thing loved, nevertheless there is a compenetration of intellect and will, such that the intellect is conscious of love itself; love therefore becomes a reductively reflexive intentional existence, or rather superexistence, with reference to the loved thing. From the reflection of the intellect upon the act of complacent love arises a deeper knowledge of the known and loved thing, a knowledge of subjectivity, which will be considered in the next chapter. From this viewpoint love has a noetic value, not that the will itself has become a faculty of knowledge, but rather that the act of love becomes a new formal means by which the intellect understands the being of the thing.

The root of psychic phenomenality

It does not seem to be to the point of this book to go into a detailed discussion of the genesis of psychic phenomenality in man. Yet some understanding of the roots of psychic phenomenality permits a further understanding of the dynamism of the act of existence itself.

First to be considered is knowledge, and then love, since love is in some manner a consequence of knowledge. As has already been pointed out, intellectual knowledge demands that there be present in the intellect an intentional form and its correlative intentional existence. This intentional existence is itself identical with intellectual knowledge. But such intentional form and existence must not be equated with mere physical intentionality, such as is present in any activity of proportionate or limited being. For this new intentionality is spiritual--in some manner independent of the prime matter that enters into the constitution of every material thing. It is prime matter which is the ultimate principle of the limitation and incommunicability of forms, which renders form the form of this thing rather than of that thing. It is prime matter which, in requiring the extension of the material thing in parts outside of parts, prevents a material thing from ever being reflexively present, itself to itself. If there are form and existence which are in some manner the form and existence of some being other than that in which they are, if such form and existence of the other as other are at the same time a means of reflexive presence of the knower to himself, this can only be because the form and existence are spiritual. Spirituality, then, is the root of both intentionality and reflexivity in intellectual knowledge. And this spirituality of the intentional form and intentional existence means that the intellect in which such form and existence are must itself be spiritual rather than material, and therefore that the human soul in which the intellect is (or any other being in which some intellect is present, outside the domain of proportionate being) must also be spiritual, possessing its being in independence of prime matter.

It is because of the spiritual possession of the form and existence of the other as other that intellectual knowledge is an immediate union with the being of the other as other. It is because of the spiritual nature of the intellect itself, and of the being which has the intellect, that such an intellect and being has a certain reflexive auto-presence characteristic of spirit. Spirituality, then, is the root of the possibility of knowledge, a possibility which also inevitably becomes actuality, in virtue of the dynamism of existence which was considered in chapter six.

Even on the level of mere sensible awareness, some degree of semi-spirituality is necessary, if the form and existence of the other as other can become intentionally present in the sentient being. But that the spirituality here is only a semi-spirituality is manifested by the fact that only individualized forms can be present and that their presence is always non-reflexive. The intentional form is individualized because it results immediately from the activity of the sensible thing upon a material sense organ, and it is non-reflexive since it is itself extended in an extended sense faculty.

At this point it may well be asked how it is possible that non-individualized forms should first come to be present in the human intellect, since they too must be ultimately due to the activity of sensible things upon the sense organs. This question concerns not the intentional form which is the concept but rather that intentional form through which occurs the original insight eventually to be expressed in the concept. It is this question which has compelled philosophers of the Aristotelian and Thomist schools to postulate the existence of a special intellectual power, which in some manner produces such non-individualized forms in what is ordinarily called the intellect, and which does so with the help of the sense images built up by a central internal sense aided by the external senses. It is not that these still material sense images themselves can act on the spiritual intellectual power; they cannot touch the spiritual. But if they cannot touch the spiritual, still they can affect the existential state of the being in which this spiritual power is, and which is in a manner present to this spiritual power. Insofar as the sense images so affect the existential state, the spiritual power--already immediately tending toward activity and therefore constituting the ultimate root of the desire to know, and of that spirit of inquiry which is simply the clearer dynamic awareness of this desire to know--passes into activity in accordance with the modified state of the total existent. The result of this activity is precisely the production of non-individualized, spiritual (therefore intentional) forms in the intellect. The active spiritual power in the production of such forms is called the agent intellect.

Note that the agent intellect is not itself a knowing power. It does not possess the forms of the things to be known; nor does it simply appropriate to itself these forms in virtue of its simple contact with the sense images. Rather, the agent intellect is simply a power to dispose the knowing intellect, in accordance with the images with which the former power is in contact, so that the appropriate intentional form does in fact appear in the knowing intellect. This activity of disposition is itself nothing more than the emanation of intentionality in the agent intellect which constitutes its "contact" with the sense images. This emanation of intentionality in the agent intellect can constitute at the same time a disposition of the knowing intellect, insofar as the agent and knowing intellects compenetrate each other and are rooted in the same spiritual substance.

But one may ask what makes the agent intellect to "contact" intentionally the sense images, since this agent intellect is in no way "touched" by the sense images. It is necessary here to understand that the agent intellect is itself only a power of the very same substance in which the sense images are. The activity of the agent intellect is only the activity of the substance itself, through the medium of the agent intellect. It is therefore not necessary that the sense images immediately touch the agent intellect to determine it to act; it is sufficient that they touch the substance, which acts through the medium of the agent intellect, itself already in a state of dynamic tension, immediate preparedness to act when given the opportunity.

But still a further difficulty arises. May not the knowing intellect itself suffice for this "contact" with the images? It seems that the distinction of active powers according to their formal objects rules out this possibility. It is one thing to make such a "contact" with the images, and another to see the intelligibility hidden in them. But may not the seeing take place in virtue of the very contact itself? On the contrary, this intentional contact with the images is not in any way identical with the spiritual intentionality of knowledge. The intentionality of the contact is not the form of some other in the agent intellect but rather a form of the agent intellect itself, as the knowing intellect is a form of the human soul. While the formal object of the knowing intellect is the other as other to be possessed intentionally, the formal object of the agent intellect is the other to be contacted or touched intentionally. Therefore, it seems necessary to retain the real distinction between the agent and knowing intellects as powers of the human existent.

As many readers undoubtedly will know, the question of the precise relation of the human intellect to sense knowledge and of the function of the agent intellect has been a mysterious one for many centuries. It would therefore be only with temerity that I could put forth the above suggestions as anything more than an hypothesis to be subjected to criticism.

Beyond the psychic phenomenality of intellectual knowledge, there is the psychic phenomenality of love. Such love is in fact an inevitable consequence of knowledge. For by knowledge the being of the knower expands; and if the being of the knower expands, then so also must his dynamism, his tendency to activity, to union and communion, to the diffusion of being. Now, the new dynamism consequent upon knowledge, and possessing its own peculiar mode, in accordance with the peculiar mode of activity and possession which is knowledge, is the dynamism of love. The intellectual agent cannot merely know; he must also love in some manner, for better or worse.

Love is the adherence of the knower to the known good. In the act of love is a new intentionality above and beyond that in knowledge, resulting from the new dynamism of being which is consequent upon knowledge. But the situation of the human knower, and indeed of any intellectual knower, is in a way paradoxical. Since intellectual knowledge is not confined to the here and now, such knowledge can present one with alternative values to be embraced or pursued. Since in fact intellectual knowledge extends to the totality of being, it also extends to the totality of good--and therefore it reveals that each value presented is in fact a limited value, which at the same time in some manner involves the exclusion of other values. (Even God, Whom we shall come to see in Part 2 as the unlimited value, can only be known in this life as a limited value alongside of other limited values. We may know that He is the unlimited value, but we only know this in our limited and indirect way.) Therefore the dynamism of love in any intellectual agent who is not already in complete union with God is at once a multi-directional and an indeterminate dynamism. The spontaneous affective complacency which arises in us before any apprehended good may be followed up with adherence to this good or with rejection of this good in preference for other goods. Moreover, in the human existent, where knowledge is ever fluctuating and the play of passions goes on unceasingly, a choice once made is not necessarily permanent. Human choice is something fragile, a straw in the wind, unless it should be confirmed by the grace of God.

All this means that the dynamism consequent upon knowledge in the intellectual agent, the dynamism of love, is a dynamism to be moderated by acceptance or rejection, by freedom. The psychic phenomenality of love is also the phenomenality of freedom. Moreover, in the specifically human existent this phenomenality of freedom is also the phenomenality of fragility of choice, and therefore of loyalty and betrayal, of continuing tension, of anxiety and even of dread.

The supreme achievement of the dynamism of love in this life is not adherence to a good merely to be acquired, but adherence which consists in the giving of self to some better good. Since we are all limited, all our acquisition is itself also limited in its mode (unless God should communicate Himself to us in a supernatural manner); therefore we may more reasonably attempt to escape from this condition of finitude by the giving of self than by the acquisition of goods for ourselves. But we are free, so that we may either use other persons for our ends or in some manner give ourselves to others in a generous love. The phenomenality of love is therefore also a phenomenality of selfishness and generosity, of a selfishness that is doomed to frustration and of a generosity that is destined (if we give ourselves in all to God) to fulfillment, and also to a return of generosity (usually even from men, and always from God).

The dynamism of generous love, of self-giving, is a tendency to communion, a much deeper mode of union with the other than is possible in mere intellectual knowledge. By such love one somehow goes into the very depths of the being of the other, into the subjectivity of the other, in a manner to be discussed in the next chapter. This penetration of subjectivity is not a penetration merely to know, but also to taste in some manner the goodness of the other. More than this, it is an immersion of oneself in this subjectivity of the other, a forgetfulness of oneself in the goodness of the other. It is total immersion and forgetfulness of self in the goodness of the other which constitutes the fullness of communion or intersubjectivity. The phenomenality of generous love is, then, also the phenomenality of communion and intersubjectivity. This communion and intersubjectivity will be considered in more detail in the next chapter.

Existence and consciousness

In the preceding section, the root of intellectual love was seen to be in intellectual knowledge and the root of intellectual knowledge in spirituality, or independence of matter. But existence itself is intrinsically independent of matter; if it were not, then it would be intrinsically dependent upon matter. But if it were intrinsically dependent upon matter, then there could never be psychic phenomenality or the phenomenality of consciousness, since this is itself a mode of existence. But if existence itself is intrinsically independent of matter, then it must be said, in virtue of the dynamism of being, that existence of itself tends in some manner toward consciousness. Either a being is or has consciousness, or in some manner it tends to become what is or has consciousness. Existence itself in its higher degrees, in spiritual things, becomes consciousness. The world of the non-conscious must be said to achieve its highest fulfillment when it enters into the consciousness of higher beings. And these higher beings reach their own highest fulfillment precisely in the consciousness which is knowledge and love. All being and all existence, then, is for the sake of knowledge and love. Knowledge and love are not mere offshoots of evolving reality; in some manner they are at the very heart of reality. And if there is a pure existence, it is also a pure knowledge and a pure love.

Chapter 8

EXISTENCE AND SUBJECTIVITY

The contrast between objectivity and subjectivity has already been seen in chapter one. Again this contrast appeared in chapter six when it was seen that activity, as an exercised act, must be the act of subjectivity and not of mere objectivity, that the agent must be not only an object but also a subject. In this chapter, first, a metaphysical analysis leads to a deeper understanding of the subjectivity of the existent. Second, a psychological account is presented (in the line of philosophical psychology and the metaphysics of knowledge and love) of the ways in which we become aware of the subjectivity of ourselves and of other things. Third, some further remarks are made about the subjectivity of proportionate and limited being.

Metaphysical analysis

In the course of the analysis of activity in chapter six, the dimension of subjectivity also appeared. To conceive the agent as a mere passive potency to which further act is simply added from outside, as is form to matter, would be a serious mistake. While the agent is in potency for the activity, this agent is also in some manner the "spring" or depth from which activity flows. This "flowing from" is what is meant by "exercise," when it is said that activity is an exercised act. Such exercise is of necessity unique and incommunicable; it can only be the exercise of this act by this thing. This exercise of act is subjectivity, as opposed to objectivity, which is mere possession of act. That which exercises the act is the subject, and the subject is unique and incommunicable in its exercise of act.

Activity presupposes that the agent is not a mere object but a subject. But this means that, before there can be an active subject, there must first be an existent subject--a subject the subjectivity of which is somehow constituted by existence itself. Therefore it cannot be correct to say that existence only gives being to objectivity; this existence is also the existence of a subject.

But existence cannot be the existence of a subject rather than a mere object unless existence itself is an exercised act. In fact, it is this very exercise of existence which constitutes the subjectivity of the existent and renders each existent unique and incommunicable, in some manner apart from every other existent and on its own in the world.

Therefore, when existence is given to the objective essence to be possessed, it also is exercised, in virtue of the new existential state of this objective essence, a state which is itself correlative with and in some manner due to existence. This existential state is precisely the state of having existence, the possession of existence as a dynamic act which needs not merely to be possessed but also to be exercised. Resulting from this state of having existence is therefore the further state of exercising existence--and this state of exercise of existence is the very subjectivity of the existent. The fact that the objective essence no longer is merely held in being by the existence which it possesses, but now makes this existence its own, means that the existent now has the fullness and interiority of the subject and not the mere exteriority of objectivity. Of course, in all this it must be remembered that the succession of states or moments is only the result of our conception (or rather, meta-conception); in fact, the possession and exercise of existence must be simultaneous.

Subjectivity, then, is constituted by objectivity in this existential state, or rather this double existential state. But the objectivity here must be the objectivity of substance. Accidents can never exercise their own existence, for they are only beings of substance. If an accident were to exercise its own existence, it would thereby be constituted as both a subject and a substance.

At this point it is interesting to note that accidents, at least those accidents natural to the thing and not superimposed on it from outside, emanate from the substance in a manner analogous to that in which activity emanates from the subject. This emanation consists in the exercise of the accidental existence by the substantial subject. Of course, every accident has an accidental existence exercised by the substantial subject in which it is; but only in the case of natural accidents can this exercise properly be called an emanation.

This analysis has brought into focus the existential state of exercising existence as the very subjectivity of the thing; this is the subjectivity of the existent, formally considered. This existential state in turn depends upon the prior existential state of having or possessing existence; the latter state is not subjectivity formally considered, but it is the immediate root of subjectivity. Both of these states are in themselves non-objective; both therefore present a problem of conceptualization to the scientific metaphysician. Again the meta-concept will have to be an a priori construct, as indeed must be the meta-concept of any existential state. Attention is here focused upon the meta-conceptualization of the existential state of exercising existence, which is the subjectivity of the existent formally considered.

Meta-conceptualization of subjectivity

This existential state of exercising existence is identical with what scholastics have called subsistence, the formal constitutive note of the subject as such. However, many scholastic philosophers have thought to treat this subsistence as if it were itself some objective note in things. In fact, as has been seen so many times already, existence and subjectivity are necessarily transobjective aspects of being. Nevertheless, one can form a meta-concept of subsistence, a meta-concept which, again, does not express the reality of subsistence but rather only designates and signifies the reality of this existential state. Again, the definition of the meta-concept is by means of a proportionality. Since the exercise of existence has already been compared to the exercise of activity, the following formula may be written (in keeping with the system of notation already used):

$$\text{Subjectivity} = X = R_{OE}, \text{ where } R_{OE} \sim R_{OD}.$$

In keeping with this formula, the subject itself, as subject, may be defined simply as OX, where X is defined as in the preceding formula.

Psychological analysis

It is time now to consider in some detail how it is possible to come to any direct consciousness or knowledge of subjectivity in things. This was briefly considered in chapter one, but the fuller treatment there promised must now be given.

There is certainly given a knowledge of oneself as a subject, in one's subjectivity. This knowledge, necessarily non-objective in its mode, arises in virtue of the essential reflexivity of spirit and its consequent auto-presence. I am not only conscious of something other than consciousness itself, but I am also conscious of my consciousness itself precisely as my consciousness, as an activity flowing forth from my subjectivity, exercised by me as a subject.

This is also true in the case of the love which is consequent upon intellectual knowledge. This love is not only intentional but consciously intentional, since it is an intentionality of spirit and in spirit; the act partakes in the reflexivity of spirit. Moreover, because of the spiritual compenetration of intellect and will, the act of the will is immediately present to the intellect as well. Now this act of love, thus a doubly conscious act, is known as an activity flowing forth from subjectivity, as an exercised act of subjectivity; for this is the whole being of such an act. Again, then, there arises an awareness of oneself as a subject.

Even deeper than the activities of knowledge and love are the habits or virtues which dispose us to act with ease in one manner or other. These virtues are essentially inclinations of the subject to some kind of activity. It is therefore impossible to become aware of such existential habits or tendencies without at the same time coming to a deeper awareness of subjectivity.

Below all the habits or virtues superadded to the human subject, there is the fundamental dynamism arising from his nature. It is the profound awareness of this fundamental dynamism and of some of its implications which enables even the unlearned person to understand, however obscurely, that some course of action befits his nature (and is therefore moral) while some other course of action goes contrary to his nature (and is therefore immoral). But since this dynamism is not the dynamism of a mere nature but of a subject having such a nature, awareness of this dynamism is at the same time an awareness of oneself as a subject.

But it is possible to probe even more deeply. Prior to every activity, and in a way even prior to the dynamism which is the tendency toward activity, is existence itself. Now in fact, the existence of the human existent is first of all the existence of his spiritual soul, a spiritual existence. But if it is a spiritual existence, then it too must be exercised in a conscious manner in virtue of the reflexivity of spirit. Everything in spirit is consciousness and light in virtue of this reflexivity. Of course, in man this consciousness and light is at a minimum, since in man the spiritual soul is also the form of prime matter. The intrinsic multiplicity of prime matter is a principle of non-reflexivity; for reflexivity is the total presence of a totality to itself and is therefore grounded in the complete unity of this totality. But still, even in man, this reflexivity of spirit cannot be completely eliminated; if it were to disappear completely, this could only mean the absence of spirit altogether. In an obscure manner, then, at the base of all human consciousness, concomitant with all human activity, there is a mysterious awareness of one's own exercise of his own substantial existence, of himself as a subject. And just as substantial existence grounds the ultimate unity of the existent me, so also this obscure awareness of the exercise of substantial existence grounds the ultimate unity of the conscious me.

So much for the awareness of oneself as a subject. But there seem to be insuperable obstacles to any such awareness of the subjectivity of other persons and things. I am a privileged observer of my own subjectivity, since I know it from the inside. But I know other things only from the outside. If even in the case of existence I can know of other things only that they are, how can I ever hope to penetrate into the mystery of the subjectivity of the other, that unique and incommunicable exercise of existence in the other?

And yet the situation is not altogether hopeless. There seems to be a new mode of awareness arising out of love, which in fact is an awareness of the subjectivity of subject-things. This is not to say that the will is itself a faculty of knowledge, but rather that the intellect sees things in a new way, insofar as they attract the will; and in this new awareness is an understanding of the subjectivity of these things.

That love does somehow lead us deeper into the being of the other than does mere knowledge has been understood best by poets and mystics. But in fact philosophers such as Saint Thomas Aquinas, John of Saint Thomas, Jacques Maritain, Gabriel Marcel, Erich Fromm, and Martin Buber confirm the findings of Saint Augustine, Saint John of the Cross, and many others that love unifies us with the other more than does mere knowledge. By love we somehow embrace the other, not in that in which this other is like others so much as in that in which this other is unique and incommunicable, in its transobjective depth in which is the source and spring of all its activity as well as its existence, in that heart of the other which constitutes it as independent and autonomous in its existence and activity, and which we call the subjectivity of the other. And when this love is mutual love between persons, it is also a communion of hearts or subjectivities, the highest form of intersubjectivity--friendship.

But even below this level of friendship there are other types of intersubjectivity arising out of love. The poet enters into an intersubjective communion with things. There is an ordinary human intersubjectivity which arises in our regard for our fellow men, even if this regard does not always rise to the height of friendship.

Such intersubjectivity is not a mere physical union; it is spiritual and conscious. But the consciousness of intersubjectivity cannot be accounted for merely by the general consciousness which we have of the intentionality of the will. For this intentionality of the will which is directed toward the other, not as mere object, but as subject, itself somehow presupposes the presence of the subject as subject in a conscious manner; the will cannot tend toward anything except insofar as it is known in some way. And yet mere knowledge, as has already been seen, does not seem to account for intersubjectivity. We seem to be on the horns of a dilemma.

However, a resolution of the dilemma can be achieved with the aid of the Thomist doctrine concerning "affective connaturality." Once any being is apprehended as a possible or actual good, the will is moved through this knowledge to the passion of complacent love. This passion in the will is an intentional form, like the object itself, since it has ultimately been produced by the object. Insofar as it has this intentional form, the will is said to be connaturalized with the thing; this is affective connaturality. There is of course still a further degree of affective connaturality if the initial complacency is followed up by a free adherence to the good in question. But only the first complacency is considered in the following discussion, it being understood that the more intense degrees of intersubjectivity in fact require more than this initial complacency.

It was said that the will is moved by knowledge. How can this motion take place? Among Thomists there has been an argument about this point, with Cajetan defending an efficient causality of the intellect upon the will and John of Saint Thomas defending a "metaphorical motion." At first sight, the view of Cajetan seems promising, since efficient causality is at least easier to understand and since we must account for a real intentional modification of the will. But in fact this view is full of difficulties. The passion of love is produced by knowledge, but it is also produced by the will itself. Moreover, in some manner it must be produced by the thing itself even more than by the knowledge, since this love is a love for the thing itself and not merely for the knowledge of the thing. Moreover, the influence of the thing itself upon the will is not an influence of efficient causality but one of final causality. Even if one were willing to accept a mysterious transformation of the final causality of the thing itself into an efficient causality of the act of knowledge of the thing upon the will, still, on this hypothesis, it would seem that it is not so much the thing as the knowledge of the thing which moves the will. But, to go even further, one may well ask what has become of the distinctive character of final causality, if it is to be reduced, even in the intellectual order, to an efficient causality of knowledge upon the will. And beyond all this there is still the problem of understanding how the intentional form of knowledge in the intellect can efficiently produce anything at all so real as the passion of the will.

In the face of these difficulties, it seems well to consider the view of John of Saint Thomas that the influence of knowledge upon the will is a "metaphorical motion," a motion of final causality itself. This causality is more a causality by the known thing than by the knowledge of the thing, but it cannot exist apart from knowledge. And yet this causality cannot be simply located in knowledge; for it is a causality which influences the will, not simply by producing the passion in the will, but in some manner by being this passion. This passion, considered precisely as in dependence ultimately upon the loved thing, is the final causality of the final cause. This same passion, considered as flowing from the will itself as from an efficient cause, is also the effect of the final causality of the known thing. These are, of course, only two ways of looking at what is really identical, namely, the passion of love itself. The passion of love is an induced activity in the will; but the influence which induces this activity, though dependent on something other than the will, is not distinct from the very activity itself.

Why is it necessary that the causality of the final cause not be in knowledge alone but in the very passion produced in the will? If this causality consisted in knowledge alone or some aspect of knowledge, then everything would be desired precisely insofar as it were known. The final cause is a cause of desire, not so much by producing desire as by being desired. This is why the motion of final causality is only a metaphorical motion.

But if this causality of the final cause is in the passion of the will, as the causality of the final cause it must somehow be exercised by the final cause itself. This exercise of influence is in the thing as representatively present in the intellect, and consists in the contact between the intellectual representation and the will. The contact, therefore, is not entitative or physical but merely representative, and arises in virtue of the spiritual compenetration of intellect and will that has been spoken of several times already.

The exercise of such contact, formally by the intentional representation of the thing and fundamentally therefore by the thing which is represented, is both the "attraction" (final causality) and the specification (formal) of the act of the will. The will itself acts as an efficient cause under such contact (which is an existential state of the will), in virtue of the natural dynamism of the will with respect to the good.

Through the intentionality of the passion of love that has been induced in and produced by the will, the will tends toward the real thing itself through the medium of its intentional representation in the intellect. It is the intentionality of knowledge which guarantees the continuity of the intentionality of the will all the way to the real thing itself. But it was said earlier that this tendency of the will is a tendency toward the very subjectivity of things, and therefore presupposes in some manner a cognitive attainment of the subjectivity of things. This cognitive attainment has still not been explained, but such an explanation is now more possible.

The affective connaturality of the will with the loved thing consists in the tendency of the will. But presupposed to the connaturality itself is the connaturalization of the will by the "metaphorical motion." This metaphorical motion of final causality is exercised fundamentally by the thing itself insofar as the thing exercises its existence and activity; this constitutes the real attractiveness of the thing, for it is existential act to which all things tend. But the metaphorical motion is exercised formally in the representative contact already spoken of. Clearly, this formal exercise of final causality in representative contact is ultimately dependent upon, grounded in, the fundamental exercise of final causality which is the exercise of existential act in the real thing itself. The thing as represented, therefore, is vicarious with reference to the real subjectivity of the thing, so far as the exercise of final causality is concerned. It may even be said that the subjectivity of the thing is now vicariously present in the intellect, exercising final causality in the formal sense. But it is present only insofar as the object in the intellect is actually connaturalizing the will by the metaphorical motion which induces the passion of love in the will. Thus, the subjectivity of the other is known in the very moment of the affective connaturalization of the will. (This moment, of course, endures so long as the other is being regarded with a degree of affectivity.)

The will then, in tending toward the subjectivity of things, is not making any blind existential leap. It is not only true that the intellect understands that there are subjects, from the evidence of the activity of things as exercised act. The intellect also understands, in a vicarious manner, the very subjectivity of things at the moment of the connaturalization of the will. Moreover, this vicarious subjectivity is referred to the real thing itself through the prior knowledge of the intellect that the thing is a subject. Therefore, as connaturalized, the will tends toward a subjectivity which already revealed itself as subjectivity in the very connaturalization of the will.

Being and subjectivity

If existence is by its nature an exercised act, then it follows that every being insofar as it is a being has subjectivity, either in itself or in some other being. Accidents are of subjects; and every substance is also a subject, endowed with a certain degree of interiority and independence and autonomy in its existence and activity. And there is in the universe a hierarchy of subjectivity, in accordance with the hierarchy of degrees of the dynamic act of existence, and therefore also in accordance with the hierarchy of degrees of the static formal acts which determine the potency of essence for existence. Interiority and independence and autonomy are not very evident in the lowest levels of material existents, but they become progressively more manifest as one moves up the scale. At the human level, where spirit appears, subjectivity becomes selfhood, the subjectivity which has reflexive interiority (self-consciousness), self-possession, and freedom. The human subject, because of his special dignity, is also called a person. And with self-consciousness comes the conscious awareness of isolation and loneliness in each human existent, and the need for communion with others, for intersubjective union, for the transcendence of one's limitation, through knowledge and love and friendship.

Chapter 9

EXISTENCE AND CREATEDNESS

In the course of the analysis of the dimensions of being, ample evidence has already been uncovered to conclude to the createdness of all proportionate and limited being, its dependence for existence upon some transcendent and infinite being. But the explicit reasoning must be left to Part 2. Still, there is another more immediate awareness of the createdness of proportionate being, one which is given without analysis or discursive reasoning. This awareness is most obscure, most frequently lost sight of in the midst of all the stirrings of analytic and discursive reason. And yet there are many testimonials to the fact of such an immediate awareness, testimonials which themselves are frequently confused and distorted attempts to express what is radically unconceptualizable and ineffable. Here is to be found yet another distinct dimension of being, deeper than all the others, at the very root of existence. Here the intuition of createdness is considered first, and then the psychological account of it. Afterward, a brief observation will be made concerning the relevance of this intuition to the metaphysical investigation of being.

The intuition of createdness

The intuition of createdness is given without analysis or discursive reasoning; yet often enough some analysis and reasoning is necessary in order to clarify just what this intuition has given. For the intuition itself is so obscure that hasty conceptual attempts to formulate its content, in however indirect a manner, are likely to distort it in one way or another. Therefore, after a brief description of some ways in which the intuition may take place, there follows a short analysis to show that it is in fact an intuition of createdness, and not of a pan-theist datum or of any other form of monist being.

One manner of approach to the intuition was already seen in chapter one. Below the superficial sameness and diversity of phenomena, below even the deeper sameness and diversity of essence, there is existence. Now although each thing seems to have its own existence, and even to exercise this existence as the existence of an independent subject, still even more deeply existence is <u>one</u>, one perfection. It is the diversity of existences that is relatively superficial; at bottom there must be unity. There are existences, but there is also existence. There are many subjects; but there is also one subject. There are finite selves, and there is the infinite self. One is sometimes able to see in the finite things before us that which transcends any one of them and is in all the others as much as it is in this one. From this viewpoint there is indeed a temptation to affirm the identity of all things in one being.

A similar intuitive knowledge may be gained from reflection upon one's own subjectivity. Ordinarily, one is not thus preoccupied directly with the evidence of his subjectivity; but it is possible for him to withdraw from all the activity that distracts him from his selfhood and to focus upon this self. But at the same moment as this withdrawal and concentration and recollection are achieved, there appears not only the self but also that which is in all other things as well; and all of this is unified in one experience of self which is also experience of Self.

And if he can retain this deep awareness of self and Self as he returns to the knowledge of other things, he discovers that the same Self is somehow revealed in the revelation of other things to him. If he did not understand this revelation before, it was because he was too taken up with the distinctions and diversities and uniqueness of these things. But now he can see that, even while they are not the same, still the Same is found in all of them.

Obviously, such an intuition strongly suggests that the real is fundamentally one in a monist or pantheist sense; frequently this is just how the intuition is interpreted. Yet even a little reflective thought shows that this cannot be the case. The distinctions and diversities of things have already been seen quite clearly, and whatever sameness is now seen in things must be understood in the light of these distinctions and diversities. Clearly, the sameness is at another level than that at which these things are; for they are diverse. It must be then that this sameness is behind things, prior to them, containing them in a supereminent way, with all the multiplicity and diversity of things reduced to unity and sameness. Moreover, if this sameness and unity is in fact immediately revealed through the contemplation of the diverse and multiple, there must be some immediate union between them, not of identity but of dependence--the being of the multiple and diverse is immediately dependent upon the being of the One and the Same. This dependence in being is the createdness of things.

Psychological analysis of the intuition

The intuition of createdness is an awareness of existence itself, precisely as immediately dependent upon an infinite existence. In previous chapters the manners in which one becomes aware of existence have already been considered. There was seen the immediate awareness of our substantial existence, which arises in virtue of the very reflexivity of spirit itself. It was also seen that we live intentionally the existence of other things in our intelligence. It is necessary now to see that one's own substantial existence, lived in the reflexivity of spirit, is also intentional with respect to Existence itself, is a medium through which is understood in some manner infinite existence. It is intentional because it exists in the spiritual soul of man and is at the same time in immediate dependence upon the pure existence. It is at the same time consciously (though obscurely) lived and exercised, and therefore gives a conscious (though obscure) union with pure existence. But this union is not an immediate vision of the pure existence. It is a consciously lived union in which pure existence is only attained in the most inadequate manner through the intentionality of consciously lived existence. It may be said that here pure existence is not seen in itself through the finite existence, but rather is confronted (most inadequately) in another, namely, in finite existence itself. In understanding my finite existence as dependent, I understand it as referring beyond itself to a pure existence of which I have some obscure apprehension in my apprehension of finite existence; but this is not at all to have a vision of pure existence in itself, for which no finite intentional medium could ever suffice.

But this pure existence is discovered not only in the lived intellection of substantial existence itself; it is also found in the existence of other things as intentionally lived in the intelligence of the knower. Here too is an existence in the spiritual soul of man and also immediately dependent (as will be seen in Part 2) upon the pure existence; therefore this existence is not only intentional with respect to the known finite thing but also intentional with respect to the pure existence itself. Again there results a conscious union (though obscure) with pure existence, not seen in itself, but seen in this finite intentional existence.

Whether one looks into one's own subjectivity or into the being of other things precisely as known to him, he finds not only the finite existence but also in some manner the infinite existence. Everywhere, if one only learns to listen, there is immediate presence of pure existence in its activity of giving existence to things. Such conscious union with pure existence, however dark and inadequate it be, is nevertheless akin to sense experience, since it is a knowledge of this pure existence as acting here and now upon the knower in producing the influx of existence in the knower. It can therefore be called an <u>experience</u> of the pure existence or absolute being. Since this union with pure existence is in a way a supreme natural fulfillment of the tendency of the human spirit to ever greater degrees of intentional existence (whereby it acquires the being of all things and becomes all things), this union must be a cause of joy to the human spirit, a fruitive union. It may therefore truly be called a natural mystical experience. If this joy in absolute being is not found in most men, it is because they are so taken up with the many and the diverse in reality as to lose sight of the all but sub-conscious experience of the One and the Same in all things. Nor is it easy for one to quiet all the faculties, the stirring of which is natural, in order to discover the Self through the self. But in fact, this discovery of the Self through the self is an all but necessary prerequisite for the discovery of the Self in the intentional living of the being of other things, unless one has already learned from elsewhere how to look beyond the things to that absolute being of which they are only the sacrament.

Createdness and metaphysics

Createdness has been listed as a distinct dimension of being; for it is given through a new type of experience and is really distinct from the dimensions of existence, activity, subjectivity, and psychic phenomenality, insofar as it contains an explicit reference to transcendent being or pure existence. In a certain sense createdness is identical with finite existence, but still it says more than does mere existence. It can become known through an analysis of finite existence, since it is implicit in finite existence; but it also becomes known in the special experience just described. It is true that this special experience takes place in our experience of existence itself, but the former is somehow more than the latter. Some special conditions are required for the explicit intuition of createdness which are not required for the mere awareness of existence. Therefore it seems that there is a distinctive manner of presentation for createdness. Moreover, the distinction between existence and createdness is grounded in a certain diversity in reality itself, namely, the diversity between finite being and infinite being. For these reasons, it seems justifiable to list createdness as a distinct dimension of being.

But should createdness be added to the meta-concept of being? Clearly this cannot be done, unless this meta-concept is to be permanently restricted to the domain of limited being. Also, because of the obscurity of the intuition of createdness, it seems just as well to reserve a detailed consideration of it for much later in the development of metaphysical science, when the obscure intuition can be confirmed by the evidence of analysis and discursive reason.

But even if the evidence of createdness is obscure, it still plays an important role in the dynamism of metaphysical progress, stimulating the metaphysician to inquire about the reality of transcendent being. All the loose ends which have resulted from the analysis of being and activity thus far, which suggest further inquiry transcending proportionate and limited being, all these are gathered together and set in a stronger light by the intuition of createdness.

Chapter 10

THE META-CONCEPT OF BEING RECONSIDERED, AND A SUMMARY OF CATEGORIES AND CAUSES

Now that the dimensions of being have been considered, some formulae can be added to the expression of the content of the meta-concept of being and of existence. One may ask whether these formulae should not be taken to designate properties of being rather than portions of the fundamental intelligibility of being itself. But the distinction between the transcendental properties of being and being itself is a difficult one to define. It seems necessary that some recognition should be given in the very definition of being itself to its multi-dimensionality; but then it becomes difficult to maintain a clear division between being itself and the transcendental properties of being. It seems best to include some reference to each of the seven dimensions of being in the meta-concept of being itself, and then later to speak of the diverse transcendental aspects of being, setting aside altogether the use of the term "property." In fact, as will be seen, there is a great multiplicity of such transcendental aspects of being. All of them, of course, are identical with being itself in reality; they emerge as distinct from each other only because of the limitation of the human intellect with its inability to comprehend the intelligible richness of being all at once.

The meta-concept of proportionate being (now extended to all limited being) included one general formula and five sub-formulae:

$$R_{OE} \sim R_{PA} \quad \left[\begin{array}{l} R_{OE} \sim R_{MF} \\ R_{OE} \sim R_{SA} \\ R_{OE} \sim R_{AS} \\ R_{OE} \sim R_{OD} \\ R_{O(O+E)} \sim R_{-OO} \end{array} \right.$$

The first additional formula expresses the tendency of every being toward activity. Since this tendency is present in virtue of existence itself, one may write simply (using an arrow to indicate tendency toward, and K for activity):

$$E \rightarrow K$$

The second additional formula expresses the fact that every being either is a subject or presupposes a subject of which it is. Subjectivity (Q) either is present in virtue of existence (in which case we have OEQ), or is presupposed, as in accidents, to existence (in which case we have QOE). One may therefore write the following formula:

If OE, then either OEQ or QOE.

The third formula simply expresses the general tendency of being toward consciousness, a tendency which arises in virtue of existence itself. Using C for consciousness, the following formula may be written:

$$E \rightarrow C$$

The fourth formula expresses the fact that every proportionate or limited being (composed therefore of essence and existence) is created. Clearly, this formula must be dropped in extending the meta-concept of being to include transcendent being. Of course, most of the previous formulae will also then require some further discussion, since they presuppose the distinction between objectivity or essence and existence. But for the present, using H for createdness, one may write:

If OE, then OEH.

The meta-concept of being has now grown in richness to a certain extent. But much more is to come. For multi-dimensional being presents a considerable diversity of facets under which it can be known, all in some manner distinct from each other, since none of them can itself measure up to the fullness of the intelligibility of being. Some of these facets of being will be seen in the next chapter. But first, it seems useful to complete the work of the preceding chapters by compiling a list of the diverse categories within proportionate being, the most generic modes or types of such being.

A summary of categories

A category is first of all a set of predicates which could be said of some subject or other in a proposition. Such a proposition would be a two-term proposition, with both the subject and the predicate known through objectively conceived notes. Categories, then, are sets of objectively conceived intelligible contents. According as there are diverse generic types of objective intelligible content, there are diverse generic categories. Some of these categories correspond to distinct intelligibilities in the thing, with a simple one-to-one congruence; this occurs when the categories are categories of concepts referring to the levels of objectivity in things themselves. Four categories of the objectivity which is found as such in things themselves as well as in the intellect have already been seen: substance, quantity, quality, and sensible phenomenality.

But other concepts and meta-concepts have also been seen, which are the result of a priori construction, and which are not simply congruent with the intelligibility of reality itself. For example, relations as such do not exist in distinction from their relata; and yet they are conceived as distinct from their relata. Such a category is a category of logical objectivity but not a category of real objectivity. Other categories arise from the construction of meta-concepts of existence, of activity, and of existential state. All such meta-conceptual knowledge could be grouped together under one category of the meta-conceptual in general. If the categories which are congruent with reality (*a posteriori* categories) are divided according to the diversity of formal objectivity itself, and the categories which are not thus congruent with reality, but rather are the result of a priori construction (*a priori* categories), are divided according to the diversity of methods of construction, there are finally the four above-named a posteriori categories of substance, quantity, quality, and sensible phenomenality, and the two a priori categories of relation-concepts and meta-concepts. Thus there are four categories of reality and six of knowledge of reality.

A summary of causes

Just as the list of categories in the metaphysics of existence and of multi-dimensional being is quite different from that of Aristotle, so also is the enumeration of causes. The place of the efficient and final causes in reality has already been seen in some detail. Only briefly and in passing was the exemplar, or exemplary cause, considered, which causes only by being a plan or model in the intellect of the intellectual agent, a plan or model according to which this agent acts. The exemplary cause is very similar to the final cause; but the final cause causes by being the object of appetite, while the exemplary cause causes by being the norm according to which action takes place. Clearly there is some influence over the being of the effect from the exemplary cause, but this influence is subordinate to the influence of the final cause and can be felt only through the medium of the efficient cause.

There is here a gradual extension of the scope of the term "cause." Originally, it was applied to the agent because of its influence in constituting the being of the effect. Then it was extended to apply to the end or goal because of its influence in constituting a tendency as a tendency. Now it has been extended to apply to the exemplar because of the influence of the latter in determining the mode or pattern of activity.

But still further extension is possible. Certainly the intrinsic principles of objectivity have an influence in the constitution of objective being, precisely by being parts of this objective being. Therefore the determinable or potential principle is called a material cause, and the determining or actual principle is called a formal cause. Prime matter is a material cause, and substantial form a formal cause. Substance is a material cause, and accidents are formal causes.

But even beyond the potency-act relation within the order of objectivity, there is the potency-act relation between objectivity and existential act. Here the potency is itself held in being by the act, and therefore cannot be regarded as a material cause in the same sense as is a potency within the order of objectivity. Likewise, the act here is beyond all degrees of formal act, and therefore is not a formal cause in the same sense as is such formal act. Essence then stands as a quasi-material cause, and existence as a quasi-formal cause.

Still another type of causality comes into view when one considers the very exercise of existence and activity, an emanative causality. Such emanative causality is found wherever there is exercised act of existence or activity: in every activity, in the emanation of accidents from the substance which exercises their act of existence, and in the emanation of substantial existence itself--in which consists the fundamental subjectivity of the existent.

There are, then, at least eight distinct types of cause, from the perspective of the metaphysics of existence: efficient, final, exemplary, material, formal, quasi-material, quasi-formal, and emanative.

Chapter 11

THE TRANSCENDENTAL ASPECTS OF BEING

It has already been seen that when one comes to the consideration of being as being, he reaches, not the most generic, least intelligible, most indeterminate aspect of the real, but rather that which contains in an implicit way all the perfection of every being, actually and determinately. The meta-concept of being, therefore, far from being devoid of content, is in fact a plenitude of all possible content. And yet this meta-concept itself still represents only a limited view of being as being. Because of the weakness of the human intellect, the intelligible richness of being as being must be known in a plurality of other meta-concepts, each of which focuses indeed upon the intelligibility of being as being, but each of which brings to light a new aspect of this being as being, an aspect contained implicitly in what was already known through the first, proper, meta-concept of being as being, but needing to be made explicit in a diverse meta-concept.

Since these new meta-concepts are in fact meta-concepts of being as being, they are implied by the proper meta-concept of being itself; but since they signify what is not explicitly known in the knowledge of being simply as being, they are in fact distinct meta-concepts, and require new acts of insight into being as a basis for their formulation. Still, since they are but new formulations referring to the same being, they must be said to share in the transcendental nature of the meta-concept of being itself. Each of these meta-concepts is, then, a distinct transcendental meta-concept, referring to a distinct transcendental aspect of being as being.

The following discussion does not enter into the details of the construction of these transcendental meta-concepts, which must take place in a manner analogous to that in which the meta-concept of being itself is constructed. Instead it focuses directly upon the reality which is signified by each of these meta-concepts, treating then, not of the transcendental meta-concepts as such, but rather of the transcendental aspects of being as such.

How is being transcendental?

At this point it is instructive to consider in more detail just precisely what is meant when it is said that being is transcendental. Being does more than transcend the distinctions of species and of genera in things, and the distinction between phenomena and transphenomenal reality, and even the distinction between actually existent and merely possible reality; it also transcends in some manner the distinction between the real (actual and possible being) and the logical (that which, although existing in thought, could never exist in reality).

Of course, being must first of all refer to the actually real. In comparison with the actually real, all other being is only a non-being which somehow bears some likeness to actual being, and is therefore called being by some analogy. The most obvious case is that of merely possible being, being which does not actually exist but which could exist. Such a possible being has essential possibility, in that its constituent elements in the line of objectivity are non-contradictory; and it also has existential possibility, in that some adequate cause does actually exist which could either immediately or mediately bring the possible being into actual being. There are, of course, degrees of existential possibility, corresponding to the greater or lesser preparation of causes to bring into actual being the possible being in question (unless we consider the possibility of the pure act of existence acting without any intermediary causes--before the power of this pure act, all possibles are equally possible). But in essential possibility there are no degrees; either the constituent elements in the line of objectivity are non-contradictory or they are contradictory. If they are contradictory, there is no essential possibility, since one of these elements would deny what is posited by another element.

If possible beings are considered in their essential possibility, they are called being by an analogy of proportionality with actual being. Even if they do not actually have existence, still they could have actual existence; and in this their relation to actual existence is similar to that which actual being has to actual existence. Therefore, such possible beings can be included in the scope of the meta-concept of being which was elaborated in earlier chapters. A distinct type of analogy emerges when possible beings are considered in their existential possibility; but this new analogy, an analogy of dependence, can be best seen in Part 2, when the dependence of all limited being upon the pure act of existence is considered.

But even further removed from the fullness of actual reality than is possible being, there are the logical beings, beings which exist only in the intellect and which cannot exist in the real world. Why then are they called beings? In themselves they are non-beings, if they are considered in relation to actual and possible reality. But nevertheless they are thought of as if they were beings, for the intellect can understand nothing except insofar as it is in some sense. Pure nothingness cannot be the object of the intellect, at least not precisely as pure nothingness. For the intellect to understand what is not in itself a being, the intellect must make some kind of a priori construction, analogous to that which it must make in order to understand transobjective being. The understanding of any negation, such as "pure nothingness," or any privation, such as "evil" or "blindness," is due to such a priori construction. So too, relations of reason, that is, relations between the acts of the intellect itself, which therefore cannot exist outside the intellect itself, are conceived by means of constructed "relation-fictions." There is a certain similarity in the conception even of so-called real relations, which in fact do not possess being distinct from the being of the relata, and which therefore themselves must also be conceived by the construction of relation-fictions if they are to be distinctly conceived at all. But all such a priori constructions do in fact have some opposition to nothingness in the intellect itself; they are therefore possible subjects of affirmation in some manner. And if they are possible subjects of affirmation, then they must be said to have being in some analogous sense; they have a relation to existence at least as affirmed in true judgment. Such non-beings are called being by an analogy of proportionality with real being, not insofar as they can possess real existence (which they cannot), but insofar as they can be said to be by the intellect, just as the intellect says that real being is. Such logical beings have acquired special importance in the thought of recent centuries, in particular by reason of their role in the theoretical structures of modern science.

When being is said to be transcendental, this is meant first of all of actual being, but secondarily of possible being as well. However, it can even be understood to refer to the whole amplitude of both real and logical being. And if being itself is found throughout this amplitude, then so also are all the other transcendental aspects of being. However, they are here considered only insofar as they are found in actual being, it being understood that they are also found in an analogous manner in both possible being and logical being.

The meaning of being

What is that in things on which the meta-concept of being, as distinct from the meta-concepts of the other transcendental aspects of being, focuses? Being is essence-in-relation-to-existence. Existence is the specifying term of this relation; and it is from existence, as the act of being, that the name "being" is derived. But the meta-concept of being is not simply the meta-concept of existence; rather, it is the meta-concept of having existence. And it cannot focus upon having existence without reference both to that which has existence and to the existence which is possessed. Still, the reference to the essence which has existence is oblique and mainly implicit; it is existence which dominates the consideration.

It is because existence is central in the meta-concept of being, though without loss of implicit reference to essence as well, that being can be said to be the root of all the other transcendentals. For all the transcendentals in some manner derive from existence; they are only aspects of the intelligible richness of existence.

The classification of transcendentals

Because of the multiplicity of transcendentals, it may be wondered whether there is not, perhaps, some order between them, an order grounding a scheme of classification. In fact, it is possible so to group transcendentals according to order. Since every negation must be relative to some affirmation and suppose some affirmation, positive attributes must be prior to negative attributes. Since every relation presupposes a relatum, relative attributes must presuppose absolute attributes. Accordingly, transcendentals may be grouped in the following order: first, positive absolute; second, negative absolute; third, positive relative; fourth, negative relative. Within each of these divisions, still further ordered grouping is possible; but this is considered in the treatment of each of the divisions. Finally, one may consider the absolute attributes of being simply as absolute, or one may consider the absolute attributes of being precisely as grounding the relative attributes of being. The latter consideration introduces us to still another group of transcendental attributes, absolute, but now absolute precisely as the ground of the relative. This group will be considered apart, after the other four groups, since it can only appear after an understanding of the simply absolute and simply relative transcendental aspects of being.

The positive absolute transcendentals

The first positive absolute transcendental is being itself; but there are several others as well. In a previous chapter it was pointed out that existence is not a static but a dynamic act, an exercised act. Therefore every being is dynamic in its existential act. This dynamism with respect to existential act is the second transcendental aspect of being. Moreover, every being endures, has at least some duration; this is to say that every being is persistent. Now if being endures, it must tend to endure. The dynamism of being in its existential act has a correlate in the tendency of being to exist; every being tends to exist, in some sense has a drive to exist.

Further, in virtue of its dynamic existential act, every being tends to superabound in activity, a second dynamically exercised act. This adds two more to the list of transcendentals. Every being is active, through a dynamically exercised superexistential act; and every being therefore has a tendency to activity, a natural drive to superabound in its being.

But it is not enough to say that every being tends toward and exercises it own proper activity. It was seen in an earlier chapter that every being insofar as it exists tends toward consciousness in some manner, whether so as to be conscious or to become part of a conscious being or so as to enter into the consciousness of some other being. This tendency toward consciousness is a tendency toward knowledge and a tendency toward love, and thus emerge two more transcendental aspects of being. These two transcendental tendencies of being are in a way the ultimate meaning of all being and of all tendency of being; being is always for the sake of knowledge and love, except where it already is knowledge and love.

These observations open a whole new field in the investigation of being. If existence is for consciousness and tending to consciousness, then every limited being must be developing, striving, always moving on its way toward a greater share in consciousness, either toward a fuller entry into the consciousness of other, conscious being, or toward a sharing or greater sharing in the act of consciousness. This means that every being has an evolutionary character, unless there be some unlimited being already possessing the fullness of being and of consciousness. Such an unlimited being would not, could not, itself be evolutionary; but this being would then be in some sense the goal of all evolutionary striving, to be possessed as fully as possible in the consciousness of some limited intelligences, and reflected as fully as possible to these limited intelligences by the perfections of other, non-conscious limited beings.

Obviously, the theory of biological evolution finds a congenial environment in such a metaphysical view of the world; but it must be emphasized that the theory of biological evolution is still a theory, and cannot claim to have become philosophically demonstrated truth in the light of such an evolutionary idea of being. But much more than the mere theory of biological evolution is illuminated by such metaphysical evolutionism. Personal development and work, the achievement of greater degrees of civilization and culture for men, the progressive movement of history, the growth of freedom, all these now become intelligible as the movement toward the greater and greater spiritualization of the world, the fuller and fuller participation in the conscious life of knowledge and love by all being and by each being in its own way.

But it is impossible here to follow up all these themes. What is immediately relevant is that two new transcendental aspects of being may be added: the tendency of being toward knowledge and the tendency of being toward love in some manner.

Further, every being must have some essence, determining the degree of existence to be possessed by the thing. Even the pure act of existence must be said to have an essence insofar as this pure act is a determinate being with a determinate grade of being, namely, the supreme grade and the determination of infinite existence. But ordinarily, as has been seen, the determination of the degree of existence proceeds from a distinct essence or objectivity of the being. This same objectivity is also the foundation for the intelligibility of things to us, since it can be the object of insight expressible in a concept; but the foundation of intelligibility will be considered later. To focus upon the essence as determining the degree of existence is not, of course, to lose sight of existence itself. Still, the focus is not quite the same as that in the meta-concept of being itself. Therefore, there is here a distinct transcendental aspect of being, which has traditionally been designated by the word thing, despite the conventionality and colorlessness of this term. To the metaphysician, the word thing designates much more than it does to the non-metaphysician. This is the case with many other metaphysical terms as well.

Finally, since the substantial thing does not merely possess existence but also exercises it (and activity as well), this thing is also a subject. Therefore, every being, whether substance or accident, must be said to be subjective, either a subject or the being of a subject.

There may now be enumerated ten distinct positive absolute transcendentals: being, existentially dynamic, persistent, tending to exist, active, tending to act, tending toward knowledge, tending toward love, thing, subjective. There may, however, still be others, which could be disengaged by further analysis.

The negative absolute transcendental

Only one negative absolute transcendental is to be seen in this analysis of being. Every being is in itself undivided or one. This simple assertion, however, requires considerable commentary. First, it is necessary to distinguish clearly the unity of being from the merely quantitative unity considered in pre-twentieth century "mathematics."

There are two types of such quantitative unity, the unity of continuous quantity (or extension) and the unity of discrete quantity (which is the foundation of the concept of the number "one"). The unity of continuous quantity here means (contrary to traditional scholastic usage) only the unity of a multiplicity or aggregate of connected points, with determinate rules for movement from one point to another. The unity of discrete quantity is the unity of an element as opposed to a collection of elements. This second unity is somewhat closer to the metaphysical or transcendental unity than is the first; and yet it is not the same, for the unity of discrete quantity arises ultimately out of continuous quantity by the taking out and setting apart of some point or other element of continuous quantity. Note that continuous quantity, as it is considered here, is not by any means to be considered as always endowed with the mathematical property of continuity. Continuous quantity in this philosophical sense is simply the quantity that is constituted by a multiplicity or aggregate of connected points with determinate rules for movement from one point to another; such quantity may or may not be continuous in the mathematical sense. It may be said that such continuous quantity is in fact studied in modern group theory, while discrete quantity and aggregates of discrete quantity are studied in modern set theory. But neither set theory nor group theory is restricted to the study of quantitative manifolds, according to the more common view of modern mathematicians.

The unit of either continuous or discrete quantity can be said to be undivided in itself, just as can the unity of being. However, in the case of continuous quantity, the indivision is merely factual, without any intrinsic necessity--continuous quantity as such is indifferent in itself to division or to indivision. Discrete quantity is simply a point or some other element of continuous quantity. If it is a point, its indivision arises from its imperfection in the line of quantity. If it is some element of continuous quantity other than a point, its indivision is again only factual, without any intrinsic necessity.

The metaphysical unity of being is something much more fundamental than the indivision that is merely factual or the indivision that proceeds from imperfection. While the indivision of a continuous being may be a sign of the deeper ontological unity, the two are on distinct planes. The unity of being is a unity of substantial essence, a unity of substantial existence, and a unity of subjectivity.

It is from the unity of subjectivity that there flows the unity of the substance and its accidents, since it is the same subject which exercises both the substantial existence and the various accidental existences of the thing. But this subjectivity is first constituted as such through the substantial existence of the being. Therefore the unity of subjectivity presupposes the unity of substantial existence. So also, the unity of essence is derived, just as is its whole opposition to nothingness, from existence. In the light of all this, the fundamental unity of the being is the unity of its substantial existence; the actual undividedness of being is grounded in the actual undividedness of the substantial existence of the being. Note that this undividedness is not merely factual; a determinate degree of substantial existence by its very nature is undivided. Similarly, this undividedness does not proceed from imperfection but from the perfection of the act of existence. In these points metaphysical unity stands in sharp contrast with merely quantitative unity.

But, as was pointed out above, quantitative unity can in fact be a sign of the deeper ontological unity of the being. First, review briefly a few points. In every quantitatively extended being, there is prime matter--pure potency and pure multiplicity--with its multiplicity as the ultimate root of the extension of the being through quantity. While prime matter is in itself a pure multiplicity and pure diversity, the prime matter of each being is "held together" by the substantial form and substantial existence of the being, and the multiplicity of the being (proceeding from its prime matter) is organized by quantity. But this prime matter in turn is the principle of individuation of the composite substance; diverse prime matter is also diverse potency for substantial form. Now, if there is complete discontinuity between quantitative extensions, then there is also diversity between the prime matters which demand these quantitative extensions. Therefore there are diverse substances as well. Quantitative discontinuity is thus a sign of the discontinuity of being, of the multiplicity of beings. On the other hand, true quantitative unity and continuity must be signs of the continuity and unity of being; for continuous quantity is in fact <u>one</u> quantity and must therefore be of <u>one</u> being.

Correlative with unity is multiplicity. Just as there is quantitative unity and multiplicity, so also there is metaphysical unity and multiplicity, the unity and multiplicity of being. Metaphysics must consider multiplicity as well as unity, as has already happened in the discussions of the multiplicity of limited acts, the principle of individuation, and the nature of quantity. The consideration of unity and multiplicity is found in various particular forms in other sciences, as well as in rather generalized form in logic and in mathematics; but metaphysics differs from the other sciences in considering all unity and multiplicity in the light of transcendental unity, and in the light of the multiplicity that is correlative with this transcendental unity. Yet this metaphysical multiplicity is not in itself a transcendental aspect of being, since each being is in fact one rather than multiple. However, multiplicity is at the root of at least two of the negative relative transcendentals, which will be seen later, namely, uniqueness and separateness.

The positive relative transcendentals

When being is considered, no longer absolutely, but in relation to other being, new sets of transcendentals appear. First, being may be considered in relation to all other being. Positively, there emerge here the generosity of being and its tendency to union and to communion. As was seen in an earlier chapter, being tends to diffuse itself through its activity; this is the dynamic generosity of being. And through this same activity is manifested, as was seen in an earlier chapter, the tendency of every being for union and communion with other being.

Second, being may be considered in relation to the human intellect. The intelligibility of being, the knowability of being to the human intellect, was already considered earlier. This intelligibility of being is called the "truth" of being, and in this light it may be said that every being is true. But in fact there are various meanings of "true" and "truth," and it is useful now to examine them in some detail in order the better to understand the sense in which truth is a transcendental aspect of being.

The first meaning of truth is the conformity of an intellect with a thing. We are using this meaning when we speak of our judgments' being true or not true. But the same word "true" is also applied to the things themselves; from this point of view truth is the conformity or conformability of things to the intellect. Of interest at present is the sense in which every being is true, therefore the second use of the word "truth," ontological truth, or the truth of things, as opposed to logical truth, or the truth of the intellect.

There is an essential conformity of being with the intelligence of its maker, as is observed in the relation of the artifact to the artificer. In Part 2, such essential conformity will be seen to exist in all being to the supreme intelligence. This primary ontological truth is in fact a transcendental, but it cannot be properly and fully considered at present. But there is no essential conformity of being to the human intellect, since this conformity is only present insofar as the intellect is actually knowing the thing. Because the human intellect need not be actually knowing the thing (indeed, this intellect need not even exist), any such conformity of thing to human intellect arising in virtue of such an act of knowledge is only an accidental conformity and certainly not a transcendental aspect of being.

However, there is an essential conformability of the thing to the human intellect, insofar as being is intelligible, able to be known by this intellect. More generally, the conformability of being to finite intellect is the secondary ontological truth of being and a transcendental aspect of being. This conformability of being to the finite intellect is an aspect of being itself and is therefore present even if the finite intellect should not exist; being is intelligible in virtue of its very being. Similarly, the finite intellect itself is conformable to being, even if it is not actually knowing being or this being. This mutual radical conformability of being and intellect is itself strongly suggestive of some deeper common root of both being and intellect, a being which is at the same time intelligence, and which is the source of all other being and intelligence. In fact, it is only when being is considered in the light of the pure act of existence, which is also pure intelligence, that the hierarchy of truths of being and intelligence can be properly clarified. For this we must wait until Part 2.

Being can also be considered in relation to the will, or to appetite in general. The object of desire is said to be a good or to be good. This is the fundamental meaning of good, "that which all things desire," or "the object of desire." Secondarily, a being is called good if its natural "desires" are fulfilled, so that this being is perfect according to its kind. This latter good, the proper good of each thing, is clearly not transcendental, since not every being possesses its proper good.

But if the former good is considered, good according to its fundamental meaning, existence can be seen to be the good of all things. Existence is the object of desire for every appetite, for every appetite tends toward some mode of being. Therefore, since every being insofar as it is a being has existence, it follows that every being insofar as it is a being is good. Similarly, since every being insofar as it is a being tends toward activity, every being insofar as it is an agent has a secondary, superadded goodness, which is the very superexistence of activity.

A third type of transcendental goodness appears when the relation of existence to the human will in particular is considered. Since existence is an unqualified good, since the human intellect can understand universal being and existence, the human will has a certain unrestricted desire for existence, for acquiring in some manner the fullness of existence. This means that every being is somehow an object of desire for the human will. This desirability of being by the human, or more generally, by the finite will, is a transcendental, since it derives from the fundamental goodness of existence itself.

Just as in the case of the truth of things, a correlativity can be noted between the agreeableness of things to the will and the agreeableness of the will to things. This mutual agreeableness is again suggestive of some deeper common root of both being and the will, a being which is at the same time will, and which is the source of all other beings and wills. Again it is only when being is considered in the light of the pure act of existence, which is also pure will and love, that the hierarchy of goods of being and of will can be properly clarified. It is only from this more profound perspective that the special goodness of the finite will itself, which consists in a certain conformity or agreement of the will with things and with the natural order of things, can be properly understood in relation to the goodness of being. And another parallel between the consideration of truth and the consideration of good is found in that the goodness of conventional goods, such as money or precious minerals, is analogous to the truth of artifacts. The hierarchy of goodness of being and of the will is again touched upon briefly in Part 2, where it can be properly ordered under the pure goodness itself.

But before leaving the goodness of being, it is opportune to say a few words about evil. If every being is good, then evil cannot be a being. If it is not a being, then it must be a nothingness. But it is not a mere nothingness; mere nothingness as such is neither good nor evil. Therefore it is a nothingness precisely where there ought to be being, a privation of being, a lack, a wound in being. There can only be evil where there is being and goodness of being. Evil is therefore a "parasite," in some sense, of being; and it derives its power and its propagation, not from itself, but from the being of which this evil is a wound. The deformity of a human act can introduce deformity into other things only because this first deformity is the deformity of an act, which as an act is good, and only because the deformity of other things will be a deformity of those things, which, insofar as they are, are good. This reduction of evil to a nothingness in being does not destroy the profound mystery of evil and its permission by God. But it does permit at least the beginning of an understanding of the freedom of the human will to choose evil and the permission of such evil under the providence of God, as will be seen later.

Being may also be considered, no longer as the good of the finite will or as the truth to which our intellects conform, but now precisely as the good of the finite intellect. Being is the object of desire to the intellect, which seeks to know all being; therefore the actual knowledge of being gives a satisfaction or pleasure to the intellect. But that which, when seen, pleases is said to be beautiful. Therefore, every being insofar as it is being is also beautiful, in relation to the human or to any finite intellect. This is a transcendental beauty of being, and must not be confused with aesthetic beauty; aesthetic beauty is an especially satisfying radiance arising from the unity and harmony of the known in itself and with our cognitive and appetitive faculties. Ugliness bears a relation to aesthetic and transcendental beauty analogous to that which evil bears to good in general. As was the case with the truth of being and the intellect, and with the goodness of being and the will, so also the agreeability of being as beautiful with the finite intellect and of the finite intellect with being as beautiful indicates that both being as beautiful and the finite intelligence must be derived from some common root, a being in which beauty and intelligence are identified. This again is the pure act of existence, as will be seen in Part 2.

In the consideration of the truth, goodness, and beauty of being, it has been found necessary in each case to postpone to Part 2 a more adequate discussion. This means that still other modes of transcendental truth, goodness, and beauty may be expected to emerge when all being is considered in relation to the pure act of existence, which is also pure intelligence and love.

The negative relative transcendentals

When being is considered so as to see what is to be denied of it in relation to other being, the first new aspect to emerge is its uniqueness. Being is not univocal in its meaning; every being is a diverse mode of being, a unique mode of being. Even when many individuals are found to be of the same specific type, the univocity is only in the manner of conception, not in the beings themselves. There is in things, it is true, a certain foundation of similarity for the univocal concepts we form; but nevertheless each individual, in its being as an individual, is only analogically similar to each other individual, even if this other be of the same specific type.

This uniqueness of each being can be seen at four levels. First, the existence of each being is an existential act of this subject rather than of any other, therefore in itself relative to this subject rather than to any other. But the relativity of each act of existence to each essence and subject is itself identical with each act of existence. Since no two acts of existence have, or rather are, the same relativity to essence and subjectivity, each act of existence must be unique.

Second, the objectivity or essence of each individual thing is also in some manner unique. Each formal act of each being is essentially relative to this prime matter or to this susbtance, even in the case of formal acts which are specifically the same and only numerically distinct. Of course, formal acts which are not even specifically the same are even more obviously unique in relation to each other. But even in the former case of only specific likeness, since the relativity to this prime matter or to this substance is itself identical with the formal act itself, each instance of this same specific type of formal act is unique in relation to any other such instance. This is a fundamental reason why univocity in the conception of formal acts does not mean univocity in the being of such acts, but rather only analogical similarity.

Even prime matter shares in its own way in the uniqueness proper to the order of essence or objectivity. First, prime matter cannot exist by itself but only insofar as it is conjoined with some (unique) substantial form and in virtue of this union is a co-principle of an essence possessing existence. Second, since prime matter is in itself pure diversity, every instance is necessarily diverse from every other instance and therefore at least in this manner intrinsically unique. Third, each instance of prime matter is constituted in a diverse existential state in virtue of the individual hierarchy of forms and existences in each being. This points to the third uniqueness of each being, the uniqueness of its existential state.

Since the existential state of each being is determined in part by the coexistence of the various formal determinations of the being, any diversity in these formal determinations means a diversity in existential state. But in fact no two beings can have the same formal determinations. This is already evident from the fact that each formal determination is in some manner unique. But other differences of formal determinations can be pointed out. Certainly, no two knowers can have precisely the same knowledge of things, since each knows the universe from his own perspective and in his own way and in his own degree. And on the lower level of material being, each has its own individual notes, exerts its own influence on others, and is influenced in its own way by others.

And in all this it must not be overlooked that the existential state of each being is itself more than the simple sum total of formal determinations of the thing. It is the very exercise of existence and activity in the subjectivity of each thing. But it has already been seen that this exercise and subjectivity is itself unique insofar as existence itself is unique. Therefore, the existential state of each being is unique.

Fourth, just as existence in each being is a unique act, so also the superexistence which is activity is unique in each being. Every being is unique in its activity; my activity is *mine* and not of any other.

Four modes of uniqueness are distinguished, then, in every being: Uniqueness of existence, uniqueness of essence, uniqueness of existential state, uniqueness of activity. These may be regarded as four distinct transcendental aspects of being.

Parallel with these four modes of uniqueness in things are four modes of separation of beings from each other. Separation results from uniqueness, and is simply the distinction and relative isolation of each being from every other being. The distinction between uniqueness and separation may be seen by reflecting that each being by its activity strives to overcome its separation from others in some manner but by this same activity strives to preserve its uniqueness as a mode of being, insofar as it strives to preserve its being. Four more transcendentals thus are added to the list: separation in existence, in essence, in existential state, and in activity.

When being is considered in relation to the human intellect, yet another negative aspect appears, insofar as being contains an excess of meaning which the human intellect is unable to exhaust. Being is here confronted as mystery. The mystery of being arises not only from the multi-dimensionality of being and the proliferation of transcendentals which is being considered in this chapter, but also from the intelligible richness of each dimension in itself. The proper mystery of sensible phenomenality has become more and more manifest with the progress of the natural sciences of physics, chemistry, biology, etc. And with this fuller realization of the mystery of sensible phenomenality has come an even deeper understanding of the mystery of transphenomenal objectivity. The existent ists have helped to uncover more of the domain of psychic phenomena ity and have shown the possibility of fuller knowledge of the subject i its very subjectivity. With all this, the mystery of being and action h deepened more and more, and with this also the mystery of createdness. Each question that we answer raises a dozen more. Therefore, being insofar as it is being is also mysterious; and mystery is a transcendental aspect, or a set of transcendental aspects, of being. According as mystery is found in the dimensions of transphenomenal essence, existence, activity, and subjectivity, four transcendental mysteries of being may be distinguished.

Correlative with the mystery that results from the excess of truth in being is the sublimity that results from the excess of beauty in being. Being is not only beautiful; it is also sublime. This consideration yields four more transcendentals parallel to those just mentioned. Moreover, if being is mysterious and sublime, then it must also have an excess of goodness, a goodness which calls not just for love but for that special intensity of love and respect which is reverence. But if being demands not only love but reverence, then this must be because being is not only good but somehow sacred. Again four new transcendentals, parallel to those of mystery and sublimity, emerge, transcendentals unfamiliar to some but familiar to those who appreciate the mystery of being and its abysses of truth, beauty, and goodness.

And yet even if these abysses of truth, beauty, and goodness can cause ecstasy in the contemplation of being, still it must finally be acknowledged that they are at bottom unsatisfying and only serve to stimulate a desire for something still greater, a plenitude of truth, beauty, and goodness which no being or combination of beings in this life can give. Not even the pure act of existence itself, as known in this life, can give such a plenitude.

But it is possible to go even further. Even if one were to achieve the fullest knowledge possible of the pure act of existence by his natural powers, in some future state, still this contemplation would leave him with a radical desire (impossible of fulfillment to pure nature, and therefore unreasonable so far as any elicited act of the will is concerned), a radical openness to something still more. This desire and openness cannot be removed through any finite truth and goodness or even through the fullest (which would still be finite) natural knowledge and love of pure existence. This desire and openness can only be satisfied by an intuitive vision of pure existence, inaccessible to the natural powers of any finite intelligence (since finite intelligence must understand in a finite manner and through a finite intentional form). By the revelation of God we know that in fact this intuitive vision has nevertheless been offered to man as a free gift from God through grace and the light of glory, but this consideration is beyond the scope of the present inquiry.

Even if this intuitive vision had not been offered to man, there would have been a possibility for happiness and contentment in the knowledge and love of the pure act of existence, even for a certain ecstasy of knowledge and love. But this happiness would still be imperfect, with an imperfection which is a necessary condition of being for any finite intelligence, unless it be removed by the free gift of God. The imperfection is a consequence of this radical natural desire or openness which it would be irrational to elicit in an act of the will, and consists in consequent tension, as natural to man as is his possibility of happiness. Such tension is the inevitable accompaniment even of the highest happiness, so long as this happiness is only the happiness of a finite intelligence and not the happiness of God, or the happiness of God shared with others by the free gift of God.

All this comes to saying that, despite the mystery, sublimity, and sacred character of being, this being is always in some manner radically unsatisfying to the natural powers of man, that even if the mystery could be understood so far as is naturally possible, even if the sublimity could be contemplated so far as naturally possible, even if the sacredness could be adhered to in love as far as naturally possible, still there would remain in man a certain void and a certain tension. This void and this tension are, of course, even more manifest in the conditions of our present existence, where we are very far from such understanding, contemplation, and love. Being thus reveals three more aspects, its inability to satiate our ontological thirst in each of the three ways just mentioned. These three insufficiencies, in truth, beauty, and goodness, are transcendental aspects of being as it is considered in relation to the natural powers of man and of any finite intelligence. There now are revealed twenty-three negative relative transcendentals: five groups of four each, centered around the uniqueness, separateness, mystery, sublimity, and sacredness of being; one group of three centered around the insufficiency of being for the finite intellect and will.

The absolute ground of the relative transcendentals

If the relative transcendentals say something real about being, then there is something absolute in being which grounds the relative attributes; for the being of the relative is always grounded in the being of the absolute. This points to a new set of transcendental terms, which refer to the absolute foundation for the relative transcendentals. In addition to the various modes of truth, goodness, beauty, uniqueness, etc. as relative attributes, there are absolute truth, absolute goodness, absolute beauty, absolute uniqueness, etc. in every being. These absolutes are nothing other than the existence, subjectivity, and essence of absolute being. The absolute truth of being is primarily its existence, secondarily its subjectivity, and thirdly its essence; and it is similar with the absolute foundation of each of the other relative transcendentals. Since seven positive and twenty-three negative relative transcendentals have been definitely enumerated, the consideration of the absolute ground of each of the relative transcendentals must yield a total of ninety distinct new transcendental terms! At this point, let it again be emphasized that the enumeration of transcendentals here given is by no means complete. New ones appear in Part 2, and even then one may not pretend to have exhausted the possibilities. It seems impossible at this point to set any theoretical limits to the proliferation of transcendental terms. So far there is a total of 131 such terms: ten positive absolute, one negative absolute, seven positive relative, twenty-three negative relative, and ninety absolute-grounding-the-relative. But just to indicate other possibilities, it must be noted that we have failed to consider still other absolute grounds of relative transcendentals, which can be discovered through an analysis of the various tendencies which have been discovered in being, such as those toward consciousness in knowledge and love.

Chapter 12

PHILOSOPHICAL PLURALISM AND THE DIMENSIONS OF BEING

Diverse dimensions of being are of central interest to diverse philosophers. While the positivists are concerned mainly with sensible phenomenality (indeed, exclusively with this if they remain true to their positivism), the existentialists focus principally upon subjectivity and psychic phenomenality. Hume's concern exclusively with sensible phenomenality was what forced Kant to look for universality and necessity entirely on the side of the knowing subject, and later idealists to look entirely within knowledge itself. Marcel's concern for the subjectivity of things has led him to minimize the concern of other philosophers with the objectivity of things, although he has himself declared that his own thought must be integrated into the wider structures of philosophical thought. Sartre's concern in Being and Nothingness is principally with psychic phenomenality; but he has come to understand that the philosophy of Being and Nothingness must be taken as an adjunct to a more complete philosophy, so that he regards his existential thought as an extension of Marxism into the human domain.

While the early Indian Upanishads seem to focus upon the immediate reference of finite being to the Absolute Self, and therefore to center around subjectivity and the intuition of the createdness of things (although usually conceived in a pantheistic manner), Aristotle seemed to lack all sense of this subjectivity and createdness in his concern with a metaphysics (which is not yet a formally achieved metaphysics at all from the perspective of the metaphysics of existence) of transphenomenal formal objectivity. Even Saint Thomas Aquinas, who rose beyond the "metaphysics" of formal objectivity to the metaphysics of existence, and who therefore came to some discursive understanding of the createdness of things, did not seem to recognize (at least, there does not seem to be evidence in the texts) the intuitive giveness of createdness. And although he most certainly understood something of the difference between subjectivity and objectivity, he does not seem to have had the profound understanding of this which was possessed by the Indian sages or by the modern existentialists, or even by some modern Thomists such as Maritain.

Most modern scholastics continue to be occupied, as were their predecessors, with transphenomenal formal objectivity; and some would even tend to reduce existence itself to this level. Some have become strongly aware of psychic phenomenality and of subjectivity, under the influence of the existentialists and phenomenologists. What is perhaps most astonishing is the tendency of scholastic philosophers to ignore the dimension of sensible phenomenality as a proper object of intellectual knowledge, despite the four hundred years of scientific progress in the intellectual understanding of phenomena and the consequent development of positivistic philosophy. Too many scholastics seem unaware of the real multi-dimensionality of being. In opposition to the tendency of such scholastics to confine philosophy to thirteenth-century limits, or even to shrink those limits further, Maritain is an outstanding example in contemporary Thomism of the movement to broaden the horizons of Thomists so as to take into account the immense acquisitions in the intellectual life of recent centuries.

Rarely is there a philosopher who does real justice to the multi-dimensionality of being. As a matter of fact, it might be pointed out (and this must seem provoking to some, but it cannot be helped) that intellectual justice to being demands a certain moral perfection in the philosopher. For it is only when all being, and every aspect of being, is seen in its proper relation to God, Who exists at the heart of reality, that each mode of being can be given its due without any distortion and overemphasis. But men tend to focus upon that in being which for some reason especially attracts them, whether this reason be temperament, environment, education, tradition, or any other.

Such subjective influences are necessarily reinforced by two factors in human intellectual life. There is in every man, as has been seen, the natural desire for being, to know being. But at the same time there is also the necessary limitation of human knowledge; one never knows the whole of things but only some aspects or others. This means that there is ordinarily an insufficient basis for judgment concerning the totality of being, unless this judgment be preceded by a lengthy gathering of data. And this collection of data must be made by an intelligence which has somehow remained completely open to all modes of being rather than become partially closed by reason of special receptivity for some particular mode or modes. But such openness to being is rarely achieved. Heidegger has pointed out how the knowledge of some special modes of being itself commonly prevents a real understanding of universal being.

Unless one possess an extraordinary degree of intellectual asceticism, the desire for being and knowledge, as conditioned by the limitation of insight and the fact of subjective inclinations to this or that particular mode of being, ordinarily results in precipitate, and therefore faulty, conceptualization and judgment. The dimensions of being are not properly disengaged from each other, or some may be disregarded entirely. This disregard of some of the dimensions of being results especially when an attempt is made to restrict philosophy to the domain of what is known clearly. Moreover, the criterion of clarity must vary from one philosopher to another, since each knows more clearly that toward which he himself is more inclined for one reason or another. To the existentialist it is the evidence of the subject, or of the stream of consciousness, that is most clear. To the positivist it is the evidence of sensible phenomena that is most clear. To many it is the transphenomenal object that is most clear. What is in fact most clear from all this is that no knowledge should be lightly dismissed because of its obscurity, in order to give entire attention to what we happen to see most clearly. This is only to open the way to intellectual provincialism of one kind or another.

It is ignoring the multi-dimensional mystery of being that results in radical philosophical pluralism even among the great philosophers. It is awakening to this multi-dimensional mystery of being (to which Christian revelation and Christian life especially call us in many ways) that results in the carrying on and organic development of the tradition of the "perennial philosophy." This "perennial philosophy" has, in fact, flourished chiefly among Christian philosophers. But such an awakening to the multi-dimensional mystery of being is difficult even for a Christian philosopher, for the reasons already given. And yet if it does not come to Christian philosophers, it can hardly be expected in others.

But if one considers the intellectual weakness of men, even of the best of Christian philosophers, he must admit the necessity of using philosophies outside the tradition of the perennial philosophy even for philosophers within this tradition. It is necessary to supplement our limited view of being with the help of those who have looked elsewhere than we have ourselves; it is necessary to deepen even the understanding which we do have by docility to those who may perhaps have seen more of some particular domain of being, even when they have not seen other domains so well. When this is understood, one no longer seeks to refute the great philosophers but simply to understand them in their proper context within the multi-dimensionality and mystery of being. In this way, distortions are corrected so that philosophers are each rendered even more faithful to the genuine light which they possess. Thus the many fragments are gathered together into the unity of the perennial philosophy rather than thrown aside and scattered by those who pretend to possess the fullness of the truth.

Chapter 13

SOME PROBLEMS

This is the end of Part 1 of our inquiry into being. In this part, analysis has disengaged the dimensions of being, the structure of proportionate and limited being, and many of the transcendental attributes of being. But in the course of this analysis numerous problems appeared, problems which point the way to a second stage of inquiry, inquiry into the possibility of the transcendence of limited being and into the existence and nature of transcendent, or unlimited, being. At this point, it seems convenient to collect these problems so as better to focus attention upon the precise point of inquiry in Part 2.

In Part 1, there arose the notion of a pure act of existence, an existence which would transcend the entire domain of proportionate and limited being. While any limited being need not exist, even if in fact it does exist, such an unlimited existence seemingly would have to exist; for this unlimited existence is its own existence. And yet such a method of transcendence has some difficulties. There is no given experience of such a transcendent being in the domain of proportionate being; that would be a contradiction. And even if some experience of absolute being (which is the pure act of existence) should be given in the mysterious and obscure intuition of createdness already spoken of, still any attempt to reinforce this obscure knowledge by a simple consideration of the meaning of pure existence seems to be in danger of becoming a merely logical analysis without direct relevance to the real world. Such an attempt at an "ontological argument" from an analysis of the meaning of existence is analyzed in Part 2.

The intuition of createdness is a stimulus to philosophical inquiry; but since it is itself non-objective in its mode, it is not a properly philosophical knowledge. It pertains to those special modes of fruitive union with being which may be grouped together as natural "mystical" experience of being. Philosophy, on the other hand, has the purpose of giving a rational and objective account of transcendence, a scientific account.

In fact many possible methods of transcendence present themselves to the philosopher. In the light of the metaphysical analysis in Part 1, he is compelled to seek for a more complete ground for many data than can be found within the domain of proportionate or limited being.

First, the fact of becoming, and in particular the becoming of existence and of substantial form, requires further explanation. So also the fact of activity as a superabundance of any limited, a superabundance to which the limited being is itself in a way only in potency, demands more investigation. Again, the fact that every limited being is a contingent being pushes one to ask for the necessary ground of any contingent existence, which cannot be found within the domain of contingent and limited being. Likewise, the fact that the perfections of being should be in themselves unlimited but nevertheless are found in limited modes calls for explanation. And the finality of natural agents has already suggested the existence of transcendent intelligence.

Nor do these five approaches, along the lines of the Five Ways of Saint Thomas, exhaust the ways of transcendence of proportionate being. The dynamism of freedom as revealed in psychic phenomenality points toward some transcendent good. Perhaps it is possible to formulate in some properly philosophical manner the content of the intuition of unity-in-multiplicity which is the intuition of createdness. It has already been seen that the analogy of being must ultimately be founded on the reference of the plurality of analogates to some one being, some one existence, which is the pure act of existence. If there be such a thing as the possibility of non-existents, this possibility must have some transcendent ground; for there is no medium between being and nothingness, no half-being of essence apart from existence. It has already been noted that the correlation between the intelligibility of being and the drive of the intellect to understand points to some transcendent union and identity of being and intelligence and intelligibility. And similar correlations with similar implications are found concerning the appetibility and beauty of being.

There follows a preliminary discussion of the possibility, difficulty, and necessity of transcendence. Then the actual demonstrations of the existence of transcendent being are presented. After the question of existence has been answered, the possibility of further knowledge of the nature of transcendent being will be considered.

PART 2

TRANSCENDENT BEING

Chapter 14

THE POSSIBILITY AND NECESSITY OF TRANSCENDENCE

In Part 1, the first stage of the inquiry into being proceeded by an analysis of the structure of proportionate and limited being. In the course of that analysis, there emerged several problems which could not be resolved within the plane of proportionate or limited being, and which therefore raise the question of the existence and nature of transcendent being. Transcendence, as this term has been used in Part 1 and as it will be used in Part 2 as well, is the movement of the human intellect beyond proportionate and limited being to a scientific understanding of transcendent being. Non-scientific transcendence has in fact already been discovered, in the intuition of createdness. But this is to be a scientific understanding, conceptually or meta-conceptually formulated systematic knowledge. Therefore no wholly or partially non-intellectual or non-rational means of transcendence, as in supernatural faith, hope, and love, is of primary interest here, even though some are of primary importance in the life, and even the intellectual life, of the believer.

The present stage of inquiry, then, corresponds to what has traditionally been called natural theology. Natural theology is only the prolongation of metaphysical inquiry beyond the plane of proportionate and limited being. This prolongation is, as has been seen, demanded by the inadequate results of the analysis at the plane of proportionate and limited being, an analysis which raises problems which it is itself unable to resolve. At the same time, unless the preliminary metaphysical analysis has been first achieved, the problems cannot even arise; in this event, natural theology may seem a castle in the air and proofs for the existence of God only dialectical games and transcendental illusions.

General objections against the possibility of transcendence

In the long history of philosophy, a multitude of objections have been brought against the very possibility of transcendence by the representatives of the empiricist, idealist, and now the existentialist, traditions. These objections are not to be here considered in detail; but some few general remarks may be made about them, remarks which, in the light of the analysis of Part 1, should be sufficient to permit the continuation of the inquiry.

In general, the objections against transcendence all rest upon the introduction of some limitation in principle to the possibility of human knowledge, a limitation which involves either the exclusion or an inadequate recognition of one or more of the diverse dimensions of being. It has already been seen in Part 1 how such omission is in fact possible and even a serious danger for the human intellect. At this point some further observations may be added to what was said there. The narrowing of intellectual horizons is frequently induced by an attitude adopted through free choice. If one inordinately desires material wealth and material power, to "safeguard" and to expand in a way his own material being, if this desire comes to dominate his life, then it is all but inevitable that his intellectual horizon become narrowed to that of the materialist. Such a man may pretend, even to himself, to seek the truth; but he has already prejudged the truth in a manner much more profound and existential than by any mere intellectual judgment. His pretended intellectual sincerity is given the lie by the insincerity of his freely chosen being, no longer open to the truth but closed by the free choice entirely centered on the material self. On the other hand, the dominant passion may not be for material wealth and power but for the truth itself--yet not for the truth of being itself but for a truth which is tailor-made to suit the tastes of the inquirer. Once again there is a prejudice deeper than any mere intellectual judgment, again the possibility of deceiving even oneself by a pretended sincerity of the intellect which is belied by the insincerity of being.

Therefore, the radical, non-philosophical because deeper than philosophy, answer to the general objection against the possibility of transcendence is to call for complete openness to being, not merely an intellectual openness rendered false by existential attitudes, but an intellectual openness guaranteed by a genuine openness of being to being. Such openness cannot be brought about by merely intellectual means; it is a moral attitude of docility to the light.

But even with docility to the light, objections and difficulties may arise as obstacles to transcendence; for transcendence is essentially a movement beyond that domain which the intellect can consider with a certain relative facility (relative--for even there being is mysterious and the truth difficult to attain). The focal point of difficulty is the use of metaphysical theorems derived from the analysis of proportionate and limited being in order to transcend such being.

But the difficulty appears much greater than it really is, when it is presented in so bald an a priori manner. In fact, a step-by-step metaphysical analysis, such as was conducted in Part 1, brings one to the threshold of a philosophical acknowledgement of transcendent being. As will be seen in more detail, we are finally confronted with two alternatives: either we must step across this threshold and acknowledge transcendent being and thereby achieve genuine transcendence, or we must refuse to step across this threshold and thereby inescapably fail to reach an adequate ground for any being as opposed to nothingness.

It is not necessary to settle a priori the question of whether transcendent being is intelligible to us in the same manner as is proportionate or limited being. As a matter of fact, it is not intelligible in the same manner at all; but this does not really affect the simple possibility of transcendence. It is enough to know that proportionate being and limited being are themselves intelligible as opposed to nothingness, and that their opposition to nothingness does not receive an adequate ground within the domain of proportionate or limited being; these facts necessarily demand the existence of some transcendent being and therefore guarantee the possibility of transcendence. The possibility of transcendence, then, is not grounded in any a priori generalization of metaphysical theorems from the domains of proportionate and limited being to the domain of transcendent being, but rather in the absolute truth of these theorems (in particular, the principle of sufficient reason) within the domain of proportionate and limited being. It is only after transcendence has been actually achieved that the whole body of metaphysical knowledge of being is applied to transcendent being itself, in order to achieve some deeper understanding in an indirect manner of the existence and nature of such being.

The difficulty of transcendence

It has already become apparent that the achievement of transcendence through the exercise of human reason in a scientific manner may be very difficult. In fact, to achieve it to the highest degree possible may be said to be the ultimate goal and supreme achievement of natural human reason as such. The drive of the human intellect is toward being, and transcendent being is in fact the plenitude of being.

Even if there is some mysterious experience of transcendent being in the intuition of createdness, this experience is most obscure and confusing. While it can provoke us to further inquiry, it cannot itself satisfy the drive of the intellect for union with being, for clearer and more adequate awareness of being. The intuition of createdness should be cultivated and deepened, but it must be followed up by the scientific mode of transcendence. However, there are still difficulties in the way of scientific transcendence.

First, the preliminary metaphysical analysis, the gathering of data about being, is itself more difficult than are other more limited forms of inquiry; for it is always necessary to preserve that complete openness to the entire transcendental amplitude of being, even while any contraction of scope would come as a relief to the human intellect, accustomed as it is to dealing with more concretely limited modes of being.

Second, this preliminary metaphysical analysis must focus primarily on the non-objective aspects of being, such as existence and subjectivity, while the first tendency of the intellect is toward the objective.

Third, the insights of the preliminary metaphysical analysis must be formulated in a priori meta-conceptual constructs, which appear as illusions to one who has given himself to the investigation of one or more of the finite modes of objectivity.

Fourth, after all this thought already beyond our depth, we are called upon to go still further, to a domain beyond all proportionate and limited being. If the first stage of metaphysics might sometimes seem tenuous and even illusory, this second stage must seem even more so.

Clearly, if transcendence is to be achieved by the metaphysician, there is need for a sustained dynamism of the intellect, a sustained drive to know, as well as for a complete openness to being. Openness is the necessary passivity of the intellect, but inquiry is the necessary activity of the intellect. Both the openness and the spirit of inquiry can only be preserved in the midst of obstacles if there is a profound love of the truth--this is why the metaphysician is a "philosopher."

And if what has been said about the difficulty of transcendence is true, then what is to be said about the pseudo-philosophical glibness of certain apologetes who mistake Saint Paul's insistence that all can come to some natural knowledge of God for an assertion of the facility of achieving a scientific demonstration of the existence of God? When the Church teaches, in the First Vatican Council, that a certain knowledge of God's existence can be attained by human reason, she does not mean to deny the assertion of Saint Thomas Aquinas that such knowledge is in fact most difficult for one unaided by faith to gain. She does not even say that it is easy for a Christian. Indeed, the long history of controversy among Christians concerning the various proofs given for the existence of God bears out the view that such knowledge is rather difficult to achieve. Dialectical sleight-of-hand, even if backed up by good will, cannot be an adequate substitute for the reasoned scientific knowledge we seek.

The necessity of transcendence

The necessity for transcendence has arisen out of the metaphysical analysis of proportionate and limited being; it may therefore be said that this necessity arises from the metaphysical predicament of man. But there is a far deeper necessity for transcendence which arises out of the existential predicament of man. This necessity appears in two ways: we need transcendence, and God calls us to transcendence.

We need to know the transcendent being who is God, for we need God and must know Him in order to approach Him. Our need for God is more than the mere need of the intellect for knowledge; knowledge is only the first step in meeting this need. Not just intellect, but the entire human subject needs God. "Inquietum est cor nostrum ..." No limited being or accumulation of limited being can so meet this ontological need and restlessness as to make the human existent happy. And if one is tempted to mistake some limited being or beings for his happiness, there is always the evil and imperfection, the instability, of all the things in this world to frustrate him and to remind him of his radical weakness and need for something greater than all the world. Even Jean-Paul Sartre recognizes this desire and need in man; but he believes that it is doomed to final frustration and that therefore man is a "useless passion."

On the other side, God calls us to know Him and to come to Him; this is His will for us. A sign of this is that very restlessness which was pointed out in the preceding paragraph, a restlessness which arises out of our being itself, this being which has been created this way by God. But the will of God has also been revealed to us more fully by God Himself; the whole point of the revelation which reached its climax in the coming of Jesus Christ is that we are called to come to God, not just in the manner commensurate with our natural faculties of intellect and will, but even by a sharing in the intimacy of God's own life, communicated to us now by grace and later by the light of glory in the beatific vision.

It is true that God is hidden, "transcendent"; yet He has left for us ample evidence so that those who really want Him can find Him. He has even gone further and has called us to a fuller and greater life with Himself, through His revelation to Abraham, Isaac, Jacob, and the Jewish prophets, and His revelation in Christ and in His Church. God <u>is</u> found by those who seek Him; and indeed they already find Him, in a way, in their very seeking. If there is also mystery and obscurity, if God hides Himself, it is by reason of the utterly transcendent character of the divine nature and so that man may really choose or reject God in freedom. This is why even revelation is given in faith rather than in vision.

At this point, a new problem arises. Why should we trouble to search for God by reason when we already know Him by faith? Furthermore, is not Pascal's contrast between the God of philosophers and the God of Abraham, Isaac, and Jacob a valid one? Why should we bother ourselves with abstractions and reasonings when

God has already given Himself to the mind and heart of man? Abstractions and reasonings give us, not the very reality of God, but a set of ideas; but God's revelation gives us the living God. Has not the fact of divine revelation eliminated the need for transcendence in the sense above given to this phrase as a scientifically philosophical knowledge of God?

In response to these difficulties several observations may be made. First, the human intellect, like every other intellect, is made to see; its primary drive is toward an immediately intuitive insight. Where such insight is unattainable, a substitute is found in mediate, demonstrative knowledge, gained through discursive reasoning. Where neither of these is possible, the obscurity of belief is accepted in preference to mere opinion, suspicion, or even nothing at all. But wherever possible, the obscurity of belief tends toward resolution in vision, in accordance with the primary drive of the human intellect, or at least in discursive demonstrative reason. Revelation is not given in order to destroy this primary drive of the intellect but to fulfill it, even to fulfill it in a superabundant manner. Therefore the revelation of God concerning Himself should not discourage rational inquiry concerning God but rather encourage and strengthen it. We believe in order that we may understand, fully only in the future, but partially even in this life.

But even so the second difficulty remains. The God of the philosophers is only a set of ideas; the God of Abraham, Isaac, and Jacob is a living God. But Pascal's problem arises in the context of a rationalistic philosophy lacking the sense of mystery. It is true that the scientific philosophical knowledge of God, like that of being, is expressed in ideas, or meta-concepts, as will be seen later. It is also true that these ideas or meta-concepts simply fail to attain to the being of God in Himself, but refer to Him only in a most inadequate manner, so much so that Saint Thomas Aquinas says that man's highest knowledge of God in this life comes only when he realizes that he does not know Him. And still further, it is true that the philosophical relation to God is simply one of knower to known while God Himself calls us to a more personal relation. But these things do not render the philosophical knowledge of God false; God is greater than man, and man must expect to know Him only in an inadequate manner. It has already been seen that every being is mysterious, and God must be expected to be the most mysterious of all. To a philosopher with the sense of the mystery of being and of God, the deeper mysteries of revelation are, in a way, not so much a surprising intrusion upon the self-enclosed world of philosophy but rather a further unveiling of the infinite treasures of being. This does not mean that these mysteries fail to provoke wonderment--the mystery of the Trinity, the Incarnation, the Cross of Christ and its sharing by every Christian soul, each of these is an abyss of mystery and a subject of inexhaustible wonder and contemplation. But the philosopher with a sense of mystery is prepared to wonder and ever to wonder anew. Such a philosopher does not confuse his little constructed set of ideas with the inexhaustible being of God; he considers them only as a most inadequate means to gain some indirect understanding of the mystery of God.

Despair and transcendence

Below much of the intellectual objection to the possibility of transcendence is a deeper moral objection. That existential predicament of man, which has been said to constitute his most profound need for transcendence, is in fact a two-edged sword. That very mysterious restlessness and frustration of man, the presence of evil and of disappointment, which indicates our need for God, can also be taken as an indication that He does not exist. Why should there be so much and so great evil if a good God made the world? Why indeed should there even be the tiniest of evils in a world made by a good God? Evil has driven men to hope in God alone, but it has also helped keep other men away from Him. Yet the mystery of being does somehow include the mystery of evil in an inescapable manner.

But the renunciation of God in fact does not do away with the mystery of evil; this is an act of despair, not so much a solution as the abandonment of every hope of a solution. And its effect is not only to leave evil radically unintelligible but also to leave the goodness of being and the being of being equally unintelligible. It proceeds from a sickness of the heart rather than from an understanding of being, a sickness which in fact can only be healed by an understanding of the truth and a loving consent to the goodness of being and of God.

But this is not to minimize the depth of the mystery of evil. Some light will be shed upon it in the course of this inquiry, and more light will appear in the obscurity of faith. But the only existential solution for a man in this life is in union with the suffering Christ, with His love and with His acceptance of the cross as the salvation of the world.

Chapter 15

IMMEDIATE TRANSCENDENCE

All that has been said so far tends to favor the view that if philosophically scientific transcendence is to be achieved at all, it is through a process of discursive demonstrative reasoning. And yet even apart from the immediate transcendence given in the supernatural order through faith, hope, and charity, the possibility of some immediate transcendence in the natural order, transcendence which may be of value even to scientific philosophy, must be discussed.

There can, of course, be no question of transcendence in the line of sense knowledge; anything given to sense knowledge is by that very fact within the domain of proportionate being. And while it has already been seen that there is in fact transcendence in the line of intuitive intellectual knowledge, in the intuition of createdness, this transcendence takes place in a non-objective and most obscure manner and is therefore not of immediate value to scientific philosophy as such.

However, philosophers such as Saint Anselm, Descartes, and Leibniz have sought to achieve immediate transcendence through an immediate analysis of the formulated concept of pure being (we should say, in the light of Part 1, the formulated meta-concept of pure being). This type of analysis is the "ontological argument" for the existence of such pure being. Its starting point is always a formulated idea of what transcendent being would be if it existed. Since such a being would necessarily be its own existence, such a being is thought necessarily to exist.

This method of transcendence has generally been rejected as philosophically inadequate. The fallacy of confusing logical existence, contained in the meta-concept of transcendent being, with real existence is pointed out. And the very possibility (compatibility of attributes) of such a constructed meta-concept is put in doubt, until a real foundation is gained for it through some a posteriori demonstration of the existence of transcendent being.

These objections against any form of the ontological argument are in fact most serious. If there is only a constructed meta-concept without any already given foundation in reality, then whatever existence is contained in it is only logical existence. Moreover, the meta-concept of pure being does contain apparently incompatible attributes, such as complete immutability and the fullest life of intelligence and freedom, or perfect justice and perfect mercy.

And yet, what if the ontological argument is understood as a philosophical attempt to formulate some of the content of the intuition of createdness? In this intuition is given, in however obscure a manner, some awareness of transcendent being as pure being. This provides a real foundation for the constructed meta-concept of pure being, just as the non-objective evidence of existence and subjectivity provides a foundation for the constructed meta-concept of being that was seen in Part 1. Now the existence contained in the meta-concept of pure being is no longer just logical existence but a logical existence grounded in real existence; and the apparent incompatibility of notes is seen to be only apparent, since the construct does indeed have a real foundation. Of course, the same real foundation could be provided by the "evidence" of divine faith; but this would make the ontological argument a theological rather than a philosophical argument or analysis. The ontological argument may have been just this to many of its proponents; but in fact it can gain a real foundation even on the philosophical plane alone, as a philosophically analytic formulation of some of the content of the intuition of createdness.

The ontological argument does indeed seem to succeed in thus translating some content of the intuition of createdness into meta-conceptual form and, by analysis, disengaging existence as an essential predicate of the meta-conceptually known pure being. But this method of immediate transcendence is still of lesser value to philosophers than are the methods of mediate transcendence to be considered later. For a necessary presupposition of this method is a firm grasp of the intuition of createdness, a most obscure awareness in itself. In fact, it is relatively easier and more secure for the metaphysician to pursue the ways of discursive transcendence.

Chapter 16

OTHER MODES OF PRE-PHILOSOPHICAL AND NON-PHILOSOPHICAL TRANSCENDENCE

One instance of transcendence has already been seen which is both pre-philosophical and non-philosophical: the intuition of createdness. There are many other modes of pre-philosophical transcendence and pseudo-transcendence: the various common sense approaches to God by the spontaneously active undisciplined intellect.

The first pre-philosophical approach to transcendence takes place by way of the intuition of createdness at the deepest level of human consciousness, reinforced by the realization, still mainly implicit, but at a higher level of consciousness, that being must be more than finite being. But even the pre-philosophical intellect tends to formulate in diverse ways crude rational proofs, or outlines of proofs, or pseudo-proofs, of the existence of God. This is especially true in the case of the believer, who already knows God through faith but who wishes beyond this to see as far as is possible.

Perhaps the most common crude rational outline of a proof for the existence of God is an argument from design. The universe is seen as an ordered system, from its grandest galactic and supergalactic structures down to the tiniest sub-atoms. But where there is order, there must be intelligence or dependence on intelligence. Therefore there must exist a supreme intelligence, who made the order we see in the universe.

Several points may be noted about this argument. First, the order considered is simply the order of the interaction of things. There is no recognition of the deepest orders within being itself; such recognition would presuppose refinements of understanding of which common sense is incapable. Second, therefore the supreme intelligence is not necessarily a creator of being but only a designer manipulating certain materials. But, third, despite the lack of logical necessity, this supreme intelligence is nevertheless regarded as a creator and not merely as a designer. Fourth, the creation is considered to have taken place at a definite point rather than from all eternity, despite the fact that the argument itself does not justify such a leap. Fifth, it is assumed that there can be only one such intelligence.

There is a parallel situation with the other favorite argument of common sense, the argument from motion. The universe is here seen as a complex of movers themselves moved by other movers. This chain of movers extends back into the past, but it cannot extend indefinitely far backwards; for unless there be a first, none of the other movers would move at all. Therefore there must be a first mover, who made everything that is moved and who moves all other things in the entire universe.

Again several remarks may be made. First, this first mover, like the supreme designer, is not necessarily a creator of being but only a manipulator of already existing materials; common sense cannot reach with sufficient clarity the standpoint of being itself, so as to consider motion as a passage to and from being. Second, nevertheless this first mover is regarded as a creator and not merely as a manipulator. Third, the assumption that it is impossible to go backward indefinitely in time in a chain of movers is arbitrary; as a consequence of this assumption creation is again thought to have taken place at a definite point and not from all eternity, but the leap is still unjustified. Finally, it is again assumed that there can be only one such first mover.

An interesting parallel may be noted in the criticisms of these two arguments. Both fail to penetrate deeply enough into being to achieve knowledge of a creator-God. Nevertheless, both claim to reach a creator-God. Both arguments are historical, in the sense that they both set some limit to the procedure of "going back." And yet neither of them is really justified in setting this limit. Finally, both seem to assume that the First to which they come must be one and not many, without adequate reason being given for this assumption.

Why is it that common sense thus tends to convince itself by inadequate arguments, and not only that but also to make the same mistakes over again? Why does common sense prefer historical arguments to arguments centering on simple dependence in being? Some tentative suggestions may be made in an attempt to answer these questions.

In the light of the metaphysical knowledge so far gained, it may be said that at least four truths are implicit in even the most primitive knowledge of being and dominate subsequent speculation even on the common sense level. First, to understand being is to understand being as opposed to nothingness. Second, to understand the being of this world is to understand being which is continually changing, which is always coming into being and passing out of being. Third, to understand being is to understand that being is itself more than finite being, that finite and multiple being is essentially relative to infinite and unique being. Fourth, to understand being is to possess, in however obscure a manner, that intuition of createdness already spoken of so often.

The attempts of common sense to formulate arguments for the existence of God are dominated by these implicitly known truths; but nevertheless these truths are known to common sense only implicitly. Moreover, the procedure of unreflective common sense is hasty, confusing, global, incapable of refined discernment. Therefore, it should not be surprising to find distortions in the formulations of common sense; in fact, it would be most astonishing if such distortions were absent.

The first distortion occurs in the attempt to make an historical argument. Common sense does not see deeply and clearly enough to formulate an argument based on simple dependence in being; this is an achievement of metaphysics. Nevertheless, common sense is aware that the coming to be and passing away of things cannot be the last word to be said of them, for it understands that being is and non-being is not and that from nothing can come only nothing. It therefore sees that if there is becoming, being is somehow presupposed. But this priority of nature is seen as a priority of time by this intelligence which has not yet freed itself from the bonds of spatio-temporal being. The argument then proceeds in an historical manner; and the profound conviction that behind all being coming from nothingness there must be some being which is permanent and which has not come from nothingness, forces a close to the historical retrogression. But in fact such a close to the historical retrogression is by no means clearly necessary. The crucial point of a valid argument here is not the impossibility of unending temporal succession or of an unending chain of dependent beings going back into the past. Still, common sense, in closing the chain of historical retrogression, is, even while making an obvious mistake, being loyal to a more profound truth--that the chain of beings coming from nothingness is in fact essentially relative to a being which does not itself come from nothingness.

A second distortion occurs in the conclusion of any such argument. To conclude to the existence of one creator-God is not an easy matter, and it is really impossible outside the perspective of the metaphysics of existence. Certainly, the common sense arguments from motion and from design are not adequate; and yet the usual conclusion of such arguments is nevertheless just this one creator-God. How is it possible to understand this leap, as illegitimate in itself as is the closing of the historical retrogression? Again there are profound truths behind the obvious mistake. Common sense, as has been seen, is obscurely aware of the relativity of finite and multiple being to infinite and unique being, and also possesses in a most obscure manner the intuition of createdness. When it leaps beyond what is warranted by the formulated premisses, it is doing so under the unformulated and implicit light of such obscure knowledge. The one creator-God is the conclusion, not of the fumbling formulae elaborated by common sense, but of the entire dynamism of the human intelligence toward being, a dynamism only expressed most inadequately at the level of common sense.

So much for the pre-philosophical modes of transcendence. It is time now to say a word about some other non-philosophical modes of transcendence, modes which may or may not be pre-philosophical, depending on the knower in which they happen to exist, but which should more properly be called non-philosophical since in themselves they are indifferent to the state of philosophical development of the knower.

In Part 1, it was seen that there exists a special type of knowing which arises in virtue of the affective response of the knower to the goodness of the being, knowledge through affective connaturality. Wherever love can follow upon intellectual knowledge, there can exist some mode of such knowledge through affective connaturality. Therefore, correlative with every mode of transcendence in the cognitive order as such, there must also exist a mode of transcendence through affective connaturality. This latter transcendence is itself non-philosophical in its mode, since it is non-objective, as is all knowledge through affective connaturality. It will not be investigated further in this inquiry, although it certainly deserves consideration elsewhere.

Beyond all the degrees of natural knowledge and love of God, there is the supernatural life of faith, hope, and love. In this supernatural life is found a whole new world of degrees of transcendence. However, the discussion of such supernatural modes of transcendence is also beyond the scope of the present inquiry.

Chapter 17

THE METHOD OF MEDIATE TRANSCENDENCE

Mediate transcendence is transcendence which takes place through the exercise of discursive reason. To be scientific knowledge, it must take place through scientific demonstration. Such demonstrative reasoning, in the most general sense, is simply inference from true and certain premisses to a conclusion which is itself true and certain in virtue of those premisses. It should be noted that this meaning of demonstration is considerably wider than the Aristotelian meaning.

In order better to appreciate the method of mediate transcendence, it seems helpful first to make a few remarks concerning the general role of demonstration in metaphysics. Let it be said at the outset that demonstration is not the primary means of discovery and acquisition of metaphysical knowledge. Demonstration is primarily a means of systematization of already discovered truths, and secondarily a confirmation of some of these already discovered truths and a method to draw out in a sure manner some further implications of these truths.

Metaphysical method may be said to consist of eight steps. First, there is intuitive discovery, such as that by which one becomes aware of the diverse dimensions of being, both objective and non-objective. Second, there is analysis of the intuitively given and formulation of the results of this analysis through the construction of meta-concepts. Third, there is systematizing demonstration to organize the body of truth already acquired, according to relations of cause and effect, or more generally, of principle and principiated. Little attention has been given here to this level of demonstration, except in establishing a few general metaphysical principles such as that of identity and that of sufficient reason. Fourth, there is an examination of the already acquired truth to ascertain the presence of "loose ends" in the system, data or facts which do not have and cannot gain a sufficient reason from the already constituted body of systematic knowledge. Such at present are the facts of limitation, contingency, finality, etc. Fifth, there is a dialectical construction standing for and referring to that which, in virtue of the principle of sufficient reason, is demanded in order to give an adequate account of the being of the aforementioned "loose ends." This construction must be at first tentative, hypothetical. But the metaphysician looks forward to step six, when the existence of that which is designated and signified by some constructed meta-concept can be actually demonstrated in a definitive manner. This demonstration is an a posteriori demonstration (except in the case of the ontological argument), proceeding from the being of certain data or facts to their completely adequate cause, itself designated by the constructed meta-concept. Seventh, there is an attempt to deduce demonstratively further properties of this adequate cause and to understand better the relation of other beings to it. Finally, eighth, the metaphysician may reflect upon his knowledge of lower things in the light of their highest and completely adequate cause; it is this reflection which is the proper act of wisdom already achieved, and which therefore brings metaphysics to its fullness as a wisdom.

In Part 2, interest centers on the fourth, fifth, sixth, and seventh steps in metaphysical method. At present the particular concern is to outline the structure of a demonstration in step six. This demonstration has traditionally been forced into the mold of the Aristotelian demonstration, but in fact such a reduction is somewhat unsatisfactory. The Aristotelian demonstration is properly concerned with establishing the connection of a given attribute with a given subject, not with simple proof of existence. But here the problem is precisely to establish the existence of an adequate cause to account for given effects.

The logical structure of metaphysical proofs of existence is in fact more properly represented by a conditional syllogism than by a categorical syllogism. In this conditional syllogism, first, certain data or facts (the "loose ends" spoken of earlier) are affirmed. Then the necessary dependence of these data upon something else (represented by a constructed meta-concept) is asserted in a conditional proposition: If the data are affirmed, then that represented by the construct must also be affirmed. Finally, the conclusion is drawn through the affirmation of the construct and of that which it represents.

The construct of course differs in accordance with the difference of data to be explained. But in the next two chapters it is seen that many diverse constructs turn out to be fundamentally equivalent when their implications are explored, that they represent diverse manners of signifying and of referring to transcendent being. The possibility of such a multiplicity of formally diverse constructs with fundamental equivalence is grounded in the very richness of transcendent being and in the diversity of effects produced by transcendent being.

It may perhaps be objected that no proof of the existence of transcendent being can be given. For any such proof would require some prior understanding of the meaning of this existence of transcendent being, while such an understanding of this existence is in fact impossible for us. It is not necessary to appeal to the obscure intuition of createdness to resolve this difficulty. Rather, it is sufficient to note that the arguments to be given do not conclude to the very existence of transcendent being but only to a justifiable affirmation of this existence, justified by the existence of lower beings which necessarily depend upon such a transcendent being. And even this affirmation is indirect, being only an affirmation of the foundation of a certain construct in reality. When it is affirmed that transcendent being exists, this only means that the constructed meta-concepts of transcendent being have in fact a foundation in reality, directly in the existence of lower beings themselves essentially dependent upon transcendent being, and indirectly in the very existence of transcendent being itself.

Therefore, in philosophical knowledge of the highest being, there is close dependence upon the metaphysical knowledge of lower beings, which in turn is dependent upon the knowledge of transphenomenal objectivity to furnish the elements for meta-conceptual construction. And since the knowledge of transphenomenal objectivity itself is completely dependent upon the knowledge of phenomenal objectivity, the entire edifice of human scientific knowledge, even of divine science, must ultimately rest upon the humble evidence of sensible phenomena. Indeed, this is true even of the formulation of the ontological argument, since even there the constructed meta-concept of pure being presupposes elements of construction similar to those used in the a posteriori procedure. This close dependence of our knowledge of transcendent being upon our knowledge of lower beings, and the resulting limitations which this dependence imposes on our knowledge of transcendent being are considered in more detail in a later chapter.

Before leaving this brief discussion of the method of mediate transcendence, it is helpful to recall again and to set into relief the precise plane of intellectual activity on which we are moving. We are already in an atmosphere uncomfortably rarified for the human intellect and are about to climb to a point at which it is even more rarified. In order to reach the plane of metaphysical analysis it was necessary to pass beyond phenomena and even beyond transphenomenal objectivity into the domain of the trans-objective. This also compelled us to pass from univocal to analogical intellection. But even here there was at least the immediate non-objective evidence of the transobjective enveloping every center and cluster of objectivity.

Now, all that is to be left behind. No more centers and clusters of transphenomenal objectivity around which to focus the investigation of the transobjective. Transcendent being in itself is wholly and entirely transobjective in its being. Therefore the constructed meta-concepts referring to transcendent being must necessarily appear as illusions to one without a firm ground in metaphysical analysis, unless some wise man should have gained a far firmer grasp of the intuition of createdness than do most men, or unless God Himself should have come down to man through supernatural faith, hope, and love.

In the light of the remarks of the preceding paragraph, one may perhaps forestall certain objections usually made against the traditional modes of mediate transcendence, the set of objections which are based upon the present state of development of the positive sciences of phenomena. In these sciences there are employed certain terms which are verbally identical with certain metaphysical terms, but which are altogether different in their meaning. For example, scientists speak of causality, motion, chance, and even of finality. I have treated elsewhere in detail of the distinctions in meaning between philosophical and scientific terms, but it should be evident even from all that has been said earlier that terms referring to phenomenal objectivity ought not to be used as if they referred to transobjective reality. With this in mind, explicit treatment of objections drawn solely from the positive sciences may be omitted.

Chapter 18

PHILOSOPHICAL TRANSCENDENCE: THE FIVE CLASSICAL WAYS

The classical five ways to establish the existence of God are not here presented as they were presented by Saint Thomas Aquinas. That would be contrary to the spirit of inquiry in which this book was written. It seems better to evolve them anew in accordance with the preceding movement of this book. The five ways here given do in fact correspond in starting point, in conclusion, and in general structure with those of Saint Thomas; but this correspondence is in a sense accidental in a work in which inquiry rather than history is the dominant consideration. Some of the details of the proofs of Saint Thomas were influenced by the state of learning in his own time (for example, by Aristotelian physics), by his own historical circumstances, and by the fact that he was first of all a theologian with primarily theological preoccupations. It must not therefore be expected of the contemporary philosopher that he follow precisely in his own thought the thought of Saint Thomas.

The First Way: from the fact of becoming

If the First Way is to be understood as a metaphysical proof of the existence of God, it must consider becoming from the perspective of the metaphysics of existence. That is, it must consider becoming, not just as the mere advent of form to matter or of accident to substance, but also as the advent of new existence. Becoming here is not mere formal becoming but existential becoming. Unless this is understood, it is difficult to conclude to the existence of an absolutely transcendent being.

In accordance with traditional terminology, and for the purpose of convenience, becoming or change is referred to in this analysis as motion. The agent that has been seen to be necessary in order that any such motion take place is called a mover.

Certainly the fact of motion in our world is evident enough; numerous examples were cited in the course of the analysis of objectivity in Part 1. And the same analysis revealed that every such motion requires a mover distinct from the motion itself, distinct from the potency-act structure of the motion. Now it is necessary to say of this mover that in its actual movement of the moved, at that very instant, it thus acts either insofar as it is subjected to the simultaneous active influence of some other mover or independently of any such active influence. To set aside the latter alternative for the moment, the first possibility may be analyzed in the following manner.

It is evident that if the mover itself acts precisely insofar as it is subjected to the influence of still another mover, the same set of alternatives again arises for this new mover. Either it moves the former mover in accordance with its own simultaneous subjection to still another mover, or it moves that former mover independently of any such active influence of another mover.

But it is impossible that such a series of moved movers extend back to infinity. For every mover-itself-acted-upon is essentially an intermediary in the chain of movement. But however many intermediaries are found or postulated, no one of them nor all of them taken together can have an adequate reason for being unless there be at the top of the series a first mover which is not itself an intermediary. For an intermediary as such receives the adequate ground of its being as an intermediary from the preceding member or members of the series. Since an intermediary does not have in itself an adequate ground for its own being, still less can it contain an adequate ground for the being of the following member or members of the series. Yet the following member or members of the series, as well as the intermediary itself, do exist and therefore must somehow have an adequate ground for being. Since this adequate ground cannot be found in any other intermediary or series of intermediaries, it follows that there must be some first mover at the top of the series, a mover which exercises its active influence without any simultaneous dependence upon another mover.

Therefore, if there is any instance of motion in the world, there must be such a first mover itself unmoved. The constructed meta-concept of an unmoved mover therefore refers to a being the existence of which is absolutely required by the fact of motion or becoming.

But it is possible to analyze this construct and to show that it is in fact equivalent to a meta-concept of transcendent being, that is, that the unmoved mover can only be transcendent being. And since it has already been shown in Part 1 that if there is a transcendent being this being can only be one being, it will follow immediately that there is only one unmoved mover. In Part 1 it was shown that any limited being is, in its being, only in potency to being a mover; for the activity by which it becomes a mover is a superabundance of being, an "overflow" of being. This means that any limited being can be only a moved mover, and therefore that an unmoved mover must be unlimited in its being. But the unlimited in its being is the pure act of existence, transcendent being. Therefore the unmoved mover is transcendent being.

The Second Way: from the fact of efficient causality

The Second Way is in many respects similar to the First, and yet it is not quite the same. There is a difference in the starting point, which is reflected throughout the course of the argument. In the First Way, the focus of interest is the passing over of passive potency into act; in the Second, the focus of interest is the passing over of active potency into activity. The similarity between the two arguments lies in the fact that in both a relation of potency to act is considered; but in the first the potency is merely passive, while in the second it is the potency of an active power to its superexistential act of activity. Despite this difference, however, there is an evident isomorphism between the structures of the two arguments.

The fact of efficient causality is evident enough in the interactions of the men and things of the physical universe. Likewise evident is the existence of chains of efficient causes, even chains of simultaneously acting efficient causes, in which the causality of one member of the series is found to be exercised in simultaneous dependence upon the causality of another member of the series. A common instance of such a series is found in the use of an instrument, such as a hammer, a saw, or a pen, by man to produce some desired result. Contemplation of such a series moves us to distinguish between causality which is itself caused and causality which is itself uncaused. Caused causality is called secondary causality, while uncaused causality is called primary causality. Secondary causality is exercised in simultaneous dependence upon some other cause, while primary causality is exercised independently of any other such cause. Every secondary cause is in some manner in (passive) potency to its causality or activity.

In the light of the distinction just drawn, one may make an analysis of causality similar to the analysis already made of motion. Every secondary causality requires another cause distinct from the potency-act structure of the secondary cause and its secondary causality. This new cause itself, at the very instant of its causality, acts either in dependence upon still another cause (and is therefore itself a secondary cause) or independently of any other such cause (and is therefore itself a primary cause). Setting aside the latter alternative for the moment, we analyze the first possibility. It is evident that the same set of alternatives arises again.

But it is impossible that such a series of secondary, caused causes extend back to infinity. For every such caused cause is essentially an intermediary in the chain of causation. But however many intermediaries are found or postulated, no one of them nor all of them taken together can have an adequate reason for being unless there be at the top of the series a first, primary cause which is not itself an intermediary. This assertion is justified by reasons similar to those used in showing the necessity of a first mover in any chain of movement.

Therefore, if there is any instance of efficient causality in the world, there must be such a first uncaused cause. The constructed meta-concept of an uncaused cause therefore refers to a being the existence of which is absolutely required by the fact of efficient causality.

But the construct of an uncaused cause is in fact equivalent to the meta-concept of transcendent being; that is, the uncaused cause can only be transcendent being. And it follows from this that there can be only one uncaused cause, since the transcendent being can only be one being.

The uncaused cause is, in fact, very much like the unmoved mover, the only difference being that the unmoved mover is seen as the cause of motion in merely passive potency while the uncaused cause is seen as the cause of the causality of active power, insofar as this active power is itself in passive potency in relation to its activity. It is apparent then that the reduction of the construct of uncaused cause to that of transcendent being proceeds in the same manner as does the reduction of the construct of unmoved mover to that of transcendent being.

The Third Way: from the fact of contingency

The Third Way is analogous to the first two. The starting point is in the fact that contingent beings do exist, beings which are but need not be, which do not contain in themselves an adequate reason for their own existence. The existence of such beings is seen from the fact that many things come into being and pass away; this is a sign of their contingency, since if they were not contingent they would always have been and always persist. And it has been seen in Part 1 that any limited being is also contingent.

Since every contingent being finds the adequate ground for its own existence in some other being, one may reason as follows. This other being is either a contingent being or it is not a contingent being. If it is not a contingent being, it is a necessary being, one that needs no other being on which to depend but which is the sufficient ground for its own existence. If it is a contingent being, the same alternatives arise again. And note that the dependence of a contingent being is a dependence that is simultaneous with its being: the contingent being, so long as it is, continues to be dependent upon some other being. Otherwise, this being would no longer be contingent but necessary.

One may therefore again consider the possibility of a chain of intermediaries, this time a chain of contingent beings. But for the same reasons which were brought forth in the last two arguments, such a chain cannot extend back to infinity.

Therefore, if there is any instance of contingent being, there must also be a necessary being. The constructed meta-concept of a necessary being, then, refers to a being which actually exists.

But this construct of a necessary being is again equivalent to the meta-concept of transcendent being. For if every limited being is contingent, as has been seen in Part 1, then a necessary being must be unlimited, and therefore transcendent--the one pure act of existence.

The Fourth Way: from the fact of given limited instances of being and its transcendental perfections

There are limited beings in the world. But as was seen in Part 1, the perfection of existence (as also, therefore, the perfection of any of the transcendental attributes of being) of itself should be one and infinite. If this perfection is in fact found in a limited manner, this means that this given instance of the perfection is not self-explanatory. It somehow refers beyond itself, as a dependent perfection. But it cannot be adequately grounded in anything else in this given being itself, since all else in the being is merely in potency in relation to existence. Therefore this existence must have its adequate ground in some other being. But if this other being is limited, the same problem arises again. And it is again impossible to go back to infinity, for the same reasons as were given in the three preceding proofs. Therefore any limited being must be ultimately dependent in its being upon an unlimited being, which is the same transcendent being arrived at in each of the three preceding proofs.

This argument may be set in a more general form, so as to proceed from the reality of any limited act to the reality of an unlimited act of existence, in the following manner.

There are limited acts in the orders of substantial form, accidental form, and existence. Every such act falls into one of two general types: type one--act the nature of which demands that it be in a potency; type two--act the nature of which does not demand that it be in some potency. While it is possible to state a priori that some acts are of type one, such as the substantial forms of material things, it is not possible to place any act in type two without some kind of a posteriori justification, as for example by noting its givenness in the intuition of createdness in which being is obscurely presented as transcendent. However, one may perhaps desire some clearer justification than the rather obscure intuition of createdness. In any event, an act of type one cannot be found in an unlimited way, since potency always limits it. An act of type two could conceivably be found in an unlimited way.

No limited act accounts adequately for its own reality. For an act of itself would be one and infinite. But no limited act, as act, can be adequately grounded in its opposition to nothingness merely by being in the potency which receives it; otherwise the distinction between potency and act would be destroyed. Therefore, any real limited act must ultimately depend on some real unlimited act, either of the same or higher order. By an act of higher order is meant an act which somehow includes the perfection of another act without itself being simply of the same kind as that lower act. Consequently, if there exists a limited act, then there exists an unlimited act, of the same or higher order.

Moreover, if there is a limited act of any kind, then there is a limited existence by which this act, and its potency, are. But there is no higher order of act than existence (and superexistence). Therefore, if there is a limited existence, there is an unlimited act of existence. Therefore, if there is any limited act, there is an unlimited act of existence, a transcendent being.

The Fifth Way: from the fact of natural finality

As has already been seen in Part 1, every agent in fact does tend, by its very nature, toward some end. Moreover, it was already seen there that tendency toward an end necessarily depends upon some directive intelligence. Some instances of finality can be accounted for by the direction of finite intelligence; but there are also instances of natural finality in every agent that acts without the direction of some finite intelligence. Moreover, even the activity of finite intelligence itself tends toward a determinate end, which is first of all the very act of understanding; and this tendency is in some manner prior to this act of understanding. Therefore even the activity of finite intelligence can be considered as an instance of natural finality, which must receive its direction from some other intelligence. And once again, any supposed chain of intermediary intelligences must end in a first intelligence, a first intelligence without any intrinsic compositions of potency and act (and therefore natural finality needing determination by a still higher being). Such a first intelligence is again the unlimited act of existence, transcendent being, and the ultimate source of all determinations of finality.

The simplification of the five classical ways

It is possible to achieve a notable simplification, from a metaphysical point of view, in these five arguments for the existence of transcendent being. First, some remarks can be made about the immediate cause of existential act. No limited being can be the adequate immediate cause of any existential act of any other being. It has already been seen that such a being cannot be the adequate immediate cause of its own existential act. That it cannot be the adequate immediate cause of the existential act of any other being can be shown by a brief analysis.

Every limited being possesses only limited existential and superexistential acts. But to say that such acts are limited is to say that, as such, they lack the perfection of any other existential or superexistential act. With respect to the perfection of any other such act, they are only nothingness. Therefore the being of any other existential or superexistential act cannot possibly receive an adequate immediate ground in a limited existential act. Therefore no limited being can be the adequate immediate cause of the existential act of any other being.

But if no limited being can be the adequate immediate cause of such existential act, then it follows that there is an immediate dependence of such existential act upon the transcendent being, that every limited existential act is immediately received from the unlimited act of existence of transcendent being. From this point of view, every limited existential act can be called a participated act--immediately received from and sharing (in a finite way) in the perfection of the unlimited act of existence. In the light of this immediate participation, which is an immediate and essential relativity, in similitude and dependence, of any limited existential act to the unlimited act of existence, the five ways of transcendence already presented may be reduced to immediate simple inferences.

First, since in every motion a limited existential act is received, there is in every motion an immediate dependence upon the unlimited act of existence. Since motion exists, the unlimited act of existence also exists. The influx required from the unlimited act of existence in this case is called concurrence in the production of the effect.

Second, since in the activity of any limited agent a superexistential act is received by the agent, there is in every such activity an immediate dependence upon the unlimited act of existence. Since this secondary causality does in fact exist, the unlimited act of existence also exists. The influx required from the unlimited act of existence in this case has been called, perhaps not entirely correctly, premotion. It will here be called activation.

Third, since the existence of any contingent being is a received existence, every contingent being immediately depends for its existence upon the unlimited act of existence. Since contingent being does exist, the unlimited act of existence also exists. The influx required from the unlimited act of existence in this case is called creation and conservation, creation referring to the beginning and conservation to the continuation of the activation.

Fourth, since every limited existence is a received existence, every limited being immediately depends for its existence upon the unlimited act of existence. Since limited being does exist, the unlimited act of existence also exists. The influx here required from the unlimited act of existence is the same as that already pointed out in the last paragraph, namely, creation and conservation; but it here appears under the aspect of communication (with resultant participation by the limited being in the perfection of the unlimited act of existence).

Fifth, since every limited being tending naturally toward an end derives this tendency from its existence, and since this tendency must be received from some higher intelligence, the existence of such a being is also received. Therefore every such being is immediately dependent for its existence upon the unlimited act of existence. Since limited being tending naturally toward an end does exist, the unlimited act of existence also exists. No new influences other than those already mentioned are required from the unlimited act of existence in order to account for such tendency. But the direction of these influxes by the unlimited intelligence of this unlimited act of existence is referred to as providence and governance.

Some notes on the communication of being by limited and unlimited being

As was pointed out in the preceding section, three influences from the unlimited being are required by limited being in order that it exist and act. The influx of creation and conservation presupposes nothing on the side of limited being, since it is this influx which gives being to limited being. The influx of activation presupposes that there is in the limited being an active power disposed to act; activation, when viewed from the side of limited being, is nothing but this very activity itself of the limited being.

The influx of concurrence presupposes that the limited agent is conjoined in a dynamic union with that which is acted upon, by the very act or superexistence which is activity. The distinction between activation and concurrence disappears when there is no effect distinct from the activity itself, as in the case of completely immanent activities of intellect or will. But when the effect is distinct from the activity itself, two stages in concurrence must frequently be distinguished. In Part 1, a distinction was made between transient dispositions directly induced through activity and the permanent determinations, whether accidental or substantial, which result from such transient modifications of the existential state of the being which is acted upon. In the light of this distinction, two modes of concurrence are distinguished: first, a conferring of transient existence in the thing acted upon, a transient existence essentially dependent upon, relative to, the superexistence of the agent, and which therefore can be regarded in a way as a secondary superexistence of the agent; second, the conferring of the permanent existence of the indirectly induced effect in the thing acted upon. Of course, if the direct transient modification should not result in any indirect permanent modification, as in fact seems to be the case in the medium through which light is propagated between the stars and planets, the first mode of concurrence is found without the second.

It may perhaps seem that this account of influxes proceeding from the unlimited being does not leave sufficient room for the genuine activity of the limited being itself. But this is not the case, if the nature of these influxes be rightly understood. The fact that, in creation and conservation, the existence conferred is not merely possessed but actually exercised by the limited being can be understood if it is seen that the existential act is conferred precisely as a dynamic rather than a static act. The active exercise is necessarily posterior (logically) to the passive reception which is mere possession (and which is the very influx of creation and conservation, as viewed from the side of the creature); but this active exercise (ordinarily and naturally by the creature itself) is necessarily also present, since existence is by its nature dynamic rather than static act, and since the potency of substantial being for existence is not merely for a received existence but for an existence which it can make its own, thereby constituting itself as a subject through the active exercise of this existence.

Analogous remarks may be made regarding the influx which is activation. The superexistence here conferred is conferred not merely to be possessed but also to be exercised by the limited being, and it is conferred precisely in accordance with the existential state of the potency of the active power in the agent for such an exercised activity. Hence, what is conferred upon the agent through activation is not just a determination in the agent but an intentionality from the agent.

In the first stage of concurrence, the transient existence in the thing acted upon is conferred in accordance with the existential state of the potency of this thing. And this existential state of the potency is determined by the conjunction of the limited agent and this potency in dynamic union, through the primary superexistence of the agent. The transient existence in the thing acted upon is thus conferred precisely as correlative with and dependent upon the primary superexistence in the agent itself. Hence it is justifiably considered as in fact a secondary superexistence of the agent (but in the thing acted upon). It is therefore conferred as the immediate, direct term of the activity of the limited agent. And since in the second stage of the concurrence the permanent existence of the indirectly induced effect in the thing acted upon is conferred in accordance with the new existential state of this thing arising from the first, transient modification, this permanent existence is conferred as a mediate, indirect term of the activity of the limited agent.

The relation of the limited agent to this mediate, indirect term at first appears much like that of any active condition (a cause which does not itself produce the effect in question but only prepares the way for some other cause actually to produce the effect) to an effect. But this is not the case. An active condition might do its part without the effect's coming to pass, because of the failure of the proper cause to act. But in the case in question, the unlimited being will in fact always concur, not only in the production of the immediate, direct term, but also in the production of the mediate, indirect term. This assertion can be justified by the following considerations.

In Part 1, it was seen that existence itself is the principle of the dynamic generosity of being. Therefore this principle of dynamic generosity is above all operative in the case of the unlimited act of existence. While the principle must be qualified in its application to the unlimited act of existence, in the light of the intelligence and freedom of this being, still one general application may be simply stated. If potencies have been created, they have been created for their act; and therefore, if a potency is immediately capable of a given act, it receives that act. A potency may be more or less removed from immediate capability for a given act, and as such it does not receive that act. Yet, if the potency has immediate receptiveness for an act, it can only receive it with the help of a divine influx, as has been seen. Now, if the divine influx were not given at this point, the potency would be frustrated and would lose its intelligibility as a tendency to act. This contradiction in the being of potency would necessarily derive from a prior contradiction in the unlimited act of existence; but such a contradiction in the unlimited act of existence is impossible, since this unlimited act is pure affirmation. (The utter unity and simplicity of the unlimited act of existence will become clearer in subsequent chapters.) It follows therefore that where potency becomes immediately disposed for some act, as it does through both the primary and secondary superexistences of the agent, that act is conferred through divine concurrence, in the order of nature. This does not rule out the possibility of a miraculous intervention, whereby the potency may be fulfilled in a higher and fuller way than that called for by nature, as in the case of the hypostatic union of the Word of God with a human nature, or in the life of grace.

But it is impossible to deny that there is a difference between the first concurrence in the transient modification and the second concurrence in the permanent modification. It may be recalled that this difference was already foreshadowed in Part 1, when the problem arose concerning the communication of substantial form in activity, and concerning the communication of permanent accidental forms. If the First Way of transcendence is interpreted as focusing upon transient modifications and their ultimate sources, a distinct argument may be developed by focusing upon the permanent modifications which depend on the second kind of concurrence. The discussion in Part 1 about the communication of permanent forms may be taken as the basis for such an argument. The argument itself is presented in the next chapter.

With respect to transient modifications, then, it may be said that the whole being of the effect is completely dependent, immediately and directly, upon the influx from the unlimited agent. And yet there is clearly a far greater dependence upon the primary cause than there is upon the secondary cause. This is expressed in diverse ways. Some say that the form of the effect is due to the secondary cause, while the existence of the effect is due to the primary cause. Others say, more properly, that the becoming of the effect is due to the secondary cause, while the existence of the effect is due to the primary cause. Still others say that the suchness of the effect is due to the secondary cause, while the existence of the effect is due to the primary cause. It seems that the first manner of speaking attributes too much to the secondary cause, while the third is unnecessarily susceptible of an occasionalist misinterpretation which would make the creature only the occasion of a divine activity.

With respect to permanent modifications, it may be said that the being of the effect is partially dependent, mediately and indirectly, upon the activity of the limited agent (considered as the primary superexistence of the agent _in the agent_). But it may also be said that the being of the effect is partially dependent, immediately and directly, on the activity of the limited agent (considered as the secondary superexistence of the agent _in the thing acted upon_, which is in fact the same as the transient existence of the transient modification). Here again, however, it may be repeated that the whole being of the effect is also completely dependent, immediately and directly, upon an influx from the unlimited agent. Because of the less intimate relation between the permanent modification and the secondary cause, less intimate than that between the transient modification and the secondary cause, the third of the three formulae of the preceding paragraph, describing the relative roles of the secondary and primary causes, seems better here, provided that one avoids a simple occasionalist interpretation: The suchness of the effect is due to the secondary cause, while the existence of the effect is due to the primary cause.

One further remark may be made, concerning the _loss_ of degrees of actuality in the course of the changes in the world, such as when a living thing dies. In the light of what has already been said regarding the communication of being, the loss of some degree of being occurs when the existential state of a potency renders it unsuitable for the continued retention of a given act. At this point, the divine conservation simply ceases; this cessation may be described as a "negative concurrence."

Chapter 19

OTHER WAYS OF PHILOSOPHICAL TRANSCENDENCE

The classical Five Ways are by no means the only ways of transcendence. There are other "loose ends" left in the metaphysical analysis of proportionate and limited being and from the intuition of createdness. From these it is possible to construct new arguments for the existence of transcendent being. In this chapter, there are presented seven such arguments, which do not pretend to exhaust the possibilities.

The Sixth Way: from the ingression of permanent actuality

This way of transcendence was already suggested in Part 1 and again near the end of the preceding chapter. Its starting point is in the characteristic mode of activity of finite agents as contrasted with the permanent effects of some such activity. Correlative with the primary superexistence of such agents is a secondary superexistence in the effect, an essentially transient existence of an essentially transient modification in the thing acted upon. This new existence is essentially transient because it is essentially dependent upon the activity of the agent and therefore endures only so long as the dynamic union arising from activity endures.

But in fact the effects of activity include not only such transient modifications but also, in some cases, more permanent modifications, as in substantial changes. Such modifications persist even after the cessation of the activity, and therefore have some existence other than the transient existence induced through activity. But such a permanent existence cannot be communicated directly by any limited being, as has been said. Therefore it must be communicated directly by an unlimited being, in accordance with the existential state of the recipient. Yet this communication must be distinguished from creation; for it is accomplished in accordance with the dispositions of the recipient as already existing, and it is the communication of a determination to an existent rather than the first constitution of an existent. Only the human soul is an exception to this rule. The soul is created at the instant in which prime matter is suitably disposed to receive it, created, since analysis reveals that the human soul is not simply a determination of matter but rather itself capable of independent existence even apart from matter. The human soul is therefore communicated as itself an existent--incomplete, and needing matter for its completion, so that the full amplitude of possibilities of human existence and operation may be realized--but not simply as a determination of an already given existent.

In every case, the new permanent existence must be communicated by unlimited being, which therefore must exist.

The Seventh Way: from the evidence of unity permeating diversity

This way of transcendence was also suggested in Part 1, in the account of the intuition of createdness. In that intuition there is seen a certain unity pervading all the multiplicity of things. In some manner all things are only parts of this mysterious unity. And yet the diversity of things, a diversity of subjects, is evident enough. Therefore the unity must exist prior to the multiplicity and diversity, and this unity must somehow include the being of the multiplicity in a higher way. Otherwise, the diverse beings of the universe could not appear as parts of the underlying unity. But this inclusion of the being of all finite beings can only take place in an unlimited being, since every finite being lacks the perfection of being of every other finite being. Therefore, the all-pervading unity is the unity of unlimited being, of which every finite being is only a limited participation.

The Eighth Way: from the preexistence of limited being

We observe in the world that beings exist which have not always been. For example, each of us had some beginning in time. But in fact it is simply impossible that the perfection of any existing being not have been at any time in the past; in some manner it must always have been. Otherwise it would have come from nothingness, so far as its own unique perfection of being is concerned. But from nothing, nothing comes, unless one would destroy the distinction and opposition between being and nothingness. But even if this existent must always have been, it cannot always have been as an independent existent. Therefore it must have pre-existed in some other existent. But the being of no finite being can simply preexist in the being of any other finite being, since every finite being has only its own perfection of being and not the perfection of being of any other being. Therefore, the preexistence must have been in an unlimited being, which contains in a higher way the being of every finite being.

The Ninth Way: from the fact of essential possibility

The essential possibility of finite beings (known through the compatibility between the notes of the essence which is the potentiality for existence) is prior to the existence of these beings. Even if these beings did not exist, their essential possibility would still remain in some way. But on this hypothesis of the non-existence of finite being, the essential possibility would need some foundation in reality. But no finite being can be the adequate ground for the essential possibility of any other finite being, since the essence-structure of any finite being is uniquely related to its own unique act of existence. Such a foundation can only be provided in the unlimited being as the ultimate ground of all possibility; this foundation consists in the fact that the unlimited being is imitable by diverse finite participations in its infinite perfection. Therefore, there must exist an unlimited being as the ultimate adequate ground for the essential possibility of every finite being.

Note, however, that the primary imitability of the unlimited being is in the imitability of its existence by the finite existence. Essential possibility, as grounded in imitability, cannot simply be understood as non-contradictory essence in some kind of abstraction from existence. Rather, essential possibility is precisely the possibility of a potency for some determinate degree of existence. It is known from the compatibility of essential notes, but it consists properly in the possibility for existence which presupposes this compatibility. It is therefore useful to distinguish between proximate essential possibility, or potentiality for existence, and remote essential possibility, or compatibility of essential notes.

The Tenth Way: from the correlativity of intelligibility and intelligence

The proper object of the tendency of human intelligence is being (although its proportionate object is the being which manifests itself through sensible phenomena). Correlative with this tendency of intelligence is the intelligibility of being and of every being. Besides having this intelligibility, being itself also has a tendency, as was seen in Part 1, toward consciousness, either toward the possession of consciousness or toward entry into consciousness by way of knowledge. If consciousness is intentional in relation to being, so also being is of its nature intentional in one way or another in regard to consciousness. Either it is or has the intentionality of consciousness itself, or it tends toward the possession of consciousness, or it tends to enter into consciousness by way of knowledge. Now if such a close correlativity is found between intelligence and being, either being is ultimately grounded in intelligence, or intelligence is ultimately grounded in being; and in either case the ultimate ground must be a being which is both unlimited being and unlimited intelligence.

The last assertion may be justified one part at a time. First, the correlativity between intelligence and being consists in the double intentionality noted above, of intelligence toward being and of being toward intelligence. But the object of any intentionality must in some manner preexist in the adequate ground for the intentionality, that is, in that which gives being to the intentionality as an intentionality. Therefore, either the intentionality of being depends upon some prior intelligence or the intentionality of intelligence depends on some prior being.

Second, if the intentionality of being depends on some prior intelligence, this means that the entire being depends for its being upon this prior intelligence; for the intentionality of the being is not really distinct from its being. Therefore this prior intelligence must be such as to include in a higher way all the perfection of the being in question. But this is to say that this prior intelligence must be unlimited in its being, the pure act of existence, and therefore also unlimited intelligence.

Third, if the intentionality of intelligence depends on some prior being, this means that the entire intelligence depends for its being upon this prior being; for intelligence is intentional in virtue of its very being. But again, such dependence in being demands that the prior being be unlimited in its being.

Therefore, there exists an unlimited being which is also unlimited intelligence.

Since every being other than this unlimited intelligence is similar to it by participation, a new transcendental aspect of being here emerges, the truth which consists in the similarity of every limited being to unlimited intelligence and in the identity of unlimited being with unlimited intelligence. This new transcendental truth of being is the fundamental truth, from which truth as knowability of being to the finite intellect derives, and is therefore called the primary ontological truth of being. And the truth of every finite being, in both the primary and the secondary meanings, itself is derived from the truth of the unlimited being in its identity with unlimited intelligence. This truth of the unlimited being is accordingly the supreme, uncreated truth; and all other truth, primary or secondary, logical or ontological, the truth of nature or the truth of artifacts, is created truth.

The Eleventh Way: from the correlativity of appetibility and will

The Eleventh Way is analogous to the Tenth. Besides the intelligibility of being, there is the appetibility or goodness of being. Since intelligibility and appetibility, intelligence and intellectual appetite or will, go along together, all that has been said regarding the mutual intentionality of being and consciousness-as-intelligence has a parallel when we consider being and consciousness-as-intellectual-appetite. Therefore by such considerations one may conclude that there exists an unlimited being which is also unlimited will and love.

And since every being other than this unlimited will and love is similar to it by participation, another new transcendental aspect of being here emerges, the goodness which consists in the similarity of every limited being to unlimited will and love and in the identity of unlimited being with unlimited will and love. This new transcendental goodness of being is the fundamental goodness, from which is derived goodness as desirability of being to the finite appetite and will, and is therefore the primary ontological goodness of things. And the goodness of every finite being, whether primary or secondary, is itself derived from the goodness of the unlimited being in its identity with will and love. This goodness of the unlimited being is therefore the supreme, uncreated goodness; and all other goodness, primary or secondary, the goodness of being or the goodness of the will-in-conformity-with-being, natural good or conventional good, is created good.

The Twelfth Way: from the correlativity of beauty and intelligence

This way is analogous to the two preceding, and need not be developed at all. It is enough to indicate the possibility of developing such an argument, and to point out that in it again emerges another new transcendental, a transcendental beauty which consists in a certain similarity of every limited being to the unlimited joy in intelligence and in the identity of unlimited being with this unlimited joy in intelligence. This is the primary ontological beauty of things. The beauty of every finite being, whether primary or secondary, is itself derived from the beauty of the unlimited being in its identity with joy in intelligence. This beauty of the unlimited being is therefore the supreme, uncreated beauty; and every other beauty is created beauty.

Chapter 20

KNOWING THE NATURE OF TRANSCENDENT BEING

Once the existence of transcendent being has been definitely ascertained, there arises the further question of what can be said about its nature. This question itself can be asked at two levels, that of names (how do we speak about God? how do we use words about Him?) and that of knowledge (how do we think about God? how do we use concepts, or meta-concepts, about Him?). But since names are used in accordance with their meaning, which in turn arises from the way in which we know the diverse realities to which the names are applied, it is sufficient to confine the present analysis to the ways in which we form and apply concepts, or meta-concepts, to God.

In fact, such formation and application of meta-concepts to transcendent being has already taken place, in the twelve ways of transcendence that have been given in the preceding chapters. But it is necessary now to examine in detail the manner of understanding there employed, in order to proceed more clearly and safely in understanding the nature of transcendent being. This understanding of the nature of transcendent being is nothing else but the scientifically philosophical attempt to answer, so far as is possible for human intelligence in this life, the question: What is God?

At the very outset, severe limitations are revealed in regard to such knowledge. Since God is not known to the senses (which attain only the phenomena of material being), since He is not the object of the intellectual insight which leads directly to the formation of a concept (such insight is only of essences), since our only immediate awareness of Him is in the most obscure intuition of createdness, any scientifically philosophical knowledge of God must be through the medium of constructed meta-concepts. Such meta-concepts do not express anything of the very being of God (anything of what He really is, in His own being) but rather merely signify and refer to it (pointing out that He is in such a manner or other). Just as in the case of the other meta-conceptual constructs of metaphysics, the elements of such constructs as are applied to God must themselves be ultimately drawn from the knowledge of transphenomenal objectivity, the objectivity which is manifested through the sensible phenomena. In other words, all such knowledge of God depends in some manner upon sense knowledge and our intellectual knowledge of material things.

Two possible procedures may be employed to establish that various meta-concepts are to be applied to God. It is possible to reason a posteriori to some of the attributes of God, as was seen in the proofs for the existence of God. In these proofs, certain attributes of God appeared, such as that He is a necessary being, the supreme intelligence, the supreme truth, etc. But an even more fruitful method is to discover such attributes through an analysis of the meaning of the pure act of existence or transcendent being. This method is primary in the treatment of the divine attributes in subsequent chapters. Of course, even this analysis is ultimately based on a posteriori knowledge, since it can proceed only in the light of the metaphysical knowledge gained from the investigation of limited being.

But before beginning the analysis of divine attributes, certain obscurities still need to be cleared up concerning the reference of constructed meta-concepts to God. First, it seems that such meta-concepts simply fail to tell us anything about the being of

God; for they are always necessarily finite, while the being of God is transcendent. In answer to this, it must be said that such meta-concepts would simply fail to give knowledge about God if they were referred directly to God. But instead they are referred to God through the medium of creatures, which depend upon God and are participations in the perfection of His being. Even in the ontological argument, the meta-concept with which the argument must begin refers to God through the medium of the knowledge of participated being out of which this meta-concept was constructed. Because creatures have an analogical resemblance to God by their participation in His being, as is explained in more detail below, such constructs derived from the knowledge of creatures can refer to God in some manner.

And yet these general remarks do not explain how such constructs refer to God, but only the possibility of such reference. A further step may be taken by distinguishing, in any such construct, the content and the mode of signification. The content is a certain intelligibility, but here a still further distinction must be made. In such a meta-concept, there is an expressed intelligibility, itself directly derived from the transphenomenal objectivity of proportionate being, and a signified intelligibility, the metaphysical intelligibility designated and referred to by the construct as a construct. Obviously, our direct concern here is not with the expressed intelligibility but with the signified intelligibility. Any attempt to apply the expressed intelligibility to the being of God could only be by way of metaphor, since this intelligibility refers to some formal perfection in the line of objectivity, which cannot be realized as such in the being of pure existence. Even with respect to signified intelligibility, it must be certain that there is question of a metaphysical perfection that does not imply any necessary limitation in its mode of realization. For example, "to be a creature" is a metaphysical perfection; yet it implies a necessary limitation (finiteness and dependence), and therefore should not be applied to the being of God. Terms such as this, which imply some necessary limitation in their mode of realization, can again of course be applied to God in some metaphorical sense, but not in a proper sense as signifying a perfection formally realized in God.

Besides the content, expressed or signified, of the construct, there is also, as has been noted, its mode of signification. The mode of signification is the manner in which the content is represented. In all human concepts and meta-concepts, the mode of signification is material and finite. The perfection expressed or signified is always represented according to its mode of being in material and finite things. Obviously, when the application of any meta-concept to God is considered, it is necessary to disregard and to ignore its necessary finite and material mode of signification.

But even when the mode of signification is set aside and attention is focused only upon signified content which does not imply any necessary limitation in its mode of realization, even here a further difficulty remains. The fact is that the content, even if it could be realized in an unlimited way, is still considered according to its finite modes of realization. When the meta-concept of being is applied to God, it is still the meta-concept of being which has been derived from a consideration of finite beings. In this meta-concept, existence is understood precisely as the act of essence, and therefore as a limited act, an act proportioned to some determinate essence. Even granting, then, that existence can be found in an unlimited way, it does not seem that we can know existence according to this mode of realization. But in this case, the meta-concept of being, and with it all other meta-concepts (which resolve in one manner or other into that of being), cannot be predicated of God. Therefore again it seems that our meta-concepts simply fail to tell us anything of the being of God, except by way of metaphor.

If then, the meta-concept of being, or any other meta-concept, is to be referred properly, and not merely by way of metaphor, to God, it is necessary for such a meta-concept to undergo an internal readjustment of meaning according as it is diversely predicated of creatures and of God. Such readjustment is already familiar even in the predication of being of diverse creatures, but with predication about the divine being a new type of analogy of being appears.

The meaning of the meta-concept clearly cannot remain identically the same, as in a univocal concept. First, it has already been seen in Part 1 that this meta-concept never remains identically the same even as it is predicated of diverse creatures. But the being of God is much more distant from the being of creatures than the being of one creature is from the being of another creature. Second, univocity is in principle impossible except in concepts referring to the objectivity of things, since every act of existence is simply unique; indeed, even in such concepts referring to the objectivity of things, the univocity exists only in the content as conceived and not in the content according to its actual mode of realization in things. Third, at the very heart of the meta-concept of being is the essence-existence relation; but this relation is altogether diverse in God and in creatures, since God is pure existence while every creature posesses an essence distinct from its existence.

However, the meaning of the meta-concept of being cannot be simply diverse, according as it is said of God and of creatures, as in two entirely distinct concepts which happen to be named by the same name. If being had such an equivocal meaning, there would be no possibility of learning anything at all about God from the being of creatures, not even His existence; nor would there be any possibility of using names about God, since the meaning of such names would refer only to the being of creatures. However, this is most certainly not the case; for already a good deal has been learned about God from the twelve ways of transcendence discussed in the two previous chapters.

Therefore, the meta-concept of being must be subject to analogical adjustment as it is said of both God and creatures. However the required adjustment for predication about God cannot be accounted for in terms of the treatment of the analogy of the meta-concept of being in Part 1. The adjustment must take place according to the actual analogy of being between creatures and God, an analogy which is more than a simple unity-in-diversity of various essences in relation to existence. It is necessary, then, to make some observations regarding the actual, real analogy of being between God and creatures and regarding the consequences which this has for any logical analogy in the meta-concept of being.

The fundamental point of diversity between limited and unlimited being is seen in the gulf between finite and infinite existence. At the same time, the fundamental point of similarity between limited and unlimited being is in the likeness of finite existence to infinite existence which arises from the utter dependence of finite existence on infinite existence as its proper cause; this is to say that the similarity arises from the participation of finite existence in the perfection of unlimited existence. Therefore, the fundamental analogy of being between God and creatures is the analogy of participation, the analogy between the unparticipated act of existence and the diverse participated acts of existence which confer actuality upon all that is in finite being.

It is only because there is such an analogy of participation of finite to infinite being that there can be a real analogy of proper proportionality between the various finite beings. The diverse finite acts of existence are similar to each other, even while each remains unique, in virtue of their participation in the perfection of the one infinite act of existence. And the diverse essence-principles of finite beings are similar to each other only insofar as they each exist in virtue of some one of the diverse, yet similar, finite acts of existence. Therefore the similarity of the diverse essence-existence composites to each other, in which consists the real analogy of proper proportionality between finite beings, is ultimately grounded in the analogy of participation of finite being to infinite being. But note that this real analogy of proper proportionality cannot be extended to include the infinite being itself, since this being is not itself an essence-existence composite.

However, even if there is no real analogy of proper proportionality between creatures and God, there is still a logical analogy of proper proportionality between creatures and God, an analogy in our meta-conceptual modes of knowing creatures and God. This logical analogy arises from the fact that our meta-conceptual knowledge of God is derived from and in accordance with the mode of the knowledge which we have of creatures. Since our meta-concept of existence is of existence as an act of essential potency, our meta-concept of pure existence is also of existence as an act of essential potency; therefore our meta-concept of unlimited being is a meta-concept of an essence-existence composite. But it follows from this that the meta-concept of unlimited being is similar to the meta-concept of any or all finite being, containing both an essence-term and an existence-term. This is the logical analogy of proper proportionality between creatures and God.

But obviously there is still more to be said about the meta-concept of unlimited being; for, if one were to stop here, there would be no adequate distinction drawn between the meta-concept of limited being and the meta-concept of unlimited being. It is therefore necessary that some special qualification be introduced into the meaning of the meta-concept of being insofar as it is to be applied to the being of God. The nature of this qualification is suggested by the following considerations. When the meta-concept of being is applied to diverse finite beings and to diverse degrees of finite being, the existence-term is understood to vary in proportion to the variation of the essence-term. The greater the degree of perfection of the objective content of the essence-term, the greater the degree of existence possessed and exercised by the thing. However, there is no limit, no maximum of essential or existential perfection, to be reached in following this method of variation. It is already known, from the analysis of limitation in Part 1, that the maximum can be reached only by diminishing the content of the essence-term to zero, at which point the content of the existence-term becomes either zero or unlimited. And yet, in the latter case, the perfection of the essence-term has not been lost. All along, such essential perfection was derived from the perfection of the existence-term, since existence gives actuality to all that is in the being; therefore the perfection of essence is already present in some manner in the perfection of existence, and therefore in the unlimited perfection of existence is also contained in a supereminent manner the unlimited perfection of essence as well.

In the light of the analogy of participation which really exists between God and creatures, it is evident that the method of qualification of the meta-concept of being so that it can be applied to the being of God is just that outlined in the preceding paragraph. The content of the essence-term as distinguished from the existence-term is diminished to zero, and the content of the existence-term becomes unlimited, not because God has no essential perfection but rather because this perfection is found in a supereminent manner in the very perfection of the act of existence itself. God is still known as an essence-existence composite; but the essence has no determinate content of its own as really distinct from existence, for such a content would result in the limitation of the act of existence. But if the essence-term no longer has any determinate content of its own, it can just as well be dropped from explicit consideration, even though the existence continues to be known by us as if the act of some essence. The meta-concept of the unlimited being then is the meta-concept of existence, necessarily considered as if the act of some essence, but nevertheless known, in the light of the qualifications already made, to be in this special case apart from any essence distinct from itself, and therefore known to be unlimited rather than limited existence.

Clearly, this knowledge continues to be unsatisfying, necessarily inadequate as a knowledge of God, a consideration of divine existence as if it were the existence of a creature, even though it is known to be in fact more than the existence of a creature. But this is a necessary limitation in the knowledge of God which can be gained by any intellectual creature, a limitation arising ultimately from the infinite gulf between the being of such a creature and the being of God, unless God should bridge this gulf through a gift of supernatural grace.

It is possible now to express in a concise way the qualification which must be introduced into the meta-concepts of being and its various metaphysical perfections in order that they may be applied to give knowledge of God. First, the perfection of existential act which is designated in such a meta-concept as that of being must be affirmed of God and therefore retained in the content of the meta-concept; for every existential act has its proper cause in the unlimited existential act of God. Second, the limitation or imperfection in the mode of realization of such perfection and act in the creature, arising from the presence of an essential, limiting potency, must be denied of God; and therefore this potency is ignored in the content of the meta-concept as it is referred to God. Third, in consequence of the negation which has just taken place, the perfection of existential act in question is affirmed of God in an unlimited way, and therefore understood in the meta-concept as unlimited, even though it is necessarily considered as if it were the act of some essence. These three steps in qualification of the content of any meta-concept insofar as it is to be referred to God are nothing but the ways of affirmation, negation, and eminence, well-known in traditional philosophy, as seen now from the perspective of the metaphysics of existence.

This method of affirmation, negation, and eminence may be applied to any metaphysical meta-concept which does not already imply some necessary limitation in the mode of realization of that to which it refers. This ultimately means that the method can be applied to any metaphysical meta-concept which designates some aspect of the perfection of existence as such, for example, to any of the notions designating some transcendental aspect of being. This also means that the method can be applied to any metaphysical meta-concept which designates some aspect of the perfection of intelligence and will; for it was seen in Part 1 that existence tends to become conscious existence and consciousness, and that therefore pure existence must also be pure consciousness.

But, again, the method of affirmation, negation, and eminence cannot be properly applied to the knowledge of content which necessarily implies some limitation in its mode of realization. Such content can be said of God only by way of metaphor.

Chapter 21

A PARENTHESIS -- A BRIEF RECONSIDERATION OF THE META-CONCEPT OF BEING

At this point it is necessary to reconsider briefly the meta-concept of being as such. If this meta-concept is to be applied to God as well as to creatures, it is necessary to make explicit in the formulation of the meta-concept the possibility of such an application to God. This possibility is clear once it is understood that existence in itself is independent of essence and can be found without essence. This understanding does not remove the fact that we necessarily conceive, or rather meta-conceive, existence as the act of essence; but it does indicate that existence need not necessarily be the act of essence. This independence of existence with respect to essence can be designated in the following formula, to be added to the nine already enumerated in the elaboration of the meta-concept of being in chapter ten. Again the dash is used to indicate denial.

If O, then E. But - (if E, then O).

It seems well now to set down together the nine sub-formulae under the one general formula, which together signify the content of the meta-concept of being as such. See chapter four for an explanation of the general formula and the first five sub-formulae (with X used for E); and see chapter ten for an explanation of sub-formulae 6-8.

$R_{OE} \sim R_{PA}$

(1) $R_{OE} \sim R_{MF}$
(2) $R_{OE} \sim R_{SA}$
(3) $R_{OE} \sim R_{AS}$
(4) $R_{OE} \sim R_{OD}$
(5) $R_{O(O+E)} \sim R_{-OO}$
(6) $E \rightarrow K$
(7) If OE, then either OEQ or QOE.
(8) $E \rightarrow C$
(9) If O, then E. But - (if E, then O).

Chapter 22

THE ATTRIBUTES OF GOD

The various names which can be said of God, the meanings of these names expressed in meta-concepts, the diverse aspects of God to which these meta-concepts refer, these are all called the attributes of God. The investigation of the divine nature is nothing but the search for the divine attributes and the relations between them. In this chapter, a divine attribute is understood to be an aspect of the divine being known through some determinate meta-concept.

If God is the pure act of existence, as has been shown in previous chapters, then in one way all the attributes are one without distinction; for they must all be identical with the divine existence. However, because of the richness of the divine being, which is an abyss of intelligibility surpassing the comprehension of any creature, and because of the weakness of our intellectual power, it is necessary for us to express even our limited knowledge of the divine being in a multitude of distinct meta-concepts. This distinction of meta-concepts is made in accordance with the distinction of divine perfections as they are found reflected in creatures, since every formulation of our knowledge of God is made in terms of our knowledge of creatures.

The distinction of divine attributes, then, depends very closely upon the metaphysical analysis in Part 1 of existence and its perfections. The analysis is divided into four parts, treating first of the fundamental attribute of God (which also reveals His fundamental name), then of the absolute attributes of God as the supreme being, next of the absolute attributes of God as the supreme consciousness, and finally of the relative attributes of God which arise from the fact that He created the world.

The fundamental attribute and name of God

The fundamental attribute (from which comes also the fundamental name) of God must be that aspect of the divine being which is known as the root of all the other attributes. But since all these attributes are ultimately attributes of being, their root must be that which most properly designates the being of God as distinct from and as surpassing every creature. But it has been seen that the transcendence of God appears insofar as He is known as the pure act of existence. Moreover, since all the perfection of every being is ultimately contained in or derived from its act of existence, all the perfection of God, all His attributes, must be contained in and derived from His being the pure act of existence. Therefore the fundamental attribute of God is precisely His existence; and His fundamental name is Existence or He Who Is or some other phrase conveying the same meaning.

The attributes of God as the supreme being: the modal attributes

If we consider God as the supreme being, two distinct sets of attributes appear. The first set simply contrasts the being of God with the being of creatures, by removing from God certain limitations and consequences of the limitations of creatures; these attributes we call modal attributes, since they reveal to us the contrast between the mode of being of God and the mode of being of creatures. They deepen our understanding of the meaning of pure existence, and thus they prepare the way for the deeper understanding of the manner in which all the transcendental aspects of being are realized in God. Although these modal attributes are negative (they are denials of certain restrictions that are found in created being), nevertheless a greater positive understanding of the pure act of existence is in fact gained from their consideration.

Six such modal attributes may be considered here. The first of these has already appeared much earlier. Since the pure act of existence is not limited by any potency, it must be infinite. But this infinity is not simply a relative infinity, an infinity in some particular line of perfection. The actuality of any and every perfection must be derived from the act of existence. The act of existence therefore contains in some manner such perfections; and the pure, infinite act of existence contains every perfection, actual or possible, in the unity of itself. Therefore, this infinite act of existence is said to be simply infinite in every line of perfection. This idea has also been expressed in calling God the transcendent being.

Secondly, since the pure act of existence is not a composite of act and potency in any manner, it must be utterly simple, devoid of any composition whatever. The parts of any composite being must be related as act and potency, since they would otherwise be distinct in their being, a plurality of beings rather than one, except for integral parts, the quantitative parts of extended being. Such integral parts are not fully actual but are contained only potentially and virtually in the extended being. Nevertheless, even the multiplicity of integral parts has its ultimate root, as was seen in Part 1, in the multiplicity of prime matter, the ultimate potential principle in material things. Therefore a multiplicity of integral parts also presupposes a composition of potency and act, which has already been seen to be impossible in the pure act of existence. Therefore, the pure act of existence cannot be composed of integral parts, just as it cannot be composed of potency and act. Therefore, the pure act of existence must be completely simple.

Thirdly, the perfection of no other being is simply outside of or beyond the being of the pure act of existence; in this pure act all such perfections are present in an even fuller way than in whatever other being may have this or that perfection. Since nothing can be simply outside of or beyond the being of God, God can be circumscribed by nothing; this impossibility of total or even partial circumscription is called the immensity of God. But this immensity should not be confused with the omnipresence of God, which is considered below, under the relative attributes.

Fourthly, in Part 1 it was seen that wherever change takes place, there is an act-potency composition in the changing thing. Since there is no act-potency composition in God, God cannot be subject to change of any kind; He is immutable in every respect. In his immutability He stands in contrast with every creature; even if there were a creature created in some final state which called for no further development of any kind, still the creature would be radically mutable insofar as it is composed of essence and existence and therefore intrinsically contingent and capable of being reduced to nothingness if God so willed it. God alone is absolutely unchangeable. And if He is absolutely unchangeable, then He is also, fifthly, absolutely necessary, unable to be other than as He is and unable not to be.

Sixthly, from the absolute immutability and necessity of God follow His eternity. Beings which exist in time are beings which realize their being through a succession of steps, whether continuous or discontinuous. Time is only the measure of such succession against some standard chosen because of its convenience and utility as a measure; there can be no time where there is no succession. Time, then, is founded in the duration of those things which realize their being in a succession of steps; it is itself a construct of intelligence, grounded in such duration of real things. But in contrast to that kind of duration is the duration of eternity. This is the duration of a being which possesses its fullness of being all at once, which is not realized successively because it already is all that it can be. Eternity then is consequent upon immutability and necessity. Therefore, just as God alone is completely immutable and necessary, so also He alone is eternal in the most strict meaning of that term. Other beings may have or acquire some share in eternity in proportion as they have or acquire some share of immutability and necessity.

The modal attributes, as also the other attributes of God, are not merely possessed. The relation of possession implies some act-potency composition between the possessor and the possessed. But it has already been seen that in God there is no such act-potency composition. Therefore, God not only has simplicity, infinity, immensity, immutability, necessity, and eternity but also <u>is</u> these attributes.

Implicit in every one of these six modal attributes is a seventh, the highest degree of spirituality. A being is spiritual insofar as it is independent of matter as a potential principle. But even spiritual being could have a composition of potency and act analogous to the composition of matter and form, such as the composition of essence and existence or that of substance and accident. If some being should lack any composition at all of potency and act, it is therefore at a still higher degree of spirituality, the highest degree. And therefore God is supremely spiritual.

And if spirituality is the root of conscious life, then God must also be supremely alive and conscious, as has already been seen. Analysis of the understanding of God as supreme conscious life reveals a whole new world of attributes beyond those which are consequent upon His being. These are considered in a later section of this chapter.

As was said at the beginning of this section, besides the modal attributes a second set of attributes consequent upon the being of God as being should be considered. These are the transcendental attributes, the attributes consequent upon being as being and therefore found in every being, and found in the highest grade in the supreme being. These attributes can therefore be said properly, and not just by some metaphor, of God; they refer to perfections actually present in the divine being and not merely contained in some higher perfection, though of course these perfections are present as identical with the divine being itself.

The attributes of God as the supreme being: the transcendental attributes

To present an orderly treatment of these transcendental attributes, it is enough to follow the order of their appearance thus far, beginning with the positive absolute transcendentals of Part 1, chapter eleven, and ending with the three transcendentals which appeared in the course of the Tenth, Eleventh, and Twelfth Ways of transcendence.

First are the positive absolute transcendentals. The first of these is, of course, being itself; but this has already been sufficiently considered. Second is the dynamism of being in its existential act; existence is not merely possessed but also exercised. The existence of God is pure self-affirmation, pure dynamism. The third such transcendental attribute is persistence in being; in God this is one with His eternity. Fourth is the tendency to exist; in God this is one with another modal attribute which emerged in the course of the Third Way and which was considered again in the preceding section, that is, His absolute necessity in being.

Fifth, every being is somehow active insofar as it exists; therefore God, as pure existence, must be supremely active, even pure activity. His existence already is, in some manner, that which in creatures is a dynamic superexistence; He is not only pure abundance of being but also the pure superabundance of being. And the sixth transcendental, the tendency to activity which every being has insofar as it is being, is found in God insofar as His activity is identical with His absolutely necessary existence and therefore shares in this necessity. There still remains the problem of understanding how God is also sovereignly free in His activity in regard to creatures, even though all that is in Him is pure necessity; this is considered in a later section.

Seventh, and eighth, every being insofar as it is being tends toward knowledge and love, though diverse beings do so in diverse ways; these are the tendencies of being toward greater and greater spiritualization. But God is supremely spiritual; His existence and activity are pure knowledge and pure love, supreme knowledge and supreme love, the source of all other knowledge and love, and that toward which the whole movement of progressive spiritualization in creation is somehow directed.

Ninth, every being has a determinate grade of being determined by its essence; the essence of the supreme being is that it be at the supreme grade of being through its infinite existence. While in creatures essence is a principle distinct from existence, in God His essence is precisely to exist. In creatures, essence determines the degree of intelligibility which each creature has; in God His essence as pure existence is the plenitude of all intelligibility, since all intelligibility is ultimately grounded in existence.

Tenth, every being is subjective, either a subject or of some subject. Since God's being is not possessed or exercised by anything else but rather is the pure act of self-affirmation, He is the supreme subject, in Whose depths of subjectivity is contained in a supereminent way all the perfection of every finite subject.

Besides the ten positive absolute transcendentals, there is also one negative absolute transcendental. Every being is one, or undivided in itself. In God, this oneness is the same as His utter simplicity in His mode of being.

Next come the positive relative transcendentals. Some of the divine attributes which appear here appear again when we consider the attributes consequent upon being as consciousness.

The twelfth transcendental attribute is the dynamic generosity of being. The tendency to diffuse itself must be present in the pure act of existence in the highest way; God is supreme generosity. It would be very easy, but fallacious, to conclude from this generosity to the necessity of creation. In fact, it will be seen that creation need not have taken place. This, of course, leaves the philosopher with a mystery as to how, on the hypothesis of no creation, the divine being could be said to have dynamic generosity. This mystery is only illuminated when faith accepts the revelation made by God of the diffusion of being among the three Persons of the Trinity.

Thirteenth, the tendency of every being toward activity implies not only a tendency toward the diffusion of being but also a tendency toward union and communion with other being. This transcendental is realized in God insofar as He gives Himself in diverse ways to His creatures; but again this realization is not a necessary one, since creation was not necessary. Again, the philosopher is lost in mystery until the illumination of faith regarding the union and communion of the Trinity.

Fourteenth, every being insofar as it is a being is conformable to or knowable by the human, or more generally, the finite intellect. The supreme being is therefore also the supremely knowable, even to the finite intellect. And yet the very height of its being and fullness of its intelligibility preclude any direct immediate vision of this being by any creature relying on its own natural powers. Still, God does remain knowable on the natural level, through the medium of the creatures which He has made.

Fifteenth and sixteenth, since existence and activity are the goods of all being, and every being is good insofar as it has existence and activity, God also, in virtue of His being pure existence and superabundance of existence, is good in these two manners.

Seventeenth, if every being is somehow an object of desire for the human will, this is only because the human will tends toward the fullness of existence. But this fullness of existence is God, Who is therefore the supreme object of desire for the human will.

Eighteenth, if every being insofar as it is being is beautiful, then the supreme being is in Himself the most beautiful. We are speaking here of beauty relative to the human intellect and to the finite intellect in general. But just as the truth of God is so great as to preclude direct vision of it by the unaided natural powers of any creature, so also the beauty of God cannot possibly be naturally appreciated by us for what it really is. But we can come to some understanding and appreciation of this beauty through its manifestation in the creatures of God. Only through the supernatural gift of the light of glory can we come to see and appreciate the truth and beauty of God in immediate vision, a gift which faith tells us is given only after the conclusion of our course of pilgrimage and purification.

Next come the negative relative transcendentals. The nineteenth transcendental is uniqueness of existence, which is applied to God insofar as He is the one pure act of existence. Twentieth, uniqueness of essence is found in God insofar as in Him alone is His essence "to be." Uniqueness of existential state is found in God insofar as He alone is His own exercise of existence by being the pure act of exercised existence; this is the twenty-first transcendental attribute of God. Twenty-second, uniqueness of activity is found in God insofar as His activity is identical with His infinite existence.

Twenty-third to twenty-sixth, consequent upon the four modes of uniqueness of being are four modes of separation, each of which is said of God. Despite His immensity, and the consequent omnipresence which is considered under the relative attributes following being, consciousness, and power, God still remains in some way entirely separate from His creatures in His existence, essence, existential state, and activity. He is always completely untouched by them in His immutability and eternity, despite the fact that they continually depend upon Him for all the being and activity that they have.

If every being is mysterious to the human intellect, God as the supreme being is also the supreme mystery, and this even on the natural level, even before the revelation of the further depths accessible through faith. His mystery is a mystery of essence, existence, activity, and subjectivity. Here are four more divine attributes.

Consequent upon this surpassing mystery of God is also the highest excess of beauty, the highest sublimity. And God is also not just goodness but the highest excess of goodness, the supremely sacred reality. These considerations yield eight new divine attributes, two groups of four, parallel with the four attributes of mystery.

But while union with God in knowledge and love can give a natural happiness to man which no other being can give, still the truth, goodness, and beauty of God as attainable by the natural intellectual powers of man or of any other finite intelligent being cannot satiate these powers. It is not that anything more is demanded by the nature of these powers; the whole point is that they could not naturally attain to anything more anyway. But even when they have attained all they can through their natural activity, they still remain radically unsatiated. At this point we can see a certain openness in man, an openness of nature to what itself would be beyond nature; this is the possibility of a supernatural order. The non-satiating character of being in its truth, goodness, and beauty in relation to the natural human intellectual powers is found even in the case of God; and these three attributes of being ground the possibility of a supernatural order.

In the consideration of the absolute foundation for the relative transcendentals, new sets of transcendental attributes appear. Explicit treatment of these was omitted in the treatment of the transcendentals, and explicit treatment of the corresponding divine attributes may likewise be omitted. But it is worth noting that all these distinct transcendental attributes do in fact exist and can be predicated properly of God.

Three other transcendental attributes appeared in the course of the Tenth, Eleventh, and Twelfth Ways. The first of these is the truth that consists in the conformity of every limited being to the intelligence of the unlimited being and in the identity of unlimited being with its unlimited intelligence. It is this identity of being and intelligence in God which is, simply speaking, the first truth on which all other truths depend, and according to which God is known as the supreme truth.

The second is the goodness that consists in the similarity of every limited being to unlimited will and love and in the identity of unlimited being with unlimited will and love. It is this identity of being, will, and love in God which is, simply speaking, the first goodness on which all other goodness depends, and according to which God is most properly known as the supreme good.

The third is the beauty which consists in a similarity of every limited being to the unlimited joy in intelligence and in the identity of unlimited being with this unlimited joy in intelligence. It is this identity of being and intellectual joy in God which is, simply speaking, the first beauty on which all other beauty depends, and according to which God is most properly known as the supreme beauty.

The attributes of God as the supreme consciousness

God is not only the supreme being but also the supreme consciousness, pure knowledge and pure love. When God is considered from this viewpoint, a new set of attributes appears. Some of these attributes coincide with some already seen, but they are now seen from a new viewpoint.

In us, knowledge is one perfection distinct from others and occupying its own place in our lives. But in God, the pure act of existence, knowledge is identical with the simple pure act of existence; everything in God is intelligence, intellectual vision, pure light. His own existence is the pure act of understanding. We distinguish in creatures between the intellect and the act of understanding, and apply this distinction to God; but as it is applied to God, this distinction is only due to our necessarily finite mode of conception. In God, the intellect and the act of understanding are one and the same with His pure existence.

Moreover, the primary object of the divine knowledge can only be the divine being itself. If anything else were the primary object, then God would be dependent upon that other for something of His perfection of knowledge; but in this case God would no longer be the pure act of existence but only another act-potency composite. The primary knowledge of God, then, is an auto-consciousness in reflexive self-possession. This self-consciousness of God is absolutely perfect without any obscurity, since it is the simple reflexivity of pure existence identical with itself.

But it may be pointed out that the objection made against the primary object of divine knowledge being something other than God holds also for any object of divine knowledge being something other than God. How is it possible for God to know anything other than Himself? But God does know things other than Himself, since the finality of created things is dependent upon the divine knowledge. One must consider more deeply the meaning of the exhaustive understanding which God has of Himself as the pure act of existence. If He understands Himself exhaustively (and He must, since His unlimited intellect and knowledge are identical with His unlimited being), then He understands all the infinity of diverse modes in which the being of creatures could be imitations and participations of the divine being. And if there is conjoined with this knowledge a decree actually to create some of these possible creatures, then He understands in His understanding of Himself these modes in which His being is actually imitated and participated. The understanding of all possible imitations of Himself is called His knowledge of simple intelligence; the understanding of all actual imitations of Himself is called His knowledge of vision. Note that such understanding of the being of creatures, whether by simple intelligence or by vision, is not just a generic or universal understanding but rather an understanding of every individual modality of being of every unique possible or actual individual; for the divine knowledge of the divine being and of its diverse possible or actual imitations is indeed an exhaustive knowledge. The diverse understandings in God of the diverse ways in which the divine being can be imitated by creatures (diverse in our understanding of God, though of course really identical in His being) are designated as the divine ideas; and those which are actually conjoined with a creative decree are called exemplars.

There is need for many further clarifications in the understanding of the divine knowledge when one comes to a discussion of the relation of creatures to God; but what has been said may suffice for the present.

Just as it is with knowledge, so it is with love in God. His love is identical with the simple pure act of existence; God is love. We distinguish in creatures between the will and the act of love, and apply this distinction to God; but again the application of this distinction to God is due only to our finite mode of conception. In God, the will and the act of love are identical with His pure existence.

Just as with knowledge, so with love, the primary object of the divine activity can only be the divine being itself; for if anything else were the primary object, God would be dependent on another in that respect and would therefore be another potency-act composite. This same truth concerning the divine love can be seen in the light of the dynamism of being. If every being tends to activity, then a being with intellectual consciousness tends to some activity in accordance with the being of intellectual consciousness. This activity is conscious love. Love then follows upon knowledge (or at least the possibility of love, in cases where there is free choice). Therefore, if the primary object of divine knowledge is the divine being, the primary object of divine love must also be the divine being. This primary divine love is an absolutely necessary complacency in and consent to the infinite goodness of reflexively conscious infinite being. It is necessary since the object of such love, and the one who loves, and the act of loving are all identical. It is necessary, but not coerced, since there is nothing outside God which could determine Him in any way. Since it is uncoerced, it may be said to proceed from freedom of spontaneity, though not from freedom of choice.

God also loves things other than Himself, as is clear from the fact that He creates things other than Himself. But He cannot love them apart from His love of Himself, for then they would in that respect determine the divine being. The situation parallels that in the divine knowledge of other things than God Himself. Since love follows knowledge, the exhaustive knowledge which God has of Himself, extending even to all the diverse modes in which the being of creatures could be imitations and participations of the divine being, must be followed by a proportionate love, which extends to all of these same possible imitations and participations of His being. This love is a necessary (though uncoerced) love of mere complacent regard, since there is no question yet of a creative decree. If God should will to create this or that creature, then there is a love of benevolence besides the mere love of complacency. But this creative love of benevolence is not a new line of love specified by anything other than God; it is simply God loving His own goodness as participatable, loving it so much as to will its actual communication to others through creation; it is the love of a means to the diffusion, through participation, of the good which God loves as the end, namely His own infinite goodness.

But this creative love of God is full of mystery. Since God is simple, immutable, and eternal, this love must be necessary in its mode of being in God, just as all else is necessary in the being of God. And yet this creative love is free as to its object. No creature is in any sense needed by God; God is utterly independent and self-sufficient in His being. Therefore, if God should decree to create, it is by an act of free choice. Such a free choice does not mean that any new contingent element is introduced into the divine being, for the choice has been made from all eternity. But there still remains the mystery in how God still could be the same in every respect had He chosen otherwise than He did. And a further mystery arises from the fact that the dynamic generosity of being seems, from the viewpoint of reason, to make creation necessary. It was seen earlier that in fact this principle of dynamic generosity is already satisfied by the diffusion of being among the Persons of the Trinity revealed to faith; but, now that we have seen God knowing and loving not only Himself but also all possible imitations of Himself, the difficulty seems to recur. How is it possible for creation to be a free act of God? It is necessary to examine in more detail the meaning of freedom and the freedom of God.

It was seen much earlier that being is ultimately realized in diverse subjects, each characterized by its interiority and relative independence of other subjects. But because there is a hierarchy of being, there is also a hierarchy of subjectivity. The lower subjects, those below rational beings, all have uni-directional dynamisms toward activity. Some have a wider range of possibilities, such as those endowed with the power of sensation, than do others; but even then the interiority and independence of subjectivity is insufficient to remove the need for some natural determination of unique goals of every individual activity.

But in intelligent beings there is not only subjectivity but selfhood--subjectivity with reflexive interiority, conscious self-possession, and freedom. The dynamism of the self can be multidirectional; for since intelligence can grasp being and goodness as such, movement toward any merely finite good or good apprehended as finite is possible but not demanded by the dynamism consequent upon the being of intelligence. This is to say that the dynamism of the self as self is free (with freedom of choice) with respect to finite good.

This last point deserves more detailed explanation. If being is dynamic precisely insofar as it is, and if intelligence expands our being through the intentional assimilation of any or of all the being of the universe of being, then each apprehension of being by the intelligence brings to the intelligent being a new possibility and a new tendency to activity. But intelligence also understands being and goodness as such, from which arises a conscious tendency to the plenitude of being and goodness. In the light of this latter tendency, the particular tendencies to finite goods or good apprehended in a finite way are revealed as not completely gratifying the desires of the intelligent being. Therefore, it remains possible for the intelligent being to choose or to reject such goods. The manner in which this choice or rejection takes place is considered below.

The fact is that some choice or rejection must be made. For while the tendencies toward such finite goods do in fact exist in us, some of these goods seem to be, and even are, incompatible with each other or with movement toward what we may consider to be, or what is, the plenitude of being and goodness. How then is a choice to be made? Is there perhaps a calculus of goods according to which we always choose the greater good? But this is contrary to our genuine experience of freedom in some of our choices.

At this point there emerges the special prerogative of a self, in virtue of its reflexive interiority and self-possession, to be able to hold itself in reserve with respect to every good apprehended as finite; this is the possibility of nihilation, which moderates the dynamism of being in an intelligent agent. Freedom is thus the moderation of the multi-directional dynamism of a self through the possibility of nihilation. This is the freedom of choice, which of course presupposes the basic dynamism of the intelligent agent in which consists its prior freedom of spontaneity.

It may perhaps seem that the above account of freedom of choice places too much emphasis on negativity, in the possibility of nihilation. But in fact, the presuppositions of the possibility of nihilation are precisely the perfection of selfhood, the dynamism of the self with respect to the plenitude of being and goodness, and its multi-directional dynamism with respect to the finite. The possibility of nihilation is therefore grounded in the riches of selfhood in its unique mystery.

And now it is necessary to apply the above remarks on the subject of freedom in the intelligent agent to obtain a better understanding of the freedom of God. It was already pointed out earlier that the principle of the dynamic generosity of being, as it is applied to the supreme being, intelligence, and love that is God, seems to suggest that creation had to take place, that it was a necessary act. But the dynamic generosity of being in God, while resulting necessarily in the diffusion of being among the three Persons of the Trinity, is moderated by the possibility of nihilation as regards the creation of finite being. Therefore, such creation is "natural" to God (in virtue of the dynamic generosity of being), and yet it is in no way necessary to Him (because of the possibility of nihilation).

But the dynamic generosity of being in God is in fact infini-directional, since in His exhaustive knowledge He contemplates and in His love complacently regards an infinity of possible creatures. Yet it is not possible for Him to create all possible creatures, since not all of them are even compatible with each other. Therefore the possibility of nihilation is a necessary condition for order in the divine plan, and that there may be this order rather than any other possible order. Moreover, had God willed from eternity not to create at all, or to create a different order of things, He would still have remained identically the same as He is now that He has willed to create the actual order of things which we see and in which we live. His infini-directional dynamism is always infini-directional, moderated only by nihilation, which is not a positive determination and which therefore neither adds nor subtracts anything from the being of God. Thus it is that the freedom of God in regard to creation is in no way contrary to His immutability and eternity.

Dynamic generosity, then, in God, must not be understood as if it were a need on the part of God to create. God gains nothing through creation and would lack nothing had He not created. His generosity must not be understood as a tendency in the same sense as a tendency of a creature toward its fulfillment. Rather, the dynamic generosity of God in regard to creation must be understood as the complacent regard which God has for His own being as imitable and participable by possible creatures. This complacent regard becomes benevolent creative love unless it is moderated by nihilation, but such nihilation is indeed possible and therefore creation is by no means necessary. And yet, when all is said and done, the primary mystery is still not so much the fact that God did create but rather the fact that He did not create even more.

Besides intellect and will, knowledge and love, then, God also possesses the power to create, the power of giving being and activity to things other than Himself. This power to create is full of mystery, and the fact of creation raises problems which are so difficult that creation might well be all but ruled out as a possibility were it not for the fact that it has taken place. And yet, as has been seen, on the other hand, creation is a natural consequence of the principle of the dynamic generosity of being as applied to God. The act of creation is considered in more detail in the last section of this chapter, and the difficulties concerning the coexistence of God and His creatures in the next chapter.

Those subjects which are also selves are called, because of their unique dignity, persons; and the subjectivity of a self is called its personality. Since selfhood consists in conscious interiority, self-possession, and relative independence, God possesses selfhood or personality in the supreme grade; for He is an infinite depth of pure conscious interiority, utterly free and independent in relation to all other being. But it is only through His revelation of His own interior life that He teaches us that personality is in fact threefold in Himself, that there is a Trinity of Persons in the unity of being.

Finally, if life consists in immanent activity, activity which has both its immediate source and its immediate term within the living being, and if consciousness is the highest form of life since it has the most incorruptible mode of being and the widest scope of activity, then God, as the supreme consciousness, must be said to be supremely alive. Indeed, since God is pure existence, which is also pure consciousness, He and all that is in Him must also be pure life.

The attributes of God consequent upon the fact of creation

The first attribute consequent upon the fact of creation is obviously that of creator. It has already been seen that in fact God did create all that is and that no creature can create anything at all, and therefore that to be a creator is a proper attribute of God alone. If creation be considered as an activity of God, it is evident that this activity must be an immanent activity; for this activity like all other divine activity is identical with the divine being. Since a transitive activity would be essentially relative to its effect, while the being of God is unchanging and independent of every other thing, therefore the being of God cannot be identified with any transitive activity. Therefore every activity of God must be formally an immanent activity. God does not, even in virtue of creation, acquire any real relation to the creature. However, when the activity of creation is considered, no longer as an activity of God, but now rather as an effect in the creature, it is evidently not sufficient to describe creation as a formally immanent activity. Even while it is formally immanent, it is also virtually transitive insofar as there results from it an effect distinct from God, namely the being of the creature. And while creation does not result in any real relation of God to the creature, it results in a real relation of total dependence (identical with the received existence) of the creature to God. This situation, where God is not really related to the creature even while the creature is really related to God, is partially analogous to what we find in our intellectual knowledge of material things, where things do not have any real relation to such knowledge even while such knowledge has a real relation to things. The divine influx, then, which is called creation, is in God identical with His being and in the creature identical with the received existence of the creature.

Since, as has been seen, creation is not merely necessary at the beginning of the being of the creature but must continue as a divine influx so long as the creature exists, a distinction is made between creation (the influx considered as beginning) and conservation (the same influx considered as continuing).

But creatures do not only exist but also act. For this, new influx is required from God, influx which in God is governance and in creatures activity and the existence of the effect of activity. The remarks already made in the case of creation concerning immanent and transitive activity are equally relevant here. Governance is divided into activation and concurrence, in accordance with the distinction between the activity of creatures and the existence of the effect of such activity. When God is called governor of the universe of being, it must be understood that He governs both as an activator and as a concurrer.

If God is the creator, conservor, and governor of finite being, then He must also be present wherever there is finite being; for where the effect is present, the causality must be present, and where the causality is present, the cause must also be present. God is therefore present to all things created; this is His omnipresence.

Since creatures are created in accordance with the divine knowledge of the divine being as imitable and participable, this divine knowledge as conjoined with the creative decrees is a law in regard to the being and action of creatures. For a law is an intelligent decree made by the ruler and promulgated by him. The promulgation of this eternal law is accomplished through the creation of the universal order of determinate beings, each with its own nature and suitable mode of activity, knowable in varying degrees to every intelligent being. The "natural law" is simply the law of the right ordering of action of intelligent creatures, known or at least knowable to these intelligent creatures, in accordance with the universal order of being; therefore this natural law has been rightly called the participation of the eternal law in a rational creature. Since the eternal law is the divine knowledge as conjoined with the creative decrees of the divine being as imitable and participable, it follows that God is the eternal law of all things; under this aspect He is the ultimate ground of natural law and of all other reasonable law, and all such law derives its authority and ultimate sanction from Him. From this point of view, every reasonable and just law is grounded in the being of God; therefore the willful disregard of any such law is equivalently a refusal of consent to the being of God in some way, which is the ultimate malice of sin.

Closely related to the eternal law is the eternal plan. This eternal plan is simply the knowledge in God of the entire course of history of all creation, which unfolds gradually in the duration of creatures. It is not an advance knowledge in God, since there is no past, or future, in the divine eternity. This knowledge is at no point a knowledge of simple intelligence; it has been from all eternity a knowledge of vision, in which the whole course of every creature has been present at once to the divine eternity. This knowledge, of course, can in no way receive determination from creatures, since this eternal plan is identical with the uncreated being of God. Obviously, a difficulty at once arises concerning the knowledge of moral evil, which must arise from the free initiative of creatures, since it is contrary to the natural law and the eternal law. How can God know such evil and take account of it in His eternal plan without being in any way determined by creatures? This problem is considered in the next chapter.

The eternal plan is distinguished from the eternal law in that it is a factual knowledge while the eternal law is a normative knowledge. The eternal law decrees what things should be; but the eternal plan is a knowledge of what they actually are, taking into account the element of moral evil introduced by the free initiative of intelligent creatures. Moreover, the eternal law is a knowledge conjoined with creative decrees establishing the universal order of being and its natural tendencies; but the eternal plan, while in fact conjoined to the creative decrees, is itself as such only knowledge. When it is considered precisely as conjoined to the creative decrees, this eternal plan receives the name of providence, so called because it is, from our limited point of view, a foresight of God in ordering the affairs of the universe.

A difficulty was seen earlier concerning the knowledge of moral evil in the eternal plan; it is difficult to see how such knowledge is not ultimately determined by creatures. A parallel problem exists regarding the permission of evil under divine providence; such moral evil seems to evade the designs of God, to be a contribution made by the creature alone to the course of the world. But if such a contribution exists, then the absolute transcendence of divine providence, identical with the being of God, seems to disappear. In this case God becomes determined in some respect by His creatures and in that respect to be a finite God. But the further discussion of this problem is left for the next chapter.

Finally, since, as has been seen, there is a law governing the activity of intelligent creatures, and since such creatures may freely follow or disregard this law, it is necessary that the meaning of law be preserved through some sanction of reward and punishment. At this point there appears the order of divine justice. This justice may be considered as a special aspect of or consequence of the eternal law. But since man at least is so utterly weak and ignorant by reason of his own frailty coupled with the conditions of his existence in the world, there is need for mercy as well as justice if men are to attain the end appointed by God. This order of mercy is another aspect or consequence of the eternal law. God is both infinite justice and infinite mercy.

Chapter 23

SPECIAL PROBLEMS

Once the existence of infinite and immutable being has been established, many problems arise regarding the coexistence of finite and mutable being with infinite and immutable being, and regarding the dependence of the finite and mutable upon the infinite and immutable. In this chapter, five such problems are considered.

Can finite and infinite existence be identified with each other?

Some have suggested that the existence of each finite being may in fact be really identical with the pure act of existence, while the essence of each finite being is a limiting principle which is given its being through this pure act of existence. The existence of each finite being, on this hypothesis, would still be distinct from the existence of every other finite being insofar as this existence is the divine existence as conjoined to this essence, while that existence is the divine existence as conjoined to that essence.

Such an hypothesis cannot be regarded as simply equivalent to pantheism, since in fact it posits the essence of creatures as completely distinct from God. And it does contribute toward an easier understanding of the mysterious communication of being which we call creation. Moreover, it removes the problem, to be considered below, of the coexistence of finite and infinite existence. Finally, such an hypothesis cannot but have a certain attraction to any Christian philosopher who philosophizes as a part of his movement toward closer union with God.

And yet, if the being of the thing is derived from its act of existence, it is difficult to see how any essence could, on this hypothesis, have a being really outside the being of God. Moreover, since it is existence which is the ultimate principle of the activity of being, it is difficult to see how the activity of creatures would be distinguished from the activity of God. Though the hypothesis is not explicitly pantheistic, it reveals itself as ultimately occasionalist and pantheist when it is considered more closely.

How can finite and infinite existence coexist?

But if finite and infinite existence are really distinct, how is it possible for infinite existence to be really infinite? Does it not necessarily lack the perfection of the diverse finite acts of existence? Is it not necessarily, therefore, finite and not infinite after all?

In Part 1, it was said that an act is called infinite if it contains all the perfection of itself, and finite if it does not contain all the perfection of itself. Obviously, for any act, such as existence, to contain all the perfection of itself, it must also contain all the perfection of every possible instance, every possible limited instance, of this perfection. But it would not be proper to the abundance of perfection of such an unlimited act to contain the perfection of finite instances in the finite way in which this perfection is found in such finite instances. Therefore, when the existence of an unlimited perfection is affirmed, this perfection is not understood to contain all the perfection of every finite instance in the finite way in which it is found in each such instance. Rather, such an unlimited perfection contains the perfection of the finite instances in a supereminent manner, as identical with the infinity of this infinite perfection.

The mystery of creation, of the production of finite being from utter nothingness by the action of the infinite being, is not resolved by the above consideration; but it is at least possible to see that the factual coexistence of the infinite and finite modes of being is not an intrinsic impossibility.

How can the mutable finite depend
upon the immutable infinite?

Since every finite and mutable being is immediately dependent in all that it is upon the infinite and immutable being, the changes in mutable being must imply changes in the divine influxes and therefore in the divine activity which produces these divine influxes. But this activity is, as has been seen, identical with the divine being, the pure act of existence and superexistence. It seems therefore that the mutability of creatures implies necessarily the mutability of the divine being.

And yet this is absolutely impossible. It has already been seen in a previous chapter that the divine activity in creatures is in fact a formally immanent activity, only virtually transitive. This means that no change in the divine activity and in the divine being is demanded by a change in the term of this activity.

But does not the divine knowledge change with the changes of things? First, it must be recalled that the divine knowledge is in eternity, to which all time is at once present. Since there is no past or future for God, there can be no change in His knowledge. Second, the supposition of the question is that God's knowledge somehow depends upon things. But in fact nothing exists at all except insofar as it depends upon the divine knowledge of vision, to which the creative decree is conjoined. God's knowledge is not in any way influenced by things; it is this knowledge which determines all that there is of reality in everything other than God, and which therefore determines from all eternity every advent of being in the flux of finite reality.

It does not seem necessary to repeat these observations in regard to the divine will. Let it suffice to say that, *mutatis mutandis*, the same remarks apply to the parallel difficulty in regard to the divine will.

How does God know and permit
physical evil among His creatures?

Before considering the questions of evil in the face of divine providence, two kinds of question should be distinguished. It is one thing to ask how such evil can be known and permitted or tolerated by God, and it is another thing to ask why such evil is permitted. In this and the following section, the first question is considered in regard to physical and moral evil. Afterward, there is considered the even deeper question as to why such evil is permitted or tolerated; but these final remarks concerning the mystery of evil are left for the following chapter.

It may be recalled that evil in general is a privation of being, a lack of the perfection of being where it ought to be present. As such, then, evil is a nothingness, but a nothingness which is a wound in some being. Physical evil is such a wound in being. Moral evil is a deficiency in the manner of action of a free will. Such a will should choose action which is in accordance with the order of being, and therefore with the will of God, however this may be manifested (whether through the natural law and the light of natural prudence, or through legitimate human law, or through supernaturally revealed law, or through any other manner in which God may choose to manifest His will). When the will chooses to act in a manner contrary to such moral obligation, then its action is deficient, insofar as it lacks due order in relation to its last end.

Moral evil, then, is a physical evil as well; but not every physical evil is a moral evil. However, the distinction between these two may be made more sharp by taking as physical evil only non-moral evil. Thus every evil is either physical or moral, but not both at once. Some brief remarks may now be made concerning physical evil and its knowledge and permission by God.

Physical evil is all too evident in our world, in the pain of living things (though this is not always a simple evil), in the catastrophes which can disrupt the lives of men, in death. It is also present in the many deprivations to which so many human beings are subjected, whether by natural circumstances or even by the moral evil of themselves or other men. But if it be recalled that this evil is of its very nature a privation, one may well wonder how it is that God knows such evil? For God is pure existence, pure being without any deficiency. But if there can be no privation in God, then it seems that there can be no knowledge of privation in God, since God knows all that He knows through His knowledge of His own being.

But if God knows all possible participations in the perfection of the infinite act of existence, He must also know all the possible defective participations, insofar as they contain anything of positive being. But in knowing such defective participations in their positive being, He thereby also knows their defects. Thus He knows privations not through any privation in Himself but rather through His being considered as participable in a defective manner.

Since privations in themselves are nothingness, they do not have an efficient cause in the proper sense; nor is there anything such as a divine influx productive of such privations. Therefore they are only accidental results of the activity of efficient causes and the corresponding divine influxes. If such a privation is due to a deficient agent acting deficiently, that agent is said to be its deficient, rather than its efficient, cause. But God is in no sense a deficient cause. If there is physical evil in this world created by God, it cannot be said to have been caused by God; rather, it comes about through the interaction of creatures, when lines of activity conflict, or when an agent with an already induced deficiency acts deficiently so as to produce deficient effects. Such evil is known by God in His science of vision in the manner already described, and it must be said to be permitted by Him insofar as He creates and preserves in being the creatures from which it results. Physical evil, therefore, pertains to the permissive will of God, and in that sense may be said to be intended by Him in His providential governance of the universe.

There still remains the problem of why such evil is permitted. Why does not God make the lion to lie down with the lamb? But this question cannot be answered, to the extent possible, until after the consideration of the general question of the purpose of creation, the end toward which all things move.

How does God know and allow moral evil among His creatures?

Besides physical evil, there is moral evil, the sin of rational creatures. Moral evil involves a rejection of the divine plan, of the order of the universe established by God. This evil in itself has nothing of positive being, since God is the author of all positive being. It must therefore arise from, and consist in, the nihilation by the free will in the face of the possibility and duty of good action. It was already seen earlier how it is that freedom consists precisely in the moderation of the dynamism of being through the possibility of nihilation. In order to understand how it is that this possibility of nihilation may be used by the free creature so as to act contrary to the moral order, and thereby to make its own contribution of evil and nothingness to the unfolding of the eternal plan, a long discussion is necessary. For many problems arise concerning the freedom of the creature even while it is totally dependent for that which is in it of being and positive action, upon God. How is it possible for God to know such free nihilations, even supposing that they can take place, without His being in any way dependent for this knowledge upon creatures? How can the eternal plan take account of such nihilations even while it remains utterly transcendent and independent of creatures in its identity with the being and knowledge of God?

For this discussion it is necessary to presuppose what was said earlier concerning the nature of freedom and its foundation in the conscious self-possession of an intellectual being. With that in mind, several points can be elaborated in order to shed some light upon the mystery of human freedom and sin before the transcendent being, knowledge, and love of God.

The elements of choice and deliberation in the finite self

The possibility of nihilation of the dynamism of the self toward finite goods grounds the fundamental form of freedom of choice, that is, the freedom of exercise. The freedom of exercise is nothing but the freedom to act or not to act, to allow a tendency to fructify or to nihilate this tendency.

When a finite good is presented by the intellect, a spontaneous movement of complacency is induced in the will. There is no freedom at all about this first movement; it is an elicited act, but it is also a necessary act. Immediately consequent upon this movement is the impulse freely to choose this good. Both the primary movement and the consequent impulse are manifestations of the general dynamism of the will toward the plenitude of being and goodness.

But since no finite good can satisfy the dynamism toward the plenitude of being and goodness, since the embracing of a given finite good may in fact be incompatible with other finite goods or with what we conceive as the plenitude of being and goodness, we may freely nihilate our impulse to choose this particular finite good.

When we consider the deliberative process, which terminates in the act of free choice, a new form of freedom appears, the freedom of specification--a freedom to select one among many possible goods and lines of action. The deliberative process and the freedom of specification can be understood by reducing them to a series of instances of freedom of exercise. In this way it can be seen that the deliberative process is not simply a calculus of goods, performed so as to discover which is greater, this greater necessarily being chosen by some kind of psychological determination. Indeed, as will be seen, the deliberative process can be indefinitely prolonged, to be terminated only by a radically free act of choice or by the cessation of deliberation through distraction or through another radically free act, by which we choose not to act at all (by which we nihilate the impulse to act and consequently also the impulse to deliberate), or give ourselves up to acting on impulse alone without the guidance of reason.

In the deliberative process we have an end-in-view and weigh the various means by which we might achieve that end. Or we have a number of mutually incompatible goods in view and attempt to decide which of them would be better for us to embrace, "all things considered," that is, taking into account other things that we know we want (above all, our last end--the plenitude of being and goodness and, unless this itself is the object of deliberation, whatever concrete object it is in which we expect to reach this plenitude--this is in fact God, but unfortunately not all men realize this for one reason or another).

It is clear that the deliberative process can be concerned only with finite goods, goods with respect to which we may either nihilate or allow our dynamism toward the good to take its course. Even when God Himself is involved, however, we can still deliberate; for God is apprehended by us in a finite way--even the choice of His goodness is a free act for us. It is precisely for this choice that we are given our freedom in the first place.

Let us now follow the process of deliberation in the abstract. The process is basically the same whether we have an end-in-view and deliberate about the means or whether we envision a number of mutually incompatible goods and deliberate about which of them to choose, attempting to line them up in relation to higher goods which we already want and know we want.

Note that the very possibility of deliberation is grounded in the possibility of nihilation. If we simply gave ourselves up to movement after any good presented, there would be no deliberative process at all--this would be action like the action of brute animals.

It is only because we can at least temporarily restrain our appetities that we can pause to entertain the diverse possibilities offered at a given moment. Deliberation will continue so long as we continue to nihilate with respect to the various goods presented to view while at the same time continuing our fundamental will to deliberate. At the moment when we cease nihilating with respect to one of the possibilities, at that moment deliberation ceases and the act of free choice takes place. This cessation of nihilation with respect to one of the goods under consideration is at the same time an implicit nihilation of the will to deliberate further, since the continuation of the will to deliberate presupposes a temporary nihilation with respect to each of the goods concerned.

Deliberation may also terminate in a definitive nihilation of the will to consider all the possibilities but one, with respect to which we allow the dynamism of the will to fructify in the free choice of this possibility. Or it may terminate in a nihilation of the will to consider any of the possibilities any longer; here all the possibilities are in effect rejected.

Of course, if we are already "irrevocably committed" to a given end, the deliberation about means is in certain respects already circumscribed. But in fact there is no end to which we are irrevocably committed in this life except for the highly indefinite one of the plenitude of being and goodness. This means that the outcome of completely rational deliberation is always at bottom an act of free choice. One may say that we would not have chosen this means except that we had that end; but we would not have had that end but for the fact that it was itself first freely chosen.

Now if that end was freely chosen, then it can now be freely rejected. Thus it is that deliberation about means may lead beyond itself to new deliberations about the end which had been taken for granted. So it is that a deliberation about the means to reach God may lead to a rejection of God Himself, as when we freely choose that what we were considering as a possible means should now be our end instead. The possibility of nihilation with respect to means is also a possibility of nihilation with respect to ends--this is a ground for fear and trembling even among the children of God.

But we have digressed. To summarize the main point, the possibility of free choice and of deliberation is grounded in the possibility of nihilation. The fundamental form of freedom of choice is the freedom of exercise; the freedom of specification of choice arises when the freedom of exercise is confronted with a multiplicity of possible objects of choice in the deliberative process.

The sequence of divine activations in choice and deliberation

It has been seen that no finite self can act without being activated by the first cause. It has also been seen that the finite self can, however, nihilate by itself without any help. And yet nihilation surely can have no significance at all unless it be nihilation precisely in the face of a divine activation. Without a divine activation the finite self remains inert--there can be no refusal to act because there is not even the possibility of action. But on the other hand, a divine activation must have its effect; if nothing real is posited in the creature as a result of the activation, then the activation itself has no reality. It would seem then that under the divine activation the creature must act and that without this activation not even nihilation will have any significance. It seems then that the necessity of a divine activation for activity in effect removes the possibility of nihilation.

In order to surmount this difficulty it is necessary to distinguish, as does Maritain, between shatterable and unshatterable divine activations. Earlier, a distinction was made between the activity of an agent and the intentionality correlative with this activity, this intentionality being the application of the finite agent to action. Ordinarily, these two, the activity and the intentionality, are conferred simultaneously by the first cause. But in the case of the free will there is a special order observed in order to guarantee the possibility of genuine freedom of choice. The intentionality, or tendency *per se prima et proxima*, to activity is conferred prior to its fructification in actual activity; and the former is conferred as a shatterable activation while the latter is conferred as an unshatterable activation. Between them lies the possiblity of nihilation in the finite self.

The tendency *per se prima et proxima* to activity is none other than the impulse to choose which is consequent upon induced complacency, which was spoken of in the preceding section. To say that this is conferred as a shatterable activation means that it is really conferred as a tendency of the finite agent, but that the finite self can exercise its prerogative of holding itself in reserve, of nihilating with respect to this tendency, so that God sees the finite self as not disposed for the unshatterable activation of actual activity and does not confer it. Thus the shatterable activation has its immediate effect in the creature, but it does not necessarily bear its ultimate fruit to which it is ordered but from which it is really distinct. If the creature does not nihilate but remains open to the divine influence, then the unshatterable activation is conferred and activity takes place, the act of free choice.

It really seems unnecessary to trace out in detail the sequence of divine activations involved in choice and the deliberative process. Once the impulse to choose a particular good is seen as a shatterable activation, while the actual choice is seen as an unshatterable activation, it is necessary only to reread the discussion of the preceding section in this light.

But four points may be noted before going on to the next topic. First, it is necessary to deny metaphysical simultaneity in the conferring of the shatterable and unshatterable activations in the case just considered. Otherwise the possibility of nihilation does not intervene, and consequently neither can the nihilation itself.

Second, the nihilation is simultaneous with the shatterable activation, not with the withholding of the unshatterable activation. It is not that the nihilation takes place because the unshatterable activation has been withheld; rather, the unshatterable activation is withheld because at the instant of the conferring of the shatterable activation, the finite self held itself in reserve, nihilated. If it had not nihilated at this very instant, the unshatterable activation would have been in fact conferred.

Third, this does not preclude the possibility that the first cause may, in a certain case, elect to give both the shatterable and unshatterable activations simultaneously to the finite self, thus overcoming the possibility of nihilation altogether in the case in question. In such a case the act of choice is certain as to its production but free as to its mode, since it is elicited as the act of a finite self containing in itself the possibility of nihilation even though there was no nihilation in the case in question. The positive content of such an act is in no way different from the positive content of any other positive free act. The negative side in each instance consists in non-nihilation in fact. But it must be emphasized that the case envisioned in this paragraph would be an extraordinary case of divine intervention.

Fourth, up to this point there has been no question of moral evil, of sin. We have been dealing with free acts considered merely as free acts. While it is true that moral evil consists in a privation rather than a positive perfection, and that consequently moral evil must result from some kind of nihilation, nihilation as such is not necessarily a privation. Indeed, nihilation has been considered even in God. And certainly nihilation plays a great part in the good acting of finite selves--not only must good be done, but evil must be avoided; not only must some finite goods be embraced as means to our last end, but others must be rejected as incompatible with it.

The problem of moral evil can be met only in the light of an adequate understanding of the freedom of the finite self and of the infinite self. We have already come a long way in this matter, but there still remains a consideration of the divine knowledge and freedom in the face of finite selves.

The freedom of the finite self before divine knowledge and freedom

The primary object of divine knowledge is the divine essence; it is in His knowledge of the divine essence that God knows all the possible imitations of Himself which He can create. His knowledge of all possible creatures is called His knowledge of simple intelligence; as such it is a purely speculative knowledge. In it are known not only all possible creatures but also all possible orders of creatures, even including orders in which creatures capable of freely nihilating play a role. The multitude of possible orders to the same ends, allowing even for the possibility of nihilation by finite selves, are all considered in this knowledge of simple intelligence. But there is no knowledge here of whether the finite self would actually nihilate in given circumstances--for this would amount to saying that the freedom of the finite self is actually determined by the circumstances in which it finds itself.

As a consequence of this knowledge of simple intelligence, there is in God an infini-directional dynamism to create, arising out of His love of His own excellence and His will to share it. The infini-directional dynamism to create is moderated by the free nihilation of the divine will, so that creation is a free act for God even though it is "natural" to Him.

Thus God determines to bring into being one of the orders considered in His simple intelligence, an order in which allowance is made for the possibility of free nihilations by finite selves; this determination is the primordial will of God. Within this order are a multitude of sub-orders which collectively take into account all the possible nihilations by finite selves throughout the unfolding of the determined order. The actual sub-order decreed by God in view of the free nihilations of finite selves is according to the final will of God. This sub-order, insofar as it is creatively decreed, is known in the science of vision. Two moments then may be logically distinguished in the science of vision (though they cannot be really distinct since both exist from all eternity in the divine unity and immutability): the moment of the preliminary plan which "will" take into account the free nihilations of creatures, and the moment of the definitive plan which actually takes into account the free nihilations of creatures.

But of course the difficulty must be faced: does this distinction, even though merely logical, of two moments in the science of vision imply a determination of the divine knowledge by creatures, hence a denial of the transcendence of God with respect to all creatures? This is the crux of the problem.

But in fact the distinction does not imply a determination by creatures of the divine knowledge. Whatever there is of positive being in the activity of the finite self is seen as due to the divine activations which are determined by the divine knowledge and freedom. The free nihilations willed by finite selves are seen as their nihilations, but this does not mean that they are in any way determining the divine knowledge. This paradox arises because in fact this nihilation, as a nothingness, can only be known through the knowledge of positive being--all of which depends on God alone, since there is no positive being apart from the divine influxes.

When we know a nothingness, we construct a "being of reason" to "represent" this nothingness. But God does not thus construct in order to know nothingness as if it were a being; He sees nothingness precisely for what it is (or rather, for what it is not). And He does not know this nothingness, "made" by the finite self, immediately in His divine essence. Rather, He knows it as in the creature itself, the positive being of which He knows through His own essence. He knew the possibility of such nihilation from all eternity in His knowledge of simple intelligence; the actuality can only be known in the science of vision--but only as outside God, as a terminus materialiter attractus, as Maritain says, insofar as He knows the positive being of the creature through His own essence.

It was said earlier that free nihilation by the finite self does not necessarily require the first causality of God, but that the creature itself may have the first initiative in such nihilation.

Now we are saying that this free nihilation, as known by God, cannot determine the divine knowledge. But if these things are so, then it is possible to distinguish the two moments of the science of vision and still guarantee the transcendence of the eternal plan. God does not depend on our nihilations in order to constitute His eternal plan; He simply takes them into account in freely decreeing this plan creatively.

It was already said above that the free nihilations of creatures cannot be foreseen in the knowledge of simple intelligence--only the possibility of nihilation can be thus foreseen. And with respect to the science of vision, nothing can be foreseen; for God sees as present all time "unrolled" before Himself from all eternity. Here, He sees the free nihilations of creatures; but this does not constitute either an increment or a diminution in the divine knowledge. He sees these nihilations in the finite self precisely as receiving the shatterable activation and simultaneously freely holding itself in reserve. As a consequence of this free nihilation by the creature under the shatterable activation decreed by God, the decree of the unshatterable activation, which had been conditional, is withheld.

One may perhaps object to the distinction between diverse moments in the science of vision. But so long as the radically impenetrable mystery of divine knowledge be acknowledged, it seems quite permissible to make such a distinction--so long as we also guarantee the transcendence of God, as I believe has been done. After all, even the distinction between the knowledge of simple intelligence and the science of vision is a distinction made according to the necessities of human conceptualization, rather than according to the mystery of God Himself in Whom knowledge is identified with an absolute oneness and simplicity of being (notwithstanding the Trinity of Persons). This is all the more true when one comes to the scientia media of futuribles, the difficulties of which may be averted by the distinction just drawn in the science of vision itself in the light of the previous discussions of nihilation by the finite self. (But this is not to eliminate the principle of the scientia media, but only an alteration and transposition.) The problem is always one, not of plumbing the depths of divine knowledge, but of conceptualizing it as best we can in our own inadequate human way. This conceptualization must be such as to safeguard, on the one hand, the transcendence of God, and on the other, the fact of human freedom. It seems possible to safeguard both in the light of the conception of nihilation as presented by Maritain. It now remains to consider the problem of free moral decision and sin.

Moral decision and sin

Through the habitual knowledge called synderesis we know that we must act so as to preserve the true hierarchy of values under the infinite good Who is God; we should love finite goods precisely insofar as they lead us to our true last end and avoid them insofar as they are in any way incompatible with our last end. Moreover, we know that our free action as a consequence should always be governed by the consideration of this hierarchy of values as it finds expression in the moral law. These necessities known by synderesis, however, are not physical but moral necessities; there remains the possibility of sin.

But the possibility of sin presents problems. Sin is violation of the order of things laid down by God; therefore it cannot be willed or caused by God. Therefore it cannot be a positive being or possess any positive being qua sin. Therefore it must be a privation, a defect in activity--produced by a free nihilation which ought not to have taken place. It is a defect in activity considered precisely as flowing from the agent, a defect traceable to a free nihilation by the finite self.

The sin of simple omission does not present any special difficulty, considered in this light. Here the defect arises simply because, although the proper course of action has been seen, the agent does not act. In this non-action the finite agent has the first initiative. All that is required in the finite agent is the freedom to nihilate.

But the sin of commission presents special difficulties. The sin of commission is not a simple nihilation; a positive act is elicited--therefore an act requiring an activation by the first cause. Clearly, the sin cannot consist in the positive act as such; for sin is not caused by God. Therefore it must consist in a defect in the activity--that is, a lack of due order of this act in relation to the moral law, the hierarchy of values, and our last end. But this defect must not be traceable to any deficient causality of God but rather to a deficiency in the finite agent. The deficiency in the activity must mean that there is a deficiency in the finite agent itself. But this deficiency in the finite agent cannot be a deficiency of nature; otherwise the sinful act would not be a free act. This deficiency must be introduced through a free nihilation.

Where is this free nihilation? It is not in the will as immediately eliciting the sinful act. For in this act the mistake is that the will does not nihilate when it should. The intellect presents a possible course of action as "good," although not conformed to the moral law--and the will does not nihilate as it should but instead allows its dynamism toward the good full play. Clearly, there is already a deficiency in the intellectual presentation itself, although this does not necessitate the will. This deficiency in the intellectual presentation consists in the lack of consideration of the true norm of moral action, the failure to consider this possible course of action under the light of the moral law. Such a lack of consideration is not in itself wrong; we need not and cannot always be considering the relation of all possible courses of action to the moral law. But it is wrong, sinful, for us to decide on a course of action without an explicit or implicit recognition of the conformity of that course of action with the moral law. We know this, as was said above, through that habitual knowledge of the first principles of the moral order called synderesis. Unless we are taken by surprise, or unless some other factors remove the possibility of moral deliberation, we have a spontaneous tendency to consider our free actions, at least implicitly, in the light of what we _ought_ to do. At this point it is possible for us to freely nihilate, to refuse to consider our action in relation to the moral order. It is this nihilation which is the deficient cause of the deficiency in the intellectual presentation, which in turn is the model for our deficient activity.

The sin is a free act. My refusal to consider is free. My refusal to nihilate before the deficient intellectual presentation is likewise free. All the while, synderesis is present, convicting me of sin. I could not actually elicit the deficient positive act itself without the help of God, but it is not in this act, _qua_ positive, that sin consists. God does not cooperate in our sin; He merely fulfills the promise of help which He made in creating dynamic being. If we choose to moderate this dynamism in a disordered manner, it is our choice. God willed to create free creatures; He will allow their freedom its full scope, all the while moving all things to the ends He has appointed.

The sequence of divine activations in moral deliberation and choice

In the light of the preceding observations about moral decision and sin, a possible sequence of shatterable and unshatterable activations in the process of moral deliberation and choice may now be traced out. This outline is rather detailed, but it may be refined even further in the future.

Let us begin with the agent in a situation in which a plurality of courses of action present themselves as possibilities, as possible goods to be embraced. Unless other factors intervene to destroy the possibility of all deliberation, first is conferred a shatterable activation giving the tendency to consider the possible courses of action under the light of the moral rule.

If the finite self does not nihilate under this shatterable activation, it fructifies into the unshatterable activation which is actual consideration of the possible courses of action under the light of the moral rule. (In fact, a complex sequence of activations, shatterable and unshatterable, would ordinarily take place here in the deliberative process. But it is here envisaged only in a global way.) Then follows a shatterable activation giving the tendency to act according to the conclusions of such a consideration.

If the finite self does not nihilate under this last activation, there follows the unshatterable activation which consists in morally good action. If, on the other hand, the finite self nihilates here, the unshatterable activation is not in fact conferred; and this last nihilation may, depending on the case, be a formal sin of omission in the metaphysical sense.

But now let us return to the situation presented by the first shatterable activation giving the tendency to consider the possible courses of action under the light of the moral rule. Suppose now that under this activation the finite self freely nihilates. As a result of this nihilation, there is no consideration of the courses of action under the light of the moral rule. Nevertheless, these possible courses of action are being considered apart from the rule; and following upon such considerations are shatterable activations giving a tendency to act in accordance with such consideration apart from the light of the rule.

Under these shatterable activations, the finite self should nihilate. If it does not nihilate, there follows the unshatterable activation consisting in a positive, but disordered (because not considered in the light of the rule of action) activity--this is a formal sin of commission in the metaphysical sense. But if nihilation does take place, we are back at the original situation again and the circle of deliberation may begin anew.

Note that this is not the only possible sequence. In a situation in which one of the possible courses of action must be embraced, in which we must do one of the things in question, the very refusal to consider the possibilities under the light of the moral rule is itself already a sin of omission as well as the root of a sin of commission, unless we also refuse to do anything at all--which would constitute a second sin of omission.

Finally, in this section only the sequence of activations in *moral* deliberation and choice has been considered. If it should turn out that no moral question is involved, then of course the possibility of sin would disappear. But even then an analogous sequence of shatterable and unshatterable activations would be found.

Parenthetical note on synderesis and moral decision

In the preceding section, it was seen that synderesis convicts us of sin, even though we refuse to consider the moral rule at the instant of positive sin. This is, on the face of it, perhaps a hard saying. It compels some observations concerning synderesis.

It is necessary to distinguish synderesis *formally* considered, which is an habitual possession of the primary principles of the moral life, from the foundation of this habit in the existential tendencies of human nature--these latter may be called synderesis *fundamentally* considered. These tendencies of human nature as such become known through connaturality; this is not in itself an objective knowledge (a knowledge of something *per modum obiecti*) --it is knowledge which is not distinct from the conscious living of tendency itself. Such non-objective awareness is eventually translated into objectively formulated moral principles. And the primary objectively formulated moral principles are habitually possessed in synderesis formally considered.

Now it is not synderesis fundamentally or formally considered which can actually dominate the specification of our acts of free choice. It is necessary for such dominance that the principles found in formal synderesis be allowed to rise to actual (explicit or implicit) objective consciousness. Nevertheless, even if we should refuse to allow these principles to rise to actual objective consciousness, or if we should push them back into the preconscious, our connatural awareness of the lived tendencies which ground formal synderesis remains--registering, as it were, a mute, but still felt, protest. Thus it is that, even when we try to ignore the moral order in our act of choice, it persists in convicting us of sin, since it is woven into the very fabric of our life.

Yet it must be admitted that this connatural awareness of the moral law may be diminished or even virtually obliterated through inveterate vice. It must even be admitted that attention to it may not be properly cultivated in many instances, so that formal synderesis may not be able to develop properly. Thus it is that there are degrees of moral sensitivity, from that of moral infants or the thoroughly corrupt to that of the saints. When it is said that the connatural awareness always remains, even when we refuse to consider the rule, those who lack any moral sensitivity at all are excluded from consideration. But of course even the lack of moral sensitivity may be voluntary and culpable in its cause.

Sin before God

After viewing the fact of sin in the light of the explanation of freedom and nihilation, what can be said about sin in relation to the eternal plan and the will of God? Clearly, God is not the cause of sin; and since He is not its cause He cannot be said to will it actively. But in fact He does not will it even permissively. It is not enough to say that God merely permits those nihilations which oppose His will. In those nihilations there is a genuinely first initiative on the part of the creature. Elsewhere the initiative of the creature is not genuinely first. In all positive action the necessity of a first initiative on the part of God is evident from what has been said earlier. Even nihilations which themselves are not sinful derive from the will of God, since it was His will to create free creatures; such nihilations are permissively willed by God. Thus the creature in such a case does not have a simply first initiative, but only in that case in which it goes contrary to the will of God in a sinful act. Such a sinful act God does not permit; rather He merely tolerates and takes account of it in His eternal plan.

Viewing the eternal plan, then, from the perspective of our limited mode of conceptualization, may we not say that God--with full awareness of all the possibilities (in His knowledge of simple intelligence)--"takes a risk" in creating finite selves? In His science of vision, He is confronted with the fact of sin; He finds the terrible possibility realized, and realized over and over again. The creature actually "frustrates" the antecedent will of God; but in doing so the creature only falls under the consequent will of God. The antecedent will of God is the eternal law; the consequent will is the order of justice or mercy (itself already embraced in a way in the antecedent will) following upon the frustration of the antecedent will from some limited viewpoint by the free sinful nihilation of creatures. This frustration is not final; the eternal law transcends the limited viewpoint and embraces such frustration in a grander order still.

It is possible to view the matter in yet another way. The preliminary plan and primordial will of God are not frustrated since they are provisional; in them is included the determination on God's part to take into account the free nihilations of creatures. These are in fact taken into account in the definitive plan and final will of God.

But with moral evil no less than with physical evil, and indeed even more, the same difficulty arises again. Why does God allow it? Granted that this allowance in the case of moral evil cannot even be called permission. Granted that moral evil is in no sense at all intended by God. Still, how is it that He can allow it, and not only allow it but allow so much of it as we have in our poor world?

Again this question cannot be answered, we can hope to shed no light upon this deep mystery, until we have considered the purpose of God in creating the world. It is only in the light of that purpose that we can even hope to understand a little of the mystery of evil in the world.

Chapter 24

THE GLORY OF GOD

It is time now to consider the purpose of creation. Already enough has been seen to say in general that the purpose of creation is intimately bound up with consciousness in knowledge and love, that somehow the goal of all creation is a fuller and fuller sharing in conscious life by all things. And since all conscious life is in some manner a participation in the perfection of the divine consciousness, the goal of creation is participation in the divine consciousness in some manner.

But it is possible to make a more detailed analysis. First, note that there are in fact two ways of looking at the ultimate purpose of creation: from the point of view of God and from the point of view of creation. Analysis from both points of view should somehow converge, so that the divine purpose is seen in the process of fulfillment by an analysis of the whole course of created being. We have already considered both points of view, at least to some extent, and wish here merely to gather together some relevant materials and to extend the consideration a little further.

While the primary viewpoint is the purpose of God Himself, it is better first to adopt the secondary viewpoint, since this must come first in any philosophical order of knowing--we know creatures before we know God. As has been seen, all creatures tend in their own ways toward fuller and fuller participation in consciousness, whether by becoming more and more conscious or by entering into the consciousness of conscious beings through knowledge and love. It is evident that in the case of beings themselves conscious the tendency is ultimately toward a fuller and fuller consciousness of the richness of the divine being itself. In the case of finite beings which enter into the consciousness of conscious beings, the tendency is first toward manifestation of themselves, but finally and most important, toward some manifestation of the divine being, of which they are only reflections and "sacraments." Such creatures have being, truth, and value only in relation to the divine being; for them to "enter into the consciousness of conscious beings" is finally to reveal themselves in their essential relation to this divine being. If this revelation is not achieved, this is only because these creatures have not yet reached the fullness of that toward which they tend; they have as yet only partially entered into consciousness and still await the opportunity to convey their most precious secret. The highest function of conscious beings is to enter into some kind of conscious union with God; and the highest function of non-conscious beings is to refer, in the consciousness of some other being, to the being, truth, and goodness of the divine being, to reveal something of this richness of the divine being. This is the deeper meaning of that progressive movement to spiritualization which was discerned much earlier in this inquiry.

But now we turn to the primary viewpoint, that of God Himself in creating things. It has been seen that God is infinitely rich in Himself and can gain nothing for Himself through creation, and that therefore His creation is purely generous, directed simply toward the communication of His perfection to others. And what is at the bottom of this generosity? At the bottom is the infinite love which God has and is for His infinite perfection of being and for all the possible modes in which this being is participable. It is from the excess of this love and joy in His perfection that there "flows" His benevolently creative love. He communicates being precisely because He so knows, appreciates, and loves the goodness of being, which He is, and would share it with creatures.

But since non-conscious, non-intellectual beings are essentially "for another" without interiority of conscious self-possession, it is impossible that the created universe be comprised solely of such beings. If they are for another, then they receive the full intelligibility of their being only in relation to that other. Therefore they must be for some conscious being or beings; they must exist in order to be known and loved, and thereby to lead such conscious beings to knowledge and love of the divine being. Nor is it sufficient to point out that one conscious being is already given, namely the divine being itself. For this divine being knows all the perfection of itself without any dependence at all upon the existence or non-existence of any other beings. Therefore, when God decrees to create, to communicate being, He decrees primarily to communicate conscious being capable of knowledge and love.

These conscious beings are created by God in order that they may come to share more fully in the perfection of the divine being, not merely through their possession of physical being, but above all through their knowledge and love of all things as reflections and "sacraments" of the divine being, and therefore through their knowledge and love of the divine being itself. It is only in conscious beings that God can communicate His perfection in anything even remotely approaching the likeness of Himself; for only here can there be consciousness of the infinite perfection of God, like that consciousness which is the very being and life of God Himself.

There is then, a convergence in the considerations of the purpose of creation from the viewpoint of creatures and from the viewpoint of God. From both viewpoints, it is greater and greater consciousness of the divine being itself which emerges as the true goal of creation, consciousness of the divine being by conscious creatures, therefore the sharing of the perfection of divine consciousness with creatures.

We have been speaking of the movement of individual intellectual creatures toward greater and greater conscious union with God. But there is also a social dimension in this movement. For while the very richness of truth and goodness in the created universe is itself a source of division and disunity among finite consciousnesses, each of which has its own unique conscious relationship to being, still God is one; therefore deeper conscious union with

God must be at the same time deeper union with other finite consciousnesses in knowledge and love. The movement of progressive spiritualization in the world then is also a movement toward fuller unity of minds and hearts. The mystery of evil is in the world and is a source of division both from God and from other creatures, but the fundamental movement of being is toward some unity of knowledge and love.

But what is the true term of this movement? If the inquiry be pursued without the aid of faith, the matter is most obscure. Faith reveals to us that God has in fact destined us for a union with Himself utterly beyond the merely natural capacity of any finite consciousness, for an immediate vision of the divine being in itself enduring for all eternity. This is a share in the actual life of God Himself. Here, united in the closest intimacy of knowledge and love with God, we shall also be completely at one with all other conscious creatures who have freely chosen to love and serve God. It is precisely the degree to which we have made this free choice ourselves, with the help of divine grace, in our own lives that will determine the intensity of our own share in the fullness of divine life for eternity.

But if one should insist upon discussing the end toward which the natural movement of created being tends, that is, the natural end of the universe considered apart from the fact of the supernatural order known through faith, still some remarks can be made. First, as has just been said and as was explained much earlier, no finite consciousness by its natural powers could ever come to the immediate vision of God. Therefore, the natural end of such a finite consciousness must consist in some lower knowledge and love of God, through the medium of His creatures. Such a state has been considered in the discussion of the relative transcendentals in Part 1, chapter eleven. The happiness in that state would be a happiness in motion, insofar as it would be necessary for us continually to move from the consideration of one creature to the consideration of another, or to a deeper consideration of the same creature. And this happiness would still carry with itself a certain tension, essential to finite consciousness so long as it has not been raised to the supernatural state of the beatific vision, a tension caused by the natural (not elicited) desire of finite consciousness for the plenitude of being, together with the natural impossibility of attaining this plenitude. In this happiness in motion, there would be union with God and with other finite consciousnesses, and with all other things as well, in knowledge and love. But the radical openness to still greater union and intimacy, and therefore a consequent tension, would still remain. In fact, however, this openness of intellectual creatures has been met by the descent of God in His supernatural order, according to which He communicates Himself to us in the fullness of His own interior life.

It is possible now to bind together all that has been said in terms of the central concept of the glory of God. The glory of God is the knowledge, appreciation, love, and resultant praise of the divine excellence by conscious being. There is first the uncreated glory of God, which is the life of God Himself in Himself from all eternity, in the ecstasy of which, as we know from divine revelation, proceed the Son from the Father, and the Holy Spirit from the Father and the Son. No other than this uncreated, internal glory of God is essential to Him; no other glory can in any way increase His infinite being.

Nevertheless, He has willed that external glory also exist, by His creation and governance of conscious creatures, who themselves can know, appreciate, love, and praise the divine excellence both through their natural powers and with the help of grace. This purpose for such creatures is not any loss for them but rather their fulfillment, for in this life of glorifying God is their highest good and satisfaction. It is for this that they are made; it is this for which the whole constitution of their being cries out. But nevertheless, God lets them freely choose to accept or reject His advances; He will not force Himself upon them. If they accept, they ultimately enter into the fullness of this formal external glory of God, as faith reveals, in the beatific vision. But if they refuse, even though they "deprive" God of external glory (no loss to Him, but much to themselves), they must still offer an involuntary glory to God insofar as they manifest in themselves to all other men and angels the justice of God. This involuntary glory is no longer formal glory but rather an objective foundation for formal glory for those who will know, appreciate, love, and praise the divine excellence and justice. Such an objective foundation is called the objective external glory of God. All creatures give such objective glory to God merely by being what they are as reflections and "sacraments" of the divine excellence.

At this point it is also possible to correlate another notion with the glory of God, the notion of the service of God. This service is only the increase of the external glory of God through our becoming what He intends us to be, by our right action at every moment of our lives. Service is the work of those who have not yet reached the fulfillment of their existence, in the ultimate union with God. It is at once an increase of both the objective and formal external glory of God, but must always have as its ultimate goal the increase of the formal glory of God. Thus it is that we do or can do everything "for the glory of God."

The mystery of providence and evil

Finally, it is now possible to make a few observations concerning the mystery of providence and evil. Providence is essentially mysterious to us, since it is the wisdom of the supreme intelligence. But most mysterious of all is the permission of so much physical evil and the toleration of so much moral evil in the universe of being which has been created by the infinitely good God. God is not the cause of evil, but it still remains true that He has made the world in which so much evil exists. We wonder to ourselves how so much evil, or indeed any evil at all, can be allowed. Surely, it would seem that, in His infinite power and wisdom, God could have made a better world, one with less evil, or even one with none at all.

In attempting to shed a little light upon this mystery, it is necessary again to distinguish between physical and moral evil. First, consider physical evil, the less serious of the two, but still serious enough when one contemplates such things as the physical sufferings of animals and men, and the catastrophes of nature and of human life. Why should there be such evil in the world?

It is good at this point to ask another question. How could such evil be excluded from the world? Clearly, a certain price would have to be paid. If the lion is not to eat the lamb, if the earth is never to quake, if storms of great magnitude are not to occur, then the lion, the earth, and the atmosphere must all be something less than they are now. If they are to retain their natural dynamism and are allowed to exercise their interactions with the various beings of the universe, certain physical evils will occur. If the evils are taken away, then something of this dynamism and interaction must be taken away first. Such physical evil is precisely the price for the variety of dynamically interacting beings in the universe. But this variety is a great good; for it permits a more varied manifestation of the divine perfection, a greater degree of objective external glory of God, which in turn offers the occasion for greater formal glory of God by intellectual creatures who behold the heavens and the earth.

But to grasp properly this explanation of the presence of physical evil in the world made by the good God, it must be understood that this is not an attempt to reduce this evil to a good. It is and remains in itself an evil; it is the price of the variety of good in the universe. It may become an occasion of good, as when men bear sufferings in abandonment to the divine permissive will or when the punishment of sin manifests the order of divine justice; but in itself it is still an evil. Nothingness and privation are in their way as absolute as being, and no amount of explanation can reduce the evil of a privation to the goodness of being. Evil and suffering are absolutes and disappear only when every tear is wiped away by the vision of God. But if the presence of so many and so great evils in the world should finally convince us that it is only in God that our happiness can be found, then such evil, still not itself a good, has become the occasion of very great good indeed. In this disillusioning function physical evil has great "value" for men and for the greater formal external glory of God.

Yet still another difficulty may be raised concerning the presence of physical evil in the universe. Granted that such evil is necessary, was it not possible for God, by His providence and governance, to protect at least conscious beings from natural catastrophe, physical illness, and the other pains of life, and even from death? Certainly this was possible; and the evil, even the excess of evil, to which the children of God are exposed in the world has a certain special mystery about it. Faith tells us how it came about that we should be exposed to these evils, in the revelation of the fall of man. But this fall itself presupposed elevation to the supernatural order, the call to sharing in the intimate interior life of God; and the immunity from physical evil which went along with the gifts of divine grace was itself a special gift in no way demanded by human nature. The implication is that, had man not been raised to the supernatural order, he would not have been immune from physical evil.

But still we may suppose that God in His providence might have given special help and guidance to men, in such a purely natural order of things, that they might more easily achieve their end without the excess of suffering to which our poor world is exposed. Instead of that special natural help, He in fact offered His grace, along with certain other gifts such as immunity from physical suffering; but when this was refused, men were left without these gifts and without the special natural help as well. Yet, God did not simply leave man in this state;

in the ruin of the original order of grace and in that very excess of suffering in this world, He instituted through Christ a new order of grace, of redemption and salvation through suffering itself. In this new order, known only in faith, physical evil and suffering become transfigured; though evil remains evil, and suffering remains suffering, by these--with the grace of God and our acceptance--we are slowly transformed, freed from our immersion in self and in other creatures, and gradually filled with the divine life.

Yet, it is not enough for us to know that some physical evil is the price of the variety of good in the universe, or that this evil has the effect of saving disillusionment for men. This knowledge still leaves those who contemplate the mystery of evil with a certain ineradicable bitterness, which is itself in a way the greatest suffering of all. This bitterness in fact can only be washed away in the blood of Christ, through loving endurance and abandonment in union with His suffering. Through this love, even bitterness is transformed into sweetness and joy, despite the continued presence of evil and suffering, in feeble anticipation of the sweet joy of the vision of God.

But beyond mere physical evil, there is moral evil, the evil of sin. If physical evil is the price of the variety of the universe, moral evil is the price of the freedom which God has given to intelligent creatures. He could, of course, create such creatures in the beatific vision or with such a degree of grace that they would not sin. But if He wills to create some intelligent creatures with the real possibility of turning away from Him as much as with the real possibility of freely loving and serving Him, then He also accepts the possibility that some will in fact turn away from Him through sin. But one will ask, Why should He create such creatures at all? Why should He take the risk He does in creating them? And it is indeed a risk! God does not know the actual sins and turning away of His creatures except in the knowledge of vision, and the first initiative for this sin is not in Him but rather in His creatures. In a sense, He does not <u>plan on</u> sin's occurring, as was seen in the preceding chapter. It is this risk of God which sets the stage for the <u>real drama</u> of free creatures. These creatures do not merely execute, in the manner of puppets, certain motions so as to reach deterministically foreordained ends. Their freedom is real, and their initiative is real in their sin.

But, again, why should God take such a real risk in creating such creatures, even a risk which results in His sending of His own Son to redeem these creatures through suffering? The answer to this question is hidden in the depths of the mystery of the divine love and generosity. Why did He create us? He loves us. Why did He redeem us? He loves us. Why does He still endure us? He loves us.

But while the risk is there as regards any individual one of these creatures, still at least some are saved through the grace of God. Indeed, even if they do not freely choose God under the influence of grace all through the course of life, He can still give them overwhelming grace at the very end, if He so chooses. If no man were saved, or no intellectual creature at all, the purpose of creation would be indeed frustrated, since it is precisely the life of intellectual creatures with God, the external formal glory of God, which is the purpose of all creation. It is impossible for us to determine how many such creatures will be saved. While the principle that nature is not in most cases frustrated seems to suggest that the majority of men will be saved, still even if only one intellectual creature were to reach the fullness of union with God, all the rest would be worthwhile as a means to this end. For the slightest degree of supernatural participation in the interior life of God Himself is worth more than the whole of the natural creation. In fact, however, Christians know that many are saved; but how many is a mystery to us.

At this point, some brief observations may be made concerning still another deep mystery, that of predestination. Predestination is not, in God, a foreknowledge, since in God there is only the present; it is only called a foreknowledge from the perspective of creatures, whose duration is in some manner temporal. God's knowledge of the course of the world and of the destiny of His intellectual creatures all exists in His knowledge of vision, one with the being of God from all eternity. Such knowledge is infallible and in no way dependent on creatures, as was seen in the preceding chapter. With respect to all the positive being and goodness of creatures, this knowledge of vision is transcendently causal. Thus, those creatures who acquire being, the merits of a good life, and finally its reward, in no way determine the knowledge and will of God but rather are entirely determined, in regard to all that is good in them, by this knowledge and love. When we consider their final state of reward, this divine determination in eternity receives the name of predestination. God, in His knowledge of vision, infallibly predestines some intellectual creatures to eternal life. But since God has not the first initiative in the line of moral evil, He cannot be said to predestine any intellectual creature to reprobation.

The nihilation of a free creature, in which consists the essence of moral evil, cannot in any way determine the divine knowledge or love, since this nihilation is precisely nothing; but at the same time, the divine knowledge and love themselves do not determine the existence of this nothing in the free creature. Once this point is understood, it is possible to see how predestination is certain and entirely determining in the line of good, without there being any corresponding predestination in the line of evil.

Finally, just four more remarks may be made regarding the fact of moral evil. First, the fact of moral evil of itself serves to render intelligible much of the physical evil of the world precisely as punishment for sin. However, it does not of itself suffice completely to explain physical evil, since both the innocent and the guilty are subject to such evil. Nor does it in any way explain the physical evils in the non-human world.

Second, the remark made above concerning the disillusioning function of such evil also applies to moral evil, which itself should drive us to a distrust of ourselves and to a placing of our real hope in God.

Third, the presence of moral evil in our world is the occasion for repentance and for the manifestation of the divine order of mercy.

Fourth, just as the bitterness resulting from the experience of physical evil can only be removed through union with the suffering Christ, so also the bitterness which results from the experience of moral failure in oneself or others can only be removed through union with Christ and abandonment to His mercy. Saint Paul tells us that all things work together unto good for them that love God; and Saint Augustine adds, even sin. But this is only fully true for those who live in union with Christ.

INDEX

Imprimi potest John R. Connery, S.J., Provincial of the Chicago Province, January 11, 1965. Nihil obstat John B. Amberg, S.J., censor deputatus, July 13, 1965. Imprimatur Most Reverend Cletus F. O'Donnell, J.C.D., Administrator, Archdiocese of Chicago, July 14, 1965. The nihil obstat and imprimatur are official declarations that a book or pamphlet is free of doctrinal or moral error. No implication is contained therein that those who have granted the nihil obstat and imprimatur agree with the contents, opinions, or statements expressed.

0
D